Whine Tasting

Musings From A Conservative Living In Far-Left Northern California

TOM THURLOW

Whine Tasting
Musings From A Conservative Living In Far-Left Northern California

ISBN-10: 0615679501
ISBN-13: 978-0615679501

Library of Congress Control Number 2014920168
CreateSpace Independent Publishing Platform, North Charleston, SC

For Martina and Rachel

TABLE OF CONTENTS

INTRODUCTION

I have a huge confession to make: this is not a book about wine, wine-tasting, or even whining. Well, maybe some complaining here and there, but I wouldn't go so far as to call it whining.

This book is really a collection of my columns on politics, "strong opinions on trivial subjects," movie and event reviews, and various other silly issues that have occupied my brain for the last several years. Give or take. There is also one very serious, non-political column, concerning the passing of a good high school friend of mine, and that is the subject of the Epilogue.

But the name of this book, *Whine Tasting*, comes from the website that houses these writings, *Napa Whine Country*. "Tasting" implies a rough sampling of the writings I have put on that website since its founding in 2011. Except this "tasting" is much different from a "wine" tasting in that there is no foreign-accented person standing nearby you as you sip some wine, reminding you how great the wine tastes and urging you to pay $45 for something that tastes like a $7 bottle of wine. But if it makes you feel any better, feel free to eat some of those little oyster crackers to cleanse the pallet after reading each "sampling" here.

Of the four chapters in the book, the largest chapter has to do with politics. If I were to try and draw some common qualities among the columns in the first chapter, I would say that they have a general, conservative approach to the controversies of the day, but with a little something extra. See, I read a lot of other writers' political columns and I enjoy the rare ones that have a certain what-does-it-all-mean point to whatever topic is being discussed. Kind of like a second essay after the initial political point is made. A two-for-one!

Too many political columns nowadays just make the point that, on any given issue, conservatives are right and liberals are wrong. Well, duh! That could be done in a paragraph or two! Most published columns go on for 800 or more words.

What readers want to read is some other take on the argument, or something else that somehow relates with the reader's life. Something different. That is how I try to write.

And, whenever possible, it is important to include humor in political columns. A political column with a few chuckles in it truly sets the column apart from all others.

In practice, including humor, or attempts at humor, is not very difficult. A lot of times it is just a matter of reporting what influential people say. Soon after I started the *Napa Whine Country* website, *New York Times* columnist Paul Krugman said in an interview that a space alien invasion would help the sluggish American economy. You read that right, an invasion of aliens! I'm pretty sure that Krugman was not joking, because liberals generally don't have a sense of humor. Or did he know something the rest of us didn't know? Who knows, but it was pretty funny, even accidentally. Krugman may still have the last laugh, but I doubt it.

A few weeks after that, North Carolina Governor Bev Perdue was heard talking about delaying her state's up-coming congressional elections until after the economy improved. Like that would incentivize the politicians to work on the economy! When pressed on the issue, she claimed she had just been joking. Nice try!

And yet, get this: the one professional comedian we have in Congress, Minnesota Senator Al Franken, stopped being intentionally funny decades ago. Oh, he is still funny alright, just not on purpose.

Maybe this is what humorist Will Rogers was talking about when he said, "everything is changing. People are taking their comedians seriously and the politicians as a joke." That comment is truer today than it was when Rogers originally said it, almost 100 years ago.

Not only does it add to the entertainment value of political discussions, but a little humor helps the average attentive person cope with some otherwise depressing facts facing our country. For example, if you look forward and project the on-going deficits that our country burns through each year, you either laugh or begin thinking of moving into a cave in the mountains or something. Come to think of it, I don't know how people can digest all that is going on without a good sense of humor.

Writing with a degree of gutsiness also helps in writing unique columns, and I am definitely up to the challenge. Ask yourself: of all the ink spilled over the recent Chik-fil-A/gay marriage issue, in which the president of Chil-fil-A voiced his support for traditional marriage, what other writer besides me addressed the blandness of the food sold at Chik-fil-A? I am proud to say that mine was the only Chik-fil-A column in which that issue was broached. Gutsiness in action, right there! And I still don't hesitate to say it: the food at Chik-fil-A is boring. There, I said it again! I have visited friends in the hospital who are served spicier food than what is sold at Chik-fil-A restaurants!

Along the way there have been some successes. Congressman Paul Ryan took my advice and declined to run for president. Of course, he later ran for vice president, but I will claim at least a partial victory here.

In September, 2011, Congressman Ryan said he needed a month to think about running for president, but a few days later when he saw my column urging him not to run, he announced his non-candidacy right away. I am sure it was my column that made up his mind, and I claim full credit that Congressman Ryan remained House Budget Chairman, getting his budget passed while the presidential campaign was going on without him.

I also claim victory with the publication of my column that suggested that the Transportation Safety Agency (TSA) should conduct breast and colo-rectal exams in addition to security checks at the airport. The TSA already does all sorts of intimate fondling at airport security checkpoints, so why not? My column on the subject led the way. Well, at least it seems that way. And no one can convince me otherwise. The next time you go to the airport, consider how much more invasive a regular colo-rectal or breast exam is beyond what you have to go through already. Well, I say we give some unemployed doctors security uniforms, and have breast and colo-rectal exams done in the airport the right way, not only to search for weapons, but also for pre-cancerous lumps and polyps that may turn into some form of cancer later in life. It only makes sense, doesn't it?

Of course, sometimes readers get angry when presented with the facts. I had been cautioned against reading the comments posted below my political columns, so I should have known better. But I once made the mistake of peeking at some of the comments on one particular column I wrote for American Thinker. That column got over 250 hateful comments! And sneering, snarky comments, each one more vicious than the last! One of those jerks looked back at a prior column of mine and misinterpreted what he read, and then he called me an … Obama-supporter! Hey pal, try saying that to my face!

Meanwhile, I wondered if I could get someone else to start my car in the morning. I eventually made it to a movie theater to forget politics for a while, and wound up writing a movie review. This is when I started reviewing movies. Writing reviews of movies or of other entertainment events are fun and rarely controversial, and when I was able to get an interview with someone involved in the movie or event being reviewed, they assumed I knew what I am doing. That was fun in a sneaky, fraudulent sort of way.

And my movie reviews are roughly contemporary with the release of the movie. I say "roughly" because the earliest movie review I did was four months before the release of the movie (*The Lorax*, which I knew from the trailer was over-the-top leftist propaganda), and the latest movie review I did was about 30 years after the movie's release (*My Dinner With Andre*, which deserves to be criticized every time some network plays it). Someone please tell me: where is it written that a movie review has to be published within a decade or two of the movie's initial release?

There is also a chapter in this book entitled "Strong Opinions About Trivial Subjects." Admittedly, these columns are not entirely centered on triviality, nor do they all evoke strong opinions, but the subjects are at least non-political. I mean really, how seriously can you take forced wedding speeches or free food samples at Costco? Maybe not necessarily trivial, but the discussions in that chapter that are not centered around important stuff like government mismanagement or world domination. Yet these columns are still fun. And besides, by titling the chapter as "trivial," I am able to use that great John Malkovich quote that I found at the beginning of the chapter. Which is cool.

So, as with any other writer with a few year's worth of columns under his belt, I am publishing this book with them. Thomas Sowell did it. Charles Krauthammer also did it. Even His Eminence Mark Steyn did it. So I am in great company. I hope you enjoy it.

Oh good, this might stimulate our sluggish economy.

CHAPTER 1

POLITICS, POLITICS, POLITICS

A little government and a little luck are necessary in life, but only a fool trusts either
—P.J. O'Rourke

PERRY INDICTMENT NOT THOUGHT THROUGH

So let me see if I understand this correctly: if the Republican governor of Texas, Rick Perry, had just waved through the $7.5 million taxpayer funding for the public integrity unit of the Travis County District Attorney's office, an office led by a convicted drunk driver with an astronomical .24% alcohol level, then Perry would not now be facing "abuse of power" felony charges. Had Gov. Perry just put down his veto pen, and sent the money to this particular Democrat District Attorney, he would not be facing almost 100 years in state prison. Do you see how ridiculous that sounds?

And have you seen the video of the prosecutor in question? It would be funny if it weren't a lead prosecutor of a very important Texas county, Travis County. The video[1], which has been making the rounds on the Internet, shows District Attorney Rosemary Lehmberg at different times claiming that she was not drunk, which was obviously not true, kicking her jail cell door, calling the case against her stupid, and topping it off with a kind of "do you know who I am?" routine. That didn't work for former United States Senator Larry Craig when he was

6

busted for lewd sexual conduct in a men's restroom, so why should it work for Lehmberg? Ms. Lehmberg can even be heard mumbling "this is the end of my political career," making at least some sense in her extreme drunken state.

But she was wrong there, too! A local court later decided[2] that Lehmberg was just fine to stay where she was as Travis County District Attorney, prosecuting other drunk drivers and even available to prosecute other public officials as part of the office's public integrity unit. From that point on, any prosecution, especially any "public integrity" prosecution, led by Ms. Lehmberg was suspect.

Here's why: if anyone is arrested for drunk driving and is prosecuted by DA Lehmberg, a fair question to be asked would be "maybe she is being so hard on that defendant and his drunk driving because she wants to show that she has extra regret for being caught doing the same thing." Or "maybe she is going easy on that drunk driver because she wants to show that what she did was really no big deal." Or if she prosecutes a public official for some misdeed in office, "maybe she is being so harsh or lenient (take your pick) to compare that case favorably with her own case or to show that she really regrets what she did."

See how that works? No one is perfect, but anyone prosecuting other people for crimes or public officials for their misdeeds at least needs to be above such questions and have nothing in their background that prompts a discussion like this. And "public integrity" prosecutions are supposed to be a serious discussion of an accused public official and whether they broke the law, not some scorecard to be compared with the prosecutor's own personal past.

In context, Gov. Perry's funding veto makes perfect sense. In fact, Gov. Perry would have been irresponsible had he *not* vetoed the funding for Lehmberg's office.

"Oh, but this charge is being led by a special prosecutor, with no direct connection to the Travis County District Attorney," the defenders of this prosecution might say. But it is no secret that these charges were first suggested by Texans For Public Justice, a liberal Texas activist group that specifically targets[3] Republican office-holders. And according to the *Dallas Morning News,* the special prosecutor in this case, Michael McCrum, was almost appointed[4] to be the local U.S. Attorney by President Obama. The Travis County District Attorney's office also has a habit of criminally prosecuting prominent Republicans: first, Senator Kay Bailey Hutchison, then Republican House Majority Leader Tom DeLay, and now Republican Governor Rick Perry.

Recently, the members of the grand jury that signed onto the indictment have shown their partisan colors as well. Five members of the grand jury were shown[5] to have been consistent Democrat voters while one member was even found[6] out to be a Texas Democratic Party delegate while the Perry proceedings were going on.

If this prosecution ever goes to trial, it will be impossible for the trial jurors not to notice that this case is being prosecuted by a DA's office that was denied funding by the defendant, Gov. Perry.

Even some Democrats agree that this indictment is a bad idea. Former Obama adviser and prominent Democrat David Axelrod tweeted[7] "unless he was demonstrably trying to scrap the ethics unit for other than his stated reason, Perry's indictment seems pretty sketchy." Liberal columnist Jonathan Chait, of *New York Magazine,* calls[8] the Perry indictment "unbelievably ridiculous."

This prosecution is so bad that instead of defending it, some Democrats have invented new theories of the case. As was reported[9] in the blog *Powerline,* a Democratic party official sent out an e-mail arguing that Perry's funding veto was in part because the Travis County DA was investigating a group with close ties to Gov. Perry. However, a report in the newspaper *Austin American-Statesman,* points[10] out that the friends of Perry in the group in question were cleared long ago. So this argument is a total red herring.

In the end, this has a big possibility of backfiring on Democrats. If there is a verdict of "not guilty," it is conceivable that a similar "abuse of office" charge could be brought against the special prosecutor, which would be funny, but Gov. Perry could use the acquittal in his presidential campaign, just like Wisconsin Gov. Scott Walker will use his recall victory in his presidential campaign. Republican voters like candidates who fight, and a few battle scars on a candidate are appealing.

If, on the other hand, the jury somehow convicts Gov. Perry, the conviction will eventually be thrown out on appeal, as was the conviction against Republican Thomas DeLay a few years ago. Not only that, but Republican prosecutors in other Texas counties will begin to catch on that if Texas someday has a Democratic governor, similar criminal charges could be brought against that governor. Only a few years ago, Texas actually did have a Democrat governor, Ann Richards, and she issued a few vetoes.

It could also work out that being prosecuted for something will become a kind of rite of passage for either side: Republican governors will be criminally prosecuted by the Travis County District Attorney, while Democrat governors will be criminally prosecuted by district attorneys in any of the various Republican counties in Texas — maybe in succession!

No, this indictment against Gov. Perry was definitely not thought through. As they say in Texas, this case is "a dog that won't hunt."

August 22, 2014

WAS THE "SHIP OF FOOLS" INCIDENT A SET-UP? AND IF NOT, WHY NOT?

The last several weeks have witnessed a delicious spectacle, at least for us global-warming "deniers," as a ship filled with eco-tourists and global warming scientists boarded a ship to sail to Antarctica and record the melted ice there. The so-called[1] "Ship Of Fools" got stuck there, and another ship sent to rescue them also got stuck in what is now known to be record ice in an area that was supposed to be ice-free or at least mostly un-frozen. It is summer in Antarctica, you know.

You had to know that this would happen. In 2008, former Vice President Al Gore famously predicted[2] that "the entire north polar ice cap will be completely gone in five years." Gore is really on a roll. The "Gore Effect," as it is now known, has become a pretty reliable reverse indicator of regional weather following a specific Gore prediction or even a local appearance by Mr. Gore. The believers who got stuck in Antarctica were a repeat of similarly-intentioned activists[3] who last year got stuck sailing in Arctic ice in the Northwest Passage.

My question is this: was the Antarctica trip a set-up? It seems almost too good to be true. This expedition would seem to confirm the "denier" side of the global warming debate. Global warming theories and computer models are one thing, but when a ship of warming scientists travels to Antarctica to record melting ice there, and instead gets stuck in *record* ice, it is a little difficult to argue around that.

If this was a set-up, it would be a change in tactics. On the op-ed pages, our side's argument is practically lost before it even begins. Here is how it works. A hypothetical debate in 2008:

Warmist: "Carbon emissions in the atmosphere are so bad that within five years the polar ice caps will be entirely melted."

Denier: "That is crazy. It won't happen. There is no scientific basis for that."

Fast forward five years, and with the ice caps still there, the 2008 prediction is long forgotten or ignored by the mainstream media. And instead of a reply by the Denier, above, the entire conversation is now swept under the rug by the media. It's as if the prediction never happened. No need to discuss anything about "how the prediction turned out." Pesky details that are universally ignored.

Ed Driscoll at PJ Media has pointed[4] out that the original video clip of Al Gore making his prediction has been scrubbed from the Internet, and the only remaining video clip is from a German publication of some sort. Despite the German interpreter speaking, the viewer can still see and barely hear the famous Gore 5-year prediction.

If this was not a set-up by some global warming deniers, maybe it should have been. And there should be more like this in the future. Our side needs to counter prevalent arguments with media stunts, because scientific logic is just not working with the general public.

A few months ago a book[5] was released by James O'Keefe, a guy who makes fools of liberals, not by arguing with them, but by videotaping the proof of conservative sides of various arguments and sending the videos out into the Internet, where the videos promptly go viral.

Was the group ACORN corrupt? Of course not, replied the mainstream media. "ACORN is a virtuous organization. Pure as the wind-driven snow. Everyone knows that." An undercover O'Keefe video showing O'Keefe and a friend posing as a pimp and a prostitute, being advised by ACORN workers, begged to differ, and quickly won the argument. Following this video Congress decided to stop funding ACORN.

Same for the potential for abuse in voting without identification. Another undercover O'Keefe video[6] showed an O'Keefe assistant going to a Washington DC voting station and claiming to be (Attorney General) Eric Holder. Without asking for any identification, the poll worker quickly offers Holder's ballot.

There are other examples, but the point is that in a world where 95% of the media dismisses or ignores conservative arguments, making an argument is simply not enough. Our side has to do media stunts that show, instead of argue, the righteousness of conservative principles. And the media stunts need to be big enough to be a media story.

So the next time a global warming scientist proposes[7] to hire a ship to travel to Antarctica and study changes in the ice there, the ship should not be allowed to just sail from New Zealand to Cape Denison in Antarctica for two weeks in December and January. No. Additional ports of call in several world coastal cities should be funded, with media events and lots of fanfare along the way. There should be parties with local celebrities, corporate sponsorships, telethons to pay for more travelers, parades; the possibilities are endless!

And when the inevitable – global warming discredited — happens, the media spotlight will be more and more drawn to the reality of what was not predicted.

January 14, 2014

HEALTHCARE PRISON BLUES

Last week, country-western stars Brad Paisley and Carrie Underwood sang a little tribute[1] to the on-going disaster that is Obamacare. We thought we would check in with Johnny Cash and see if he had any song to sing on the subject. He said there was in fact a certain song that had been creeping and crawling around his head, and it goes like this:

(To the tune of "Folsom Prison Blues")

I hear the train wreck coming
it's rollin' round the bend,
and I don't see it workin' 'til I don't know when.
I'm stuck in Healthcare website,
and time keeps draggin' on.
But that train wreck keeps a rollin'
on down to San Antone

When I was just a baby, my momma told me "Son,
always have insurance, don't ever go it alone."
But when I got that cancellation letter,
I just wanted to die.
And now I get that error message,
I hang my head and cry.

I bet there's politicians gettin' fancy insurance plans.
They're probably gettin' covered for everything they need.
Well I know I had it comin' …
no insurance for free.
But those pols get their exemptions,
and that's what tortures me.

Well if they freed me from healthcare prison
and my old health plan was mine
I bet I'd move it on a little further down the line,
far from healthcare prison.
That's where I want to stay.
And I'd let my old healthcare plan
blow my blues away

November 11, 2013

MEANWHILE, ON AL JAZEERA AMERICA ...

It has been almost two months since Al Jazeera America (AJA), the American outlet of Qatar-based news network Al Jazeera, debuted in the U.S. Viewers of the network note its impressive graphics and lack of commercials, a welcomed change of pace compared to most cable news in the States. The network also employs a host of familiar faces that help bolster AJA's image as just another news network. It remains to be seen just how radical AJA will let its coverage becomes once it grows more assured of its acceptance into the mainstream. Already AJA's Sunni sponsors have let the mask slip.

Despite a petition drive[1] to exclude AJA from cable distribution, AJA's coverage is definitely on the rise. Last spring and summer, AJA went on a hiring spree, hiring producers, writers, technicians, and hundreds of other staffers. AJA also snapped up big news names like Joie Chen, David Shuster and Soledad O'Brien, and then opened 12 American bureau offices. Broadcasting began August 20.

Of course, AJA is not just another news network. AJA's parent company, Al Jazeera, is owned by the government of Qatar, the tiny, oil-rich, Sunni Muslim state in the Persian Gulf, bordering Saudi Arabia. Qatar is ruled by Shiekh Tamim bin Hamad Al Thani, who, despite his personal business dealings with Israel, is pro-Hamas, pro-Muslim Brotherhood and anti-Israel[2]. Al Jazeera's news coverage has reflected those views.

In fact, Al Jazeera is so pro-Muslim Brotherhood it recently got kicked[3] out of Egypt for instigating Muslim Brotherhood protests there. In 2008, Al Jazeera's Beirut bureau chief threw an on-air birthday party[4] for Samir Kuntar, convicted killer of an Israeli family.

Americans learned to hate Al Jazeera in the days after 9-11, when Al Jazeera first repeated the charge that American Jews were warned beforehand of the attacks in New York, then repeatedly broadcast interviews of Osama bin Laden. Al Jazeera has even described the War on Terror as "so-called," and suicide bombings as "paradise operations."

Through the years Al Jazeera has had on-air personalities who were blatantly anti-Semitic. One popular Al Jazeera show, *Shari'a and Life,* features a host who regularly criticizes[5] Shiites, Americans and Jews.

During the height of the Iraqi war years, then-Secretary of Defense Donald Rumsfeld described[6] Al Jazeera as "the mouthpiece of Al Qaeda," while President George W. Bush referred[7] to Al Jazeera as "a terrorist organization." Upon the initial invasion of Afghanistan and later in Iraq, US military forces bombed local Al Jazeera offices because of the support they had given terrorists.

Now that AJA is on the air in the US, Americans will get to judge for themselves if AJA will be an independent news network covering news items important to Americans, or if AJA possesses the dispositions of its parent company.

While the network's foreign news coverage is acceptable, the viewer gets the feeling that AJA is "up to something" whenever the news involves Israel, Hamas, the Muslim Brotherhood, or the Mideast in general.

Take for example the network's coverage of the civil war in Syria. A Pew study[8] revealed that most of the Syrian coverage by AJA was similar to most other American networks, but AJA spent much more time covering the humanitarian aspects of the story and the hardships of the rebels. And no wonder – Qatar has funded[9] the rebels.

In its domestic news coverage, AJA is clearly left-leaning. Typical of a pattern, in a recent day's news broadcast, President Obama is shown speaking and blaming Republicans for the government shutdown, then the GOP response was only paraphrased in passing by the show's anchor.

Strictly as a marketing issue, this liberal domestic news slant puts AJA in the same crowded category as most other American news channels, like ABC, CBS, CNN, NBC, NPR and MSNBC, leaving Fox alone in the right-of-center TV news coverage. Granted, AJA is only weeks old, but so far it is positioning its domestic news coverage in a pretty crowded field.

One recent episode of an in-depth news talk show on AJA, *The Stream,* revealed a definite anti-Israeli bias. The episode addressed the issue of the Israeli/Palestinian conflict, and how to get Israel to discuss peace. Special guests included members of the International Solidarity Movement[10] (ISM), which is a scandal in and of itself. The ISM is an organization, not of peace activists, but of para-militants who actively work with Palestinian terrorists and who call for armed force against Israel. ISM activists protect weapons-smuggling tunnels and have been photographed with assault weapons. Another group on the show calling itself Combatants For Peace (CFP) equates Israeli soldiers with Palestinian "combatants" (i.e. terrorists). Neither the CFP nor ISM's websites acknowledges Israel's right to exist, even with defensible borders. *The Stream* even included a former Israeli soldier, who complained of Israeli aggression against Palestinians. He was probably trying to be Israel's version of John Kerry, circa 1971.

The show featured furrowed brows and hand-wringing about how to get "both sides to stop talking past each other," and how to "open a dialogue." A stream of viewer tweets across the bottom of the screen confirmed that the viewers were of the same mindset. There was also some talk of "Israel's occupation" and the need to boycott Israel's products in order to foster peace talks.

AJA also maintains a website to supplement its on-air overage. Recently, the website reported on a study that calculated the number of deaths from the Iraqi war to be over 500,000, dramatically higher than estimates from most other studies. The website also included a letter from an inmate and hunger-striker at Guantanamo, complaining of the force-feeding he has to endure to keep him alive. Poor guy!

So what is a news-watcher to do? When it comes to foreign news coverage, most of the important news involves Middle East matters, a subject where AJA is pretty biased. For domestic news, so far AJA's coverage is similar to the coverage of several other networks.

But beyond these questions, what is the point of Al Jazeera even coming to America? Why would the Emir of Qatar go through the hassle and expense? One theory could be that AJA is some sort of pan-Arab pride project. And it is true that most significant regions of the world have at least one major news network. Some have also speculated that AJA is just a vanity project on the part of the Emir of Qatar, which is possible.

One other theory, and it is speculative but worth pondering, is that AJA may be getting into the American mainstream, slowly getting accepted, so that if there is another 9-11, a war involving Israel, or some other mass terrorist event, AJA will be there to share its pro-Al Qaeda or anti-Israel side to American viewers. Kind of an "embedded news network," ready to propagandize at a moment's notice. Given Al Jazeera's past loyalties to Al Qaeda and positions against the US and Israel, it is certainly possible.

When Al Gore sold Current TV to Al Jazeera, he is reported to have said that Al Jazeera "gives a voice to those who are not typically heard," and "speaks truth to power." Actually, in the event of a war involving Israel or another large-scale terrorist attack against Americans, AJA will be a vehicle for arguing *against* speaking truth to terrorist powers. It may in fact be terrorized Americans.

October 18, 2013

"LIFE OF JULIA" UPDATE

Remember Julia? You know, the Obama campaign cartoon figure who was helped at every stage of her life by some government program that had been begun by President Obama but scheduled for destruction by the dastardly Mitt Romney? Most Americans wondered who Julia was and why they were being asked to pay for everything in her life.

Well, elections have consequences, and thanks to President Obama's re-election in 2012, Julia's support checks are still flowing, from *you,* dear reader, to Julia, after a brief pit-stop in Washington, DC.

Or are they? We thought we would check back with Julia and see how she is holding up in this period of government shutting down and implementing Obamacare.

At 3 years old, Julia tries to go to Head Start, which is closed because of the government shut-down. Julia's mother has to care for Julia during the day, so Julia's mother loses her job. President Obama told us that he supported Head Start, and that if Mitt Romney were elected, Head Start would close. Oh well. At least Julia's mother was able to get unemployment, some welfare benefits and an Obamaphone.

In her teens, Julia takes the SAT and begins applying to colleges. Julia's high school was part of the "Race To The Top" program, implemented by President Obama. She then qualifies for a Pell Grant and enters college to pursue a Flatulence Studies degree. In a coming of age weekend, Julia has an unplanned pregnancy but terminates the pregnancy, paid in full by Obamacare. Mitt Romney would have defunded all these options to pay for tax cuts for the rich.

In four years, Julia accumulates $105,000 in student loans. After graduation, she is shocked to learn that she must either work for the government to go back to college to defer her loan payments.

Julia goes to a nearby clinic to get a free Obamacare pap smear.

One day Julia goes to the Vietnam War Memorial to heckle the veterans who are crossing the "barrycades" to pay their respects and to get arrested as acts of civil disobedience. Julia gets caught up in the commotion and gets arrested with the others. She is thrown in a jail cell worse than the men from the protest. Thanks to the Emily Ledbetter Act, which was signed into law by President Obama, Julia is able to stand up for her rights and get a jail cell equally as nice as the male arrestees. Julia makes friends with some of her cell-mates, and they share Mitt Romney horror stories.

As a relief from the stress in her life, Julia goes on vacation to the Grand Canyon, only to find that it is closed due to the government shut-down. She decides to drive to Mt. Rushmore, which may be closed, but because it is outside she figures she can at least view the monument. Instead, orange cones keep her from pulling over to the side of the road or even slowing down to get a good view. She consoles herself by looking at Mt. Rushmore from her rear-view mirror while she drives away at 65 miles per hour.

Julia heard somewhere that the Liberty Bell is at least viewable through a window, so on her way back home she drives to Philadelphia to see it. When she gets there she notices that because of the government shut-down, the Park Service has covered up the window with black felt.

Julia starts a web-development company from home, and then receives a letter from her health insurance company. Like other small business owners, Julia is outraged to learn that her health insurance premiums will increase 120% in 2014.

A sister who has type 1 diabetes relates how she appeared at her hospital to get her monthly insulin supply and was told that her insurance was cancelled and that henceforth she would need to pay $1,000 per month out of pocket for the insulin. The sister persuades Julia to let her move in and sleep on Julia's couch until the sister can "figure something out" with her finances.

Julia's web development business slows to a trickle, and without any health insurance, she looks for a job. She has a stroke of good luck when she gets a job with the IRS, which is hiring new employees to enforce Obamacare on those Americans not exempt from it. These jobs would not have been available had the dastardly Mitt Romney won the election. Julia gets a so-called "platinum health insurance policy" along with President Obama, members of Congress, their staff members, and other federal employees. Yay!

Because of the government shutdown, Julia is issued a furlough notice, but Congress agrees to continue her paychecks. She spends her days in her cramped apartment, eating Fig Newtons and watching daytime TV, nagging her sister about her sister's non-existent job search. It becomes clear that her sister has stopped bathing and has given up on finding a job. This means that the sister is excluded from the unemployment rate, which of course is not reported because of the government shut-down.

Sadly, Julia contracts an extremely rare disease that would require millions of federal dollars to pay for operations and drugs to keep her alive. A local Independent Payment Advisory Board (recklessly dubbed by Sarah Palin as a "death panel") decides that Julia's life is not worth the federal money needed to prolong it, and that Julia has nothing left to contribute to society. Nothing. Julia is given a pill to end her life. Julia's sole heir is her sister, but after estate taxes and probate fees the sister inherits nothing besides Julia's pet cat Barack.

But things could be worse, a lot worse: at least birth control pills are free.

October 10, 2013

FIVE GAME-CHANGING QUESTIONS ON OBAMACARE

"What is the airspeed velocity of an unladen swallow?" is the question that tripped up the bridge-keeper in the 1975 movie *Monty Python and the Holy Grail,* resulting in the bridge-keeper's immediate death.

Well-thought out questions about Obamacare directed at President Obama would not result in the same fate, but politically-speaking, they could be just as much of a game-changer. Maybe this is why President Obama has allowed so few questions following his recent statements concerning Obamacare. This is an unpopular law that is being promoted with empty slogans and outright lies.

But tough questions must be asked. Here are five of my suggestions:

Question 1: "Why do you refer to Obamacare as a law that is already in place when your administration has been treating it as a malleable bill for three years?" There are many examples of administrative actions taken that contradict the wording of the Affordable Care Act, but here are a few: over 1200 Obamacare waivers have been granted since the law's passage, primarily[1] to labor unions. The administration has also abandoned[2] the CLASS Act part of Obamacare, and the administration has recently announced a delay[3] of two years for the employer mandate. None of these actions have any basis in the wording of the law as passed by Congress.

So why not make a few more changes to Obamacare, especially if they are supported by the general public? Republicans in Congress only seem to be taking their cue on the changeability of Obamacare from the Obama administration itself. It is pretty inconsistent to spend three years changing a law and then claim that because it is a law, with the president's signature, that the law cannot be changed. Of course it can be changed – President Obama has been changing it on the fly for three years!

Question 2: "Why is it so wrong to bargain with congressional Republicans on a continuing resolution that changes some or all of

Obamacare when you have essentially been bargaining with your supporters on Obamacare since it passed three years ago?" This is the problem with granting waivers and exemptions from the law that is binding on the general public. Apparently it is fine to bargain with supporters of the administration – and that is what it is, an implicit bargain for continued political support — but not OK to bargain with Republicans.

I will answer my own question here, which is that the Republicans cannot threaten to withdraw political support for President Obama, because Republicans are the loyal opposition. But the question should be asked anyway. It exposes the cynicism at work here.

Question 3: "When you were a senator in 2006 and a Republican president requested that Congress raise the debt ceiling, you spoke[4] on the Senate floor that such a request showed a 'lack of leadership' and you voted against the increase. Now your aid compared[5] congressional Republicans who oppose raising the debt limit to terrorists and arsonists. Do you stand by that characterization?"

Let's face it: President Obama is asking senators and representatives to vote "yes" on something. And instead of meeting with these people and making the case for a higher debt limit, he calls them names and threatens them with blame for a "no" vote or not acting at all. Not only is this childish, but it is also unrealistic. Calling people names is not a good way to get them to do what you want them to do.

Question 4: "Why not equalize the applicability of Obamacare to everyone, including yourself, the entire executive branch, Congress, their staffs and families?" This different treatment may be the most annoying part of Obamacare.

The public has watched with disgust the shenanigans in Washington, where healthcare policies for the political class and federal workers are exempt from the healthcare laws that apply to the rest of us. Even the IRS agents who are in charge of enforcing Obamacare on the rest of us do not want to be subject[6] to it.

Question 5: "How could you have been so wrong in promising[7] a $2,500 annual drop in healthcare premiums for a typical family of four under Obamacare?" President Obama mentioned this figure many times throughout his 2008 campaign, and in the months preceding the passage of the law. President Obama may claim that he was making a good faith projection, but the reality is that when he repeatedly made this promise he was way off. Instead of going down, most[8] family's healthcare costs are going up. Way[9] up. Healthcare premiums may well replace the mortgage, food and car payments as a typical American family's top monthly expense.

So, after all these and other questions, a typical Obamacare supporter might complain of ineffective messaging – they usually do. But in this case the Obama administration has already pledged[10] $67 million to over 100 organizations to help "navigate" consumers through their health insurance options under Obamacare. Celebrities[11] have signed up to help promote Obamacare. Now NBC News has decided[12] to spend a whole week extolling the virtues of Obamacare.

Maybe NBC News can persuade me that the letter I received last week telling me of a 71% premium increase, for a worse health insurance policy, was not in fact true. Or maybe NBC News can tell thousands of employees whose hours were dropped to part-time because of Obamacare, that their demotions were for the best. Obamacare is a disaster and anyone trying to sugarcoat it or even explain it has a tough road to hoe.

Reality is difficult to hide.

October 2, 2013

OBAMACARE ON THE BALCONY

Recall from history that one of the Eastern Block's longest-serving and brutal dictators, Romanian President Nicolae Ceausescu, fell from power after a single speech[1] in front of his subjects. On December 21, 1989, President Ceausescu spoke from a balcony in Bucharest to a group of about 80,000 Romanians, during which opposition to Ceausescu's rule galvanized. A few people in the crowd began booing and jeering, totally unheard-of during Ceausescu's rule. The booing spread, then the crowd began chanting opposition slogans, and eventually charged the presidential building en masse.

The popular opposition galvanized despite unanimous support of the military and state-run media. Within three days of the speech, Ceausescu and his wife had been deposed and executed, and Romania became a newly-freed, former communist country. It was a staggeringly-swift turn of events. And it all began and gathered momentum during a single speech, now known as the Ceausescu Balcony Speech.

Metaphorically, Obamacare has just now walked onto the balcony and has begun to speak to its subjects, us Americans, who will be held captive by its new regime of laws, regulations and distortions. Despite widespread positive coverage from the mainstream media, liberal celebrities,[2] and even politicians who accuse opponents of racism,[3] doubts are coalescing. Popular support has never[4] been that strong, and people are only now coming face to face with the real problems of Obamacare, and they don't like it.

The media is starting to cover horror stories of healthcare premiums doubling and tripling, and thousands of workers getting laid off or converted to working less than 30 hours a week. Doctors are retiring[5] to avoid having to deal with it. Retired workers are losing[6] their insurance and told to go to the Obamacare exchanges for coverage. Health insurance companies are exiting[7] states. A new problem has also emerged: Americans are being told of a newly-discovered Obamacare "family glitch[8]," in which many workers will be able to keep their healthcare coverage but their spouses and children will be dropped.

The hundreds of millions of dollars spent[9] by the Obama administration to provide paid "navigators" to "get the word out," and help from liberal celebrities can only sugar-coat things so long. Within the next few weeks Americans will receive notices in the mail describing the true, terrible details of changes to their healthcare coverage.

A few lucky Americans, like some unions and members of Congress and their staffs, will be exempt from Obamacare. Agents at the IRS, who will enforce Obamacare on the rest of us, are urging[10] Congress to vote against a proposal[11] that will place them in the same healthcare boat as the rest of us. Seems like the healthcare that is good enough for the rest of us is not good enough or the IRS!

And whatever happened to President Obama's promises? Remember when he told[12] us "if you like your doctor or healthcare plan, you can keep it"? The White House doesn't want us to remember those comments. President Obama also probably wants us to forget when he said[13] that under Obamacare a typical family's healthcare premium will decrease by $2,500. The reality[14] is that for most Americans, their health insurance premiums will rise[15] dramatically, and they may not be able to keep their current insurance coverage at all.

The dynamics in Congress are just beginning to change. A few days ago the House of Representatives passed a continuing resolution to fund the government *except* for Obamacare. Even some Democrat representatives voted for it. Only a few weeks earlier, this would have been unthinkable.

While the Democratically-controlled Senate is expected to pass a resolution that will fund Obamacare, Democratic Senate Leader Harry Reid is trying his best to pass the resolution in such a way that vulnerable Democrat Senators up or re-election in 2014 do not need to publicly show their support for Obamacare. Voters back home in Alaska, Arkansas or North Carolina, for example, might not approve of their senators voting to keep Obamacare in place.

Texas Senator Ted Cruz's filibuster did not win a vote on defunding Obamacare, but he was at least successful in presenting to the general public some of the arguments against Obamacare that are usually ignored by the mainstream press, and Democrats in general are on the defense.

Yes, the bottom is falling out of Obamacare support, and like the end of Nicolae Ceausescu, it could be very quick.

September 27, 2013

2013: THE YEAR PRIVACY DIED

One civil rights attorney recently called[1] the NSA phone-gathering activities "beyond Orwellian."

If privacy were a patient, you could say that in 2013, this sick patient has finally died. Under President Obama, the federal government has seized phone and credit card records[2] and emails[3], catalogued[4] images of the front and back of mailed letters, gathered information[5] from Internet[6] searches, given IRS records to political opponents[7], and soon: medical records gathered, managed and interpreted by the helpful and omniscient IRS.

It has gotten so bad, that someday we may see the headline: "government has placed listening devices in everyone's bedroom," and such a headline would not be from *The Onion.*

Not bad for a president who only five years ago proclaimed[8] "as for our common defense, we reject as false the choice between our security and our ideals."

But wait – I thought the War on Terror was over[9], and we won it.

As Mark Steyn recently pointed out[10] in National Review Online, it is not as if all this snooping is geared towards fighting terrorism. Just look at the public statements Maj. Hassan made in public for all to see before his jihadist rampage at Ft. Hood, or the suspended immigration controls that allowed free entry and departure for the Tsarnaev brothers before their terrorist attack on the Boston Marathon.

The federal government appears to be accumulating information on citizens for reasons that have nothing to do with fighting terrorism. Sometimes the reason is to harass political opponents, like what happened to True The Vote[11], and prominent Romney donor Frank Vandersloot[12], or the information given to the groups ProPublica[13] and the Human Rights Campaign[14] on their political opponents. But for other citizens, whatever the reason, it is impossible to imagine the sum total of information the government over the past few years has amassed on all of us, to be used whenever the government deems necessary.

One NSA whistleblower, William Binney, has said[15] that everyone in the United States is under "virtual surveillance" and the NSA has dossiers[16] on nearly every United States citizen.

What if you have nothing to hide, that you have done nothing wrong, as Senator Lindsey Graham recently suggested[17] regarding his own Verizon account? This is a common rebuttal to complaints of loss of privacy. According to the former NSA analyst Binney[18], "the problem is if [the citizen] thinks they're not doing anything that is wrong, they don't get to define that, the central government does. The central government defines what is right and wrong and whether or not they target you."

So what if you want to live your life in private? What if you say "I just won't mail any letters or go online, use a phone, make any credit card transactions, make any campaign contributions, participate in politics, and just mind my own business on my own land"? Some people actually think by living without the activities government routinely snoops on, they can "escape" the surveillance and live a life of complete privacy, being "left alone." Well, think again: government use of domestic drones[19] for spying on American citizens is being considered by county and local governments, including law-enforcement agencies.[20]

In addition, hiding in plain sight is the omnipresent, watchful eyes of Google Earth[21], which will give anyone with a computer a snap-shot of your land. Some local governments have already used Google Earth to detect zoning and permit violations.[22]

It is not so farfetched to envision a day when we could see a government agent approaching you on your land and saying, "we noticed from satellite images of your land that you were planting some vegetables that are high in carbohydrates. This will cause more expenses, longer term, for the government under the Affordable Care Act."

Same for smoking cigarettes, sunbathing, barbecuing red meat, or any other activity you think you are engaging in in private on your own land. The government is now a partner in your everyday activities, and it feels it has a right to know … everything.

There really is no escape – no possibility of just being "left alone." *1984* indeed.

June 10, 2013

THE IRS AUDITED OUR ADOPTION EXPENSES TWICE

"This feels like the movie *Groundhog Day*," I told our CPA when we were notified by the IRS that our family's adoption tax expenses were being audited for a second time. And there was not anything new that

the IRS wanted to look at; just the same audit of the same expenses. All for a second time.

In 2009, my wife and I adopted our daughter Rachel from India, and immediately petitioned the local California court, which then officially declared my wife and me to be Rachel's adoptive

Our daughter Rachel, after we brought her home from India.

parents. We gave the local Social Security office all of our paperwork, but it delayed giving our daughter a social security number. A few months later, we filed our 2009 returns anyway, and the IRS audited our adoption expenses. After much shuffling of papers, the IRS notified us that our adoption tax credit would not be allowed for 2009, but could be used for 2010. The IRS even suggested a specific dollar amount.

When we filed our 2010 returns, we claimed the exact amount for the adoption tax credit that the IRS had suggested. The IRS audited our adoption expenses anyway!

This time I re-sent to the IRS not only all of our adoption expenses – the *exact* same expenses sent in the previous audit – but I added a copy of the IRS letter from the previous audit. The IRS accepted our adoption expenses and allowed the tax credit. No changes were made to our 2010 tax returns.

This saga was all in the back of my mind when I heard that the IRS was harassing various conservative groups that were applying for non-profit status. There were also reports of IRS audits expanding beyond the group itself, auditing the personal and business returns of the person filing for tax-exempt status on behalf of the conservative group. In one case,[1] an application for non-profit status by the group "True The Vote," resulted in not only hundreds of questions from the IRS, but an over two-year wait on the application. The IRS then audited the personal and business returns of the head of True The Vote, and ATF, OSHA and a state version of the EPA all piled on and inspected the family's business for good measure.

My ears really perked up when I heard that a non-profit application by a pro-life group[2] in Iowa was delayed by IRS demands that the group pledge not to protest outside Planned Parenthood clinics. The group was also asked to explain how their prayer meetings were scientifically or medically educational. IRS harassment of other pro-life groups has also been documented.[3]

Adoptive families have also been targeted. A recent IRS Taxpayer Advocate Report[4] revealed that 90% of all families claiming the adoption tax credit experienced an IRS audit of some sort, so our family is definitely not alone. I was not able to find out how many adoptive families experienced *two* successive audits, as was our family.

To be fair, because a tax credit, as opposed to a tax deduction, results in an immediate transfer of money from the federal government to the taxpayer, it would make sense that the IRS would more closely scrutinize a taxpayer filing for a tax credit. But in the case of adoptive parents, a very small amount of the credit in prior years has been disallowed (only 1.5% in 2011, for example[5]). Definitely a waste of time for both the IRS and the taxpayer.

On the other hand, it could be that standard tax enforcement was not the real reason for all these adoptive tax credit audits. Of all the adoptive parents I have met, most of them appear to have pro-life views. And that would make sense: part of the rally cry against abortion is for a pregnant woman to bring the baby to term, give birth to the baby and give the baby to a family eager to adopt. The more people like us adopt, the more credible that argument becomes, and the fewer children are aborted and adopted instead.

And those are the real losers in this part of the IRS scandal: the children. While the link to abortions is more theoretical, the link to adoptions is real and tangible. Fewer families will adopt now that the word is getting around that an adoption will likely trigger an IRS audit.

I have personally encouraged countless families to adopt a child like we did, whether the adoption is domestic or international. "There are millions of amazing children in need of a loving family," I tell them. I also advise them of the legal hoops and inches of paperwork that our family had to wade through, and the expenses involved.

The feedback is usually positive, until the family asks me about taxes. "There is a tax credit, so you will get back much of your adoption expenses. But keep track of all of your expenses, because you may be audited. Maybe even twice, like we were."

"Twice?!" After a pause, it usually goes downhill from there.

Thanks to the harassment the IRS has given adoptive parents, fewer parents are willing to go through with an adoption. Why would anyone open themselves up to an IRS audit? Shame on whomever is behind this extra, pointless auditing of adoptive families!

As for myself, I am still waiting for a *third* audit of our adoption tax credit. Our CPA is skeptical, but you never know. I didn't think we would have a second audit, but that happened. Bill Murray's character in *Groundhog Day* relived the same day more than twice, you know.

May 27, 2013

IRS SCANDAL FOLLOWS OLD OBAMA ILLINOIS PATTERN

Boy, it sure makes a primary or election contest easier when your opponent pulls out, don't you think? Barack Obama has been managing to do that since he won the Democratic nomination for state senator in Illinois in 1996, and it helps explain the IRS harassment of conservatives and Tea Party groups since 2010. Whereas once Obama targeted candidates to get them to pull out, from 2010 onward, he had the IRS and possibly other federal agencies target groups that represented a set of ideas, hoping to get those ideas to withdraw from the race. The pattern has been the same: get the opposition to leave.

In 1996, as he faced an incumbent state senator and two other challengers for the Democratic nomination for state senator in a heavily-Democratic district in Chicago, then-candidate Barack Obama directed his campaign staff to challenge the candidacy petitions of his opponents. By disqualifying signatures one by one, as one local columnist put[1] it, Obama "made sure voters had but one choice."

Then, in 2004, not only in the Democratic nomination for United States Senator from Illinois, but in the general election, Team Obama perfected the art of getting confidential documents on Obama's opponents unsealed.

First, Obama's primary opponent had to try and explain to the voters the contents of recently-unsealed divorce records, which included allegations[2] of spousal violence. The former front-runner finished third, far behind the winner, Barack Obama. Then, in the 2004 general election, Republican nominee Jack Ryan ended[3] his race for the Senate after child custody records were unsealed, revealing allegations of wild forays at sex clubs with his actress wife, Jeri Ryan.

Is it any wonder that once President Obama's signature accomplishment, Obamacare, came under scathing criticism from Tea Party groups in 2010, that the IRS suddenly began to give extra scrutiny, and in many cases deny non-profit status to groups with "tea party" or "patriot" in their name? The extra IRS scrutiny and audits were blamed[4] on a few "rogue" IRS agents in Cincinnati, but the scandal is big enough to be blamed for the harassment of over 500 conservative groups.[5] Reportedly, 63% of all Tea Party-related groups that applied for non-profit status since 2010 eventually withdrew[6] their applications, obviously limiting donations to these groups, and their ability to promote conservative ideas. Government harassment works.

With the non-profit voter integrity group "True The Vote," a delayed application for non-profit status was only the beginning. In the two years since the group applied for non-profit status, the founder and her family's business became targets[7] of other government agencies, including the FBI, the ATF, and OSHA.

And despite denials to the contrary, evidence suggests direction from the top of the executive branch. An anonymous IRS official employee from the Cincinnati office confirmed[8] that orders of singling out organizations based on political belief is something that would only "come from the top."

Old Chicago habits die hard, and during the 2012 campaign, the Obama campaign website posted[9] the names of 15 prominent donors to Mitt Romney's campaign, sending the message far and wide to investigate these people, possibly unsealing any confidential files, at the least dissuading other possible Romney supporters from donating to the campaign.

Apparently the IRS and the Labor Department took the bait and audited one of the listed Romney donors, Frank VanderSloot.[10] Within weeks of being listed on the Obama website, IRS agents audited Vander-Sloot's personal and business tax returns, and the Labor Department even investigated VanderSloot's business. VanderSloot says[11] he is not the only person on that list to be audited.

How extensive is this scandal? As far as we know today, the IRS took the lead in harassing conservatives and Tea Party groups, occasionally joined by the Department of Justice, OSHA, the ATF, and the Labor Department. If you were to add some news of spying on reporters – that was announced[12] Monday — then it all becomes reminiscent of the following exchange[13] from the 1976 movie *All the President's Men:*

Bob Woodward: Segretti told me and Bernstein that...

Deep Throat: [interrupting] Don't concentrate on Segretti. You'll miss the overall.

Bob Woodward: The letter that destroyed the Muskey candidacy... did that come from inside the White House?

Deep Throat: You're missing the overall.

Bob Woodward: What overall?

Deep Throat: The people behind all of this were frightened of Muskey and that's what got him destroyed. They wanted to run against McGovern. Look who they're running against. They bugged offices, they followed people, falsified press leaks, passed fake letters... they canceled Democratic campaign rallies, they investigated Democratic private lives, they planted spies, they stole documents... and now don't tell me that all of this was the work of one Donald Segretti.

Substitute the phrase "a few rogue IRS officers from Cincinnati" for Donald Segretti, and a few other updates, and this exchange gives a glimpse at how big and how far this scandal may go. But one thing is for sure: all of these actions are part of an old Obama pattern since his days in Illinois of doing whatever it takes to get one's opponents, be they candidates or groups, to withdraw from the competition of ideas.

May 23, 2013

THE CLINTON SCANDAL PLAYBOOK AND BENGHAZI

The punditocracy is pulling out its collective hair, wanting to know why there have apparently been multiple layers of cover-ups in the evolving Benghazi story. An early scandal from the Clinton administration, the so-called "Travelgate" scandal," may be instructive.

Recall that in the 1993 firings of employees at the White House Travel Office, a determination[1] was made early on by the new president Bill Clinton and then-First Lady Hillary Clinton, that the Travel Office workers, who served at the pleasure of the president, could be fired and that the Travel Office business, and the commissions that came with it, given[2] to a cousin of President Clinton's, Catherine Cornelius, who had a travel agency of her own.

But simply handing over government business to a relative would have been politically embarrassing, so the Clintons concocted a story whereby the Travel Office was rife with corruption and the workers there needed to be fired[3]. An audit[4] was conducted on Travel Office finances, and while the record-keeping at the office was found to have been pretty inadequate, there was no smoking gun of corruption or embezzlement. No matter. The FBI was pressured[5] to make arrests, and the local US Attorney was charged with prosecuting the employees for corruption.

White House denials of any scheme, and leaks by those involved, led to a firestorm of media criticism. Most of the Travel Office employees were eventually given other government jobs or retired. A prosecution for corruption of the head of the Travel Office, Billy Dale, ended in an acquittal[6]. Clinton's cousin was removed as new head of the Travel Office. A later report written by Independent Counsel Robert Ray concluded[7] that, while she did not make any knowingly-false statements under oath, First Lady Hillary Clinton had made a number of inaccurate statements concerning the firings and her role in them.

In retrospect, it is kind of funny that the Clintons would ever complain about corruption from anyone. Pot, meet Kettle. That kind of thing.

But the point is that the initial decision to replace government employees with the president's cousin, so that she could make commissions from arranging White House travel, was a bad decision. Everything following that decision, the firings, the made-up charges of corruption, the federal prosecution, and the denials from the Clintons that later proven to be untrue, were an effort to distract people from the initial bad decision.

Fast forward to the fall of 2012, when the State Department repeatedly denied[8] requests by officials at the American consulate in Benghazi for more security. This was the initial bad decision from which flowed all other obfuscations.

Who would make such a bad decision? In his recent congressional testimony, consulate security officer Eric Nordstrom blamed Secretary of State Hillary Clinton, pointing to a memo[9] signed by Secretary Clinton, denying additional security.

What would lead Clinton to make such a bad decision? Remember that in the summer of 2008, when her presidential campaign had ended and the Russians invaded South Ossetia, Hillary Clinton was formulating what would later be her "reset" policy towards Russia. Such a policy assumed that whatever frostiness existed between the United States and Russia had been caused by American belligerence. If only the American side would initiate a fresh "reset," then the Russians would be more accommodative to United States interests, like our policies concerning Iran's nukes.

It may be difficult to grasp, but liberals, Hillary Clinton included, actually believe that bullies like Russia, can be appeased by weakness of others, hence the "reset" policy towards Russia, and the later denial of more security for the consulate at Benghazi. Clinton probably thought that a strong American military presence at the Benghazi consulate would be provocative.

Obviously this was a bad decision. On September 11, 2012, the American consulate was attacked and overrun by terrorists in a planned, coordinated attack. While under attack, officials at the consulate called for help, which could have made it from Italy in time to help. But if provided, this military help would have highlighted the earlier, bad decision to keep security there weak, so the request for military help during the attack was denied.

When the smoke had cleared, an American ambassador and three other Americans were dead. Anything besides a narrative that this attack was a spontaneous uprising because of an anti-Muslim YouTube video would have led people to question the initial, bad decision by the State Department to keep consulate security weak to begin with. The following week, UN Representative Susan Rice appeared[10] on five television news shows to reiterate the story that the deaths were caused by a spontaneous uprising related to the video. A few days later, President Obama stated[11] at a forum hosted by Univision, and again later at the United Nations[12], that the Benghazi attacks were provoked by the video.

President Obama and Secretary Clinton even filmed their own public service announcement[13], played in Pakistan, apologizing for a private American production of the anti-Muslim video and calling for calm. This PSA later became a self-fulfilling prophecy[14], when its reference to an anti-Muslim video caused riots in Pakistan that led to the deaths of 18, and scores of injured Pakistanis.

All these actions were taken to distract people from the initial, bad decision made by Secretary Clinton to keep consulate security in

Benghazi weak. Apparently, when defending a bad decision by Hillary Clinton, anything goes. The standard operating procedure was apparent as far back as 1993.

May 13, 2013

MONTY PYTHON AND THE SEQUESTER

A friend of mine recently pointed out that there is such a thing as a Monty Python YouTube channel, apparently begun by the Monty Python members because they were tired of "getting ripped off" by unauthorized postings of their movie and TV shows. Where have I been on this? I love Monty Python, and I had no idea. The channel[1] was begun in 2008, and so far has over a quarter million subscribers.

Thanks to the Monty Python YouTube channel, the viewer can watch all the classic, hilarious Python scenes from their movies and TV shows. Comedy nirvana, with the only price being the viewing of a brief antacid commercial.

One of my favorite Monty Python movies excerpted on this You-Tube channel is the *Life of Brian,* which contains a stoning scene[2] that is actually very instructive for today's Republican party. In fact, a comment made by the person about to be stoned should be front and center in the mind of every Republican who ever proposes cuts in government spending. Sounds a little far-fetched, but let me explain.

The scene starts like this: in Jerusalem, 33 AD, a man is brought in front of a crowd holding stones, and a magistrate who reads from a scroll the defendant's name and the conviction of blasphemy, and repeats the sentence of death by stoning. The magistrate yells out the charge of "blasphemer," as the man was caught saying the name of Jehovah, and angrily points at the defendant. The defendant explains that at the blasphemy in question he was merely complimenting his wife's cooking, saying it was "good enough for Jehovah."

The crowd gasps, ready to start the stoning, and the magistrate yells "he said it again!" The prisoner says "what, Jehovah?" The magistrate shouts "hey, you're only making it worse for yourself!"

To which the man says "how can it get any worse?" Then he begins dancing and crying out "Jehovah! Jehovah!" to the outraged crowd.

But you can't really blame the guy. If ever he had any inclination to say the name "Jehovah" out loud, he might as well say it now, as many times as he wants. He is about to get stoned to death for saying that name anyway. At this point he really has nothing to lose, and it certainly won't get worse than getting stoned to death.

Fast forward to the summer of 2011, in Washington DC, when President Obama proposes, and the Republican House agrees to a series of "sequester cuts," as a way to delay definitive action on raising the debt limit that was about to be exceeded. The deadline eventually agreed to: March 1, 2013, conveniently after the 2012 elections, which would lead to automatic budget cuts unless a deal is agreed to before then. If no other agreement were made, the federal government would spend $85 billion less this fiscal year than originally planned, followed by $1.2 trillion cuts in increased spending over the next ten years, half from defense spending and half from domestic programs. Very few people thought that the sequester date would come and go without a new debt limit deal.

Well, it did. In the days shortly before the cuts in spending went into effect, polls[3] showed that most Americans blamed Republicans for the sequester. Almost immediately after the cuts went into effect, White House tours were cancelled[4], "due to staffing reductions resulting from sequestration." Republicans got the blame[5].

The sequestration was listed as the reason to cut spending in food inspections, Head Start[6], Meals On Wheels[7], schools[8] in military communities, and, most recently, the staffing of flight controllers[9], causing flight delays all over the country.

In all the sequester cuts, even though the administration made sure the public felt the pain of any spending cuts, Republicans were still blamed[10]. Yet the cuts amounted to a total[11] of 2.5% of total federal spending. Granted, with current annual deficits[12] of over $1 trillion, spending cuts are needed, or, in this case, a reduction in the growth of spending. But if this is the way to cut bloated government spending, it is small potatoes indeed, despite so much blame being thrown around. Kind of like the man sentenced to be stoned to death for blasphemy, all because he said his wife's cooking was "good enough for Jehovah."

And this is how the man about to be stoned in the Monty Python movie so closely resembles today's Republicans. For the minor misdeed of cutting spending a mere 2.5%, Republicans are sentenced to be stoned. No doubt there are some Republicans in Congress who would like to make deeper cuts – this year's federal deficit is still projected[13] to be $900 billion, you know – but others in the GOP are probably counseling them "not to make things politically worse."

But truly, how can things be any worse for Republicans? Republicans need to kick up their feet and sing "Jehovah! Jehovah!" and propose even steeper spending cuts. They are getting the blame anyway, so why not make the cuts that really need to be made?

So that is the plan, Republicans. Make the cuts that need to be made to get this budget in balance, and take your PR stoning like a man. After the blame you have gotten for these current minuscule cuts, you really have nothing more to lose. And the country will be much better off as a result.

May 6, 2013

PANIC IN DETROIT

Michigan Governor Rick Snyder has decided to appoint an emergency manager for the city of Detroit, taking control of the city's operations and putting the city through a sort of prolonged bankruptcy, the largest-ever effective bankruptcy of any American city. When I first heard the news, being a David Bowie fan who listens to talk radio, I looked forward to the talk-show bumper music of Bowie's 1973 song, "Panic In Detroit.[1]"

As part of his hit 1973 album, *Aladdin Sane,* David Bowie produced this incredible song with strange lyrics that may or may not have referred to the Detroit riots of 1967. It had some nice, raw guitar riffs and a steady drumbeat, punctuated by some strangely-accenting vocals. A truly great song! Tailor-made for this story!

But it was not to be. Talk radio has mostly ignored the subject of Detroit's bankruptcy, along with the obvious and great David Bowie bumper music that would go with it.

As for Detroit, it has been a basket case for many years. A few years ago I went to a legal conference there, and many things about Detroit didn't sit well with me, starting with the fact that from Detroit, you can walk *south* across a bridge, and enter Canada. But how bad can a city that birthed the 1959 Cadillac Eldorado, or the 1967 Ford Mustang be? During the breaks in the conference, I set to find out.

Across the city, it appeared to me as if Detroit had at one time been a very vibrant city, but had since seen a few decades of decline. The parts of the city where you don't feel safe encircle the city downtown, which was sprinkled with new government buildings. Looking at the people of Detroit, it seemed as if anyone who had any financial or business ambition was doing their best to leave.

Even a lunch at a nearby White Castle[2] restaurant offered no relief (you people in the eastern U.S. have no idea how lucky you are to have White Castle restaurants). It had the kind of plexi-glass protecting the people who worked there, like what you would see in a bank. I almost asked "how many times have you guys been held up?" But the answer was obvious: enough.

Other parts of the city were just as disappointing. A third[3] of the residential lots in Detroit are vacant or abandoned. Things have gotten so bad that the city has decided to tear down abandoned houses, but the backlog[4], 80,000 abandoned structures, is huge. Foreigners come to Detroit specifically to tour[5] abandoned houses and buildings – kind of a cynical tourist attraction. I remember driving by an abandoned house with an "auction" sign in front, and wondering if the auction was how high the owner would pay someone to take the house off the owner's hands.

After a few more failed attempts at enjoying myself in Detroit, I did what I normally do when I get desperate to enjoy a new city: I went to the "rich" part of town to hang out and people-watch. In the case of Detroit, the rich part of town in called Grosse Pointe, where rich people like Michael Moore have their mansions. And I saw something amazing: beautiful, huge, lakefront mansions, with 2+ acre front yards, going for $200,000! Yes, there is something seriously wrong with Detroit.

The great thing about successes or failures of any state or city in our country is that people can see what policies are being implemented and learn accordingly. Texas, for example, has no state income tax and a manageable regulatory environment, and the result is a strong economy with almost full employment. On the other hand, my state of California has just raised its taxes to be the highest in the country, and with the stifling regulatory burden, most everyone with any money is considering their ability to move their families and businesses out of state. California could very well be the next Detroit.

True, the main industry of Detroit, the American car industry, has had quite a decline, so the population of Detroit has been cut in half since its peak in the 1950's. Yet the city government and the public sector unions spend like the good times are still here. Detroit has a massive total debt[6] of $14 billion, including a recent $237 million deficit[7] just for last year. And the city has less than 1 million residents!

A couple years ago the city laid off[8] about 9% of its workforce, which was a good start. But pockets of union excesses still exist. A recent survey[9] found that even after a recent pay cut, teachers in Detroit are paid higher than their counterparts in richer cities like New York and San Francisco. A local columnist[10] discovered so much waste in Detroit's water treatment services that he called it "intolerable." One local reporter even discovered[11] that Detroit has on its payroll a horse-shoer, and while the city of Detroit has been dealing with horse *excrement* in its finances for many years, it hasn't had an actual horse that has needed shoeing in several decades.

At the same time, the national news on Detroit's effective bank-ruptcy seems to treat it all as if it is just one of those things; another sad chapter in the history of Detroit. And that is the real panic of Detroit: the fact that the media coverage on this development is so muted that the rest of the country will not be able to learn from it. Maybe that is the point. The mainstream, left-leaning press doesn't want us all to see where liberal policies inevitably conclude.

At least my trip to Detroit wasn't a total loss. The mandatory legal education conference was about as fascinating as always, but I got a real lesson in how dire things can get in a once-great city, now ruined by government mismanagement. And we call all still enjoy the David Bowie song "Panic in Detroit," even without any reference to the city's recent troubles. The song features[12] Mick Ronson on the lead guitar, you know.

March 4, 2013

PRESIDENT BUCHANAN REDUX

Today is President's Day, which obligates writers of all stripes to reflect on the men who have held that office. Writers on the left, when they acknowledge his mortality at all, compare President Obama to the great presidents in our nation's history. The more clear-headed among us, some call us "conservative," feel the obligation to point out the shortcomings of President Obama, charitably saying he is the worst by far of all of our nation's presidents.

Pretty standard and predictable. The late Chet Atkins had it right, when he said "once you become predictable, no one's interested anymore." Maybe that explains Atkins' totally unpredictable sideburns.

So just about every columnist on the right or left has his implicit marching orders for today, which are utterly predictable. Well, here is something unpredictable: have you ever read anything comparing President Obama to President James Buchanan, president from 1857 to 1861? No? Well, stay tuned, dear reader.

History judges presidents by, among other qualities, how much effort and success the president has at tackling chronic problems facing the country. It is for that reason that American historians rate the handful of presidents who preceded the Civil War as among the worst presidents in our country's history.

Take President James Buchanan, the "bachelor president," who served from 1857 to 1861. President Buchanan was so unhelpful to the chronic problems of states' rights versus the abolition of slavery, and the impending war among the states, that he did not even brief the incoming president-elect, Abraham Lincoln, on the status of the secessionist movement or the strength and details of Union forces.

Immediately following his swearing in as president, Lincoln had to start from scratch, researching the forces at his disposal, educating himself on military strategy and updating himself with the most recent secessionist developments among the southern states. In a short amount of time it became incumbent on Lincoln to develop a strategy to end the Civil War as soon as possible and re-unify the country.

Because he had to do the politically heavy lifting involved in ending slavery and keeping the country united, Abraham Lincoln is rated among the top presidents in United States history. And while he might have had a great time as a bachelor in the White House, James Buchanan is rated among the worst presidents. He was no help at all in solving the serious problems right at our country's doorstep.

I would argue that Barack Obama will be rated among the worst presidents in our country's history, very close to the rating of James Buchanan. My reason: deficit spending, and President Obama's demagoguing of any meaningful attempt at a course correction. These problems doom the country, possibly in an existential way. The culmination of these very real problems will probably be very ugly, either a huge inflation or Depression 2.0, if we are lucky.

Just a few years ago, President George W. Bush presided over an increase in our total debt[1] from $6 trillion to $10 trillion. During that time, the annual interest payment on our cumulative debt went from $206 billion to $252 billion every year. That was bad enough.

But under President Obama, what was once unthinkable, a trillion-dollar-plus annual deficit, has occurred in not one year but in *every* successive year of his presidency. The Obama overspending has gotten so bad that interest[2] on our debt now gobbles up 7% of our country's annual spending every year. Predictably, demand for our government bonds has dried up to the point that the biggest buyer of our debt is our own Federal Reserve, dollar bill printer extraordinaire.

This overspending can last only so long before compounded interest starts to take up a higher and higher percent of current spending. As *US News* recently put it, cumulative net interest[3] on government debt "is expected to spiral ever higher in coming years."

With an individual who spends too much, at some point almost all of his or her money goes to paying interest on past debts, without any effect at all on the principle owed. The only hope such an individual has of avoiding bankruptcy is to stop his irresponsible overspending and suddenly become extremely *responsible,* that is, under-spending and paying not only the current interest due but part of the principle owed.

This is very unlikely with the irresponsible bankrupt-bound individual, and it is also unlikely with the United States under President Obama.

Like ships passing in the night, conservatives and Obama-supporters have nothing in common when this issue comes up. The typical debate on the subject goes something like this: the conservative says "we need to do something to turn around our over-spending before it is too late." To which the Obama supporter answers "the rich don't pay their fair share of taxes," sometimes including an accusation of racism for good measure.

See, the problem with putting this off on another president who will need to do the heavy lifting of getting us out of this debt spiral, is that more and more overspending doesn't just continue a straight line of more debt. Picture a chart with the progression of time along the bottom, and the y-axis being the total debt owed by the United States. With each new year's deficits adding to the interest compounding on all of our country's past deficits, the line of total debt changes direction, and at some point the line will increase its slope, going straight up. This is called "going exponential." How it ends is anyone's guess, put it is sure to be ugly. And President Obama seems oblivious to this dire problem on our country's doorstep.

So there you have it: President Obama is so bad, he is like another President Buchanan.

Happy President's Day.

February 18, 2013

OBAMA'S POLITICAL CAPITAL

President Obama blows through his own political capital just as fast as he blows through America's financial capital. Neither case of over-spending is sustainable, and we will just have to wait to see which spending spree is forced to end first.

But this further confirms my suspicion that President Obama's brains are the most over-rated to occupy the Oval Office in generations. Take his recent nominations, which are a mess.

Last week's Senate hearings on Senator Hagel's confirmation as defense secretary were a disaster. Senator McCain pressed[1] Senator Hagel to confirm or deny Hagel's earlier statement that the Surge in Iraq was "the greatest foreign policy blunder since the Vietnam War." Senator Ted Cruz pointed out[2] that Senator Hegal, during an interview with the Al Jazeera English network in 2009 had agreed with a questioner who said that the United States appeared and acted like the world's bully. As Paul Mirengoff at the Powerline Blog wrote[3], "if he were a Broadway play, Hagel would close after one performance."

There were also a number of past anti-Semitic, or at least anti-Israel statements about which Senator Hagel was questioned. About the only thing about the hearing that was reassuring to those who take national defense seriously was that Hagel bumbled so much he sounded like he may have dementia. Let's face it, a defense secretary who suffers from dementia may not be as bad as an anti-American defense secretary who is purposefully soft on defense and unconcerned about looming problems with Iran's nuclear program.

Senator Lindsey Graham has threatened a hold on the Hagel nomination, and he should. Not only is a defense secretary an important policy position, but as has been pointed out by Republican critics that in any given foreign crisis, the defense secretary will be one of the few advisors in the room, advising the president.

Next up: a nomination battle for a Treasury secretary nominee, Jacob Lew, who has never worked in a bank except as an attorney for Citibank, and has held many different government jobs, most recently

President Obama's chief of staff. Definitely a financial industry light-weight. Lew has also been accused[4] of misleading the public on deficits. About the only thing that stands out about Jacob Lew as Treasury secretary is the fact that his signature[5] — which will appear on all of our currency – looks like a bunch of circles. Oddly enough, it doesn't appear as if Lew has had any medical training.

After that, brace yourself for President Obama's nominee for director of the Bureau of Alcohol, Tobacco, Firearms and Explosives (ATF), Todd Jones. Jones is the current acting director of ATF and has been criticized[6] by a local Democratic FBI office director as being politically well-connected but incompetent and soft on gun and violent crime prosecutions.

Past presidents have had difficult times in their second terms, but the difficulty is usually with big proposals. President George W. Bush unsuccessfully tried to pass privatization of Social Security and immigration reform in his second term. President Reagan spent his second term solidifying his victory in the Cold War and simplified the tax code, lowering the top marginal tax rate to 28%. Meanwhile, President Obama is trying to get Charles Hagel approved as defense secretary, Jacob Lew at Treasury secretary, and Todd Jones as ATF director, not grand plans by any means.

President Obama may get these nominees approved by a majority of senators. But the question is: why is he fighting these particular battles? He could have easily found better qualified nominees for these positions and fought bigger battles on some substantive legislative proposals. Why spend what remaining political capital he has on these problematic appointments? I have a theory, and here goes.

As liberal as he is, President Obama prefers to settle scores with his political adversaries even more than getting big liberal proposals passed. There were some clues dropped in the recent campaign. In one speech President Obama told[7] his audience, who booed after Gov. Romney was mentioned, "don't boo ... voting is the best revenge." This follows a slip he made a couple years earlier when he encouraged[8] Latinos to punish their "enemies," and when he warned[9] African Americans that a Republican take-over of Congress would mean "hand-to-hand combat up here on Capitol Hill."

These Freudian slips and others show the resentment that President Obama feels towards anyone who opposes him. Opposing ideas are not to be argued against; their proponents are to be personally defeated and the victory noted. Somewhere in his brain the president is keeping score, and he relishes announcing to his opponents, as he did[10] in his first term, "I won."

It is a pettiness that may work out well for the conservative cause. After all, the best way to block any future liberal proposals is to not have them proposed in the first place. The Hagel, Lew and Jones nominations, and the spending of President Obama's political capital needed to advance these nominations, may be just the ticket to stall any future liberal proposals.

February 5, 2013

THE GOP NEEDS A GENERAL GRANT

Lately there have been a number of analogies made between various liberal political positions and the abolitionist, Union side in the Civil War. No doubt this is a result of the 2012 Steven Spielberg movie *Lincoln,* and its notoriety, and the universal need to identify with the virtuous side of any historical struggle.

A few days ago, on CNN's Piers Morgan's show, columnist Frank Rich likened opposition to gun control to slave-owners in the pre-war South who did not want to give up their slaves. According[1] to Rich, "I think that in some ways the gun culture is as entrenched in the American psyche as [was] slavery."

As a gun owner, I resent the comparison. But if there are any credible analogies to be made with today's political movements and Abraham Lincoln, it is between the Union side of the Civil War and today's Republican party. Hear me out on this.

And I don't mean to simply point out that Abraham Lincoln was a Republican, which he was. Recall from history that during the Civil War, President Lincoln had a problem getting generals who would actively engage the Confederate army. "Some of my generals are so slow," Lincoln once remarked[2], "that molasses in the coldest days of winter is a race-horse compared to them."

We conservatives have a similar problem with our leaders, who hesitate to engage with President Obama and other liberal leaders.

We have just finished a month of statements from President Obama that were not only largely ignored by the Republican party, but easily rebutted if the GOP had dared to mount a formal response. In his January 14 press conference, President Obama called on congressional Republicans to raise the country's debt limit without any pre-conditions, arguing[3] that "we are not a nation of deadbeats."

Of course we are. Never before in human history has a country spent so much more money than it has brought in. Our country is so irresponsible with its spending that we have gone beyond trying to sell our debt to others. We now sell our debt to ourselves, specifically the Federal Reserve, printer of the Dollar.

Republicans were largely quiet after that press conference. A few days later, President Obama, flanked by children, signed 23 executive orders[4] concerning gun control, none of which would have stopped the Sandy Hook massacre. Yet, except for scattered objections, Republicans in Washington were silent on the orders and the spectacle of using children to stand nearby when the president signed the orders.

Then, in last week's inaugural speech[5], among other whoppers, President Obama said that "we cannot substitute spectacle for politics." No one connected the dots to the president's own spectacle a few days earlier.

Come on, Republicans! Get in the public debate and fight! Another gripe from President Lincoln comes to mind, when he wrote[6] General McClellan and said, "if you do not want to use the army I would like to borrow it for a while."

And this Republican non-engagement isn't new. Remember when President Bush and Karl Rove made the rounds, promoting their books? I heard them both on at least two conservative talk shows, where one of the first questions asked – by conservatives, mind you – was along the lines of "why did you guys stay so quiet in the second term, when such ridiculous charges were made by Democrats?" Democrats high and low had charged that President Bush and his advisors knew about the 9-11 attacks beforehand, and that they lied to the American people about weapons of mass destruction in Iraq. Either charge, if really believed by the accuser, would have resulted in impeachment proceedings. Yet the charges were repeatedly made and then ignored by the Bush White House.

"We didn't want to dignify such crazy charges with a response," was the common reply. But after the charges were made so often without a response, even today a sizable percent of Americans actually believe these charges.

Or take the recent presidential election, in which President Obama's campaign aired the ad "Stage7," portraying Gov. Romney as an uncaring corporate raider. The ad ran in battleground states totally unanswered for almost two months. Is there any wonder why Romney was seen by the voters as less sympathetic than President Obama?

Contrast all this Republican silence with President Clinton, who deserves some cynical credit for his rapid response to all the scandals that erupted during his presidency. Within a few minutes of each new scandal eruption, the Clinton White House had a denial, complete with a media smear of the accuser and counter-revelations. As a result, relatively few Clinton scandals occupied the public's attention. (Of course, the operative term there is "relatively.")

We Republicans need a General Grant, or better yet, a series of General Grants. Ulysses S. Grant was promoted to lead Union general by President Lincoln because Grant repeatedly engaged the enemy. Grant knew that the Union had major advantages in troops and equipment. Grant also knew that if the Union army repeatedly engaged the enemy, even if the Union forces incurred more casualties, the Union would eventually win the Civil War. And this is what happened.

Just like the advantages held by the Union forces in the Civil War, today's conservatives have many advantages over liberals. America is

Library of Congress

General Ulysses S. Grant

still a center-right country. Capitalism works, and economies built on less than capitalism have clearly failed. Americans want a safety net for fellow citizens who cannot support themselves, but Americans don't like that so many have been dependant on government support for so long.

Other liberal policies, like Obamacare, gun control, union card-check, and bloated government, are losers with the voters. As in the Civil War, the more conservatives engage President Obama and liberals on these issues, the more the natural advantage, the inherent popularity of conservative principles, leads to victory.

So there you have it: if any side of the current political divide is allowed to identify itself with the movie *Lincoln,* it should be the conservative side. We have the advantages but we have problems getting our leaders to engage.

In fact, the conservative movement is even more aligned with the more entertaining recent Abraham Lincoln movie, *Abraham Lincoln: Vampire Hunter.* After all, we conservatives are battling ideas that have already died. But that is an argument for another column.

February 4, 2013

ACKNOWLEDGE THE PLAN

We need to answer the Mayor Bloomberg-inspired, self-righteous online video[1] of celebrities who "demand a plan" to end gun violence. The original online video, filmed mostly in black and white, features emotional, self-righteous actors who "demand a plan" for the mass shootings that have occurred. The subtext clearly called for banning guns.

There is already one great answer to this video[2]. It is another online video that has been making the rounds on the Internet. It repeats the original "Demand A Plan" video except it contains footage of violent movies from most of the same actors who demand a plan to end gun violence. The footage of these movies shows guns blasting and blood splattering. It also includes some very foul language, you know, the crass, insistent things that people usually say when they have a gun pointed at someone else. The video ends with a graphic song, and the words across the screen, and I will try and keep this G-rated, "Demand celebrities [have intercourse with themselves]."

The hypocrisy of most of the celebrities in the video is very low-hanging fruit. Only a quick Internet search is needed to discover the actors' history of making violent, gun-filled movies. And there is a helpful website[3], Internet Movie Firearms Database, which details the pistols, rifles or shotguns used by celebrities in various shoot-'em-up movies or TV shows.

For example, after a brief search, I was able to find that two of the actors in the "demand a plan" video were also involved in the 2010 movie *The Town*. Question: what was anyone from that movie doing in a public conversation on gun violence? *The Town* was so violent that a Time magazine review[4] called one of the characters in the movie "trigger happy." No one associated with that movie, like Jon Hamm and Jeremy Renner, should be part of any discussion concerning gun violence. Maybe these actors thought no one would research their previous movie credits, but now that the news is out it looks pretty hypocritical.

And couldn't Jamie Foxx have at least waited a little longer after sounding[5] so excited about getting to "kill all the white people" in the movie *Django Unchained?* Foxx made that comment on *Saturday Night Live* only a few days before the Sandy Hook massacre, and less than a month later he is "demanding a plan" to end gun violence. Well, here's one plan, just off the top of my head: stop making movies that glorify gun violence. Take your celebrity role seriously and stop making millions of dollars acting in movies where a happy ending means that one or more people gets shot.

But there is yet another "plan" that should be promoted, and that is the plan of arming more good guys in schools, shopping malls, and other public places so that if and when a bad guy shows up to commit mass murder, a good person with a gun will be there to cut short the killing.

There are already many examples of this plan working to save lives. Just a few days before the Sandy Hook shooting, in Clackamas Town Center, outside of Portland, Oregon, a gunman[6] entered a crowded shopping mall and started shooting people. A shopper there with a concealed-carry permit drew his gun and pointed it at the gunman. When the gunman saw that someone there might shoot back, he ducked into a stairway and killed himself. Although two people were killed in that episode, the presence of a good guy with a gun greatly limited the body count.

Almost the same thing happened[7] at a movie theater in San Antonio a few days later, except the good gal with a gun, an off-duty sheriff's deputy, actually fired a shot that ended what could have been a mass shooting.

The San Antonio movie theater incident was almost an exact repeat of what happened[8] in 2007 in Trolley Square Mall in Salt Lake City, Utah. In that case, a gunman started shooting people in a crowded shopping center, and he killed five people before an armed off-duty police officer shot the gunman dead. That officer is credited with saving many lives. Simply put, in these shootings, and in many others, lives were saved because a good person with a gun was there to fire back.

This point needs to be the gun-rights answer to the "demand a plan" crowd. Our side needs to make its own video, filmed in the same black and white, in which gun-rights celebrities (there are some), with the same concerned expressions, invoke the locations of gun massacres that have been stopped short by other people with guns, whether they are private citizens with concealed-carry permits, off-duty deputies, or a police officer who happens to be there. Then the plea, "how many other massacres could have been stopped?" needs to be made.

One gun-rights celebrity is rocker Ted Nugent, who recently wrote an open letter to Vice President Joe Biden. In his letter[9], Nugent argued that "gun-free zones" are really "modern killing fields" and they should be banned. Nugent also argued that concealed-carry permits should be authorized for qualified citizens, including school officials, so that they can "protect themselves, their loved ones and innocents."

He's right. We need to make the argument back to those who seek to ban guns, and we need to drive home the point that gun massacres have been and will continue to be ended by good guys with guns. Lives can be saved by teachers, fellow shoppers, security guards, and off-duty police officers who have a gun when a bad person shows up and starts shooting.

Demand a plan? The plan is obvious: get more guns into the hands of good people so that they can stop the bad guys who will always be able to get a gun. It is time we acknowledge this.

January 9, 2013

SILVER LININGS

As 2012 comes to a close, there is much to worry the average American conservative, and it would be easy to dwell on the negative. And granted, thanks to Supreme Court Chief Justice John Roberts and the election results, the incredibly wasteful and innovation-squelching Obamacare will soon be fully implemented. Medical care in the United States will no longer be the best in the world, and it will soon begin to resemble the substandard medical care found in Canada or England.

Other government freebies that were so freely thrown-about in President Obama's first-term will now be frozen in place, if not expanded. Countries that neighbor the bullies in Russia will soon find out the details of the flexibility that President Obama pledged to Prime Minister Medvedev in front of an open microphone a little over a year ago. And even those countries can console themselves that they are not Israel, surrounded by countries pledged to destroy it, including Iran, which cannot wait to develop a nuclear weapon and send it straight to Jerusalem as soon as possible.

But as Johnny Cash sang in one of my favorite songs, "there is a silver lining behind every cloud," and I have noticed a few silver linings in the American political scene. So here they are, in no particular order:

First, President Obama, recently re-elected, is even more of a lame-duck than other re-elected presidents. During the recently-concluded presidential election campaign, President Obama was entirely lacking in any second-term agenda. His answer to the main issues for the voters, the economy and jobs, could be summed up with a quick one-liner: "it is all Bush's fault, and without me it could have been worse."

History has shown that lame-duck presidents have a hard enough time enacting any new legislation at all, but when, as with Obama, he campaigned on *no* new agenda, he is even more of a lame-duck president than others. In fact, because of his agenda-less campaign, President Obama was a lame-duck president before he even got re-elected.

That means that President Obama has no mandate to promote or pass anything new. After concluding the "fiscal cliff" matters and raising of the debt ceiling, both of which are left over from his first term, the second Obama term will revert to a caretaker presidency.

Things can always change, like if there is a vacancy on the Supreme Court, or if there is a world war involving the United States. But absent those possibilities, President Obama's days of greatly influencing the future of this country are behind us.

Even President Obama's re-election rhetoric was misleadingly moderate. While his instincts are liberal, he dare not admit it. Who could forget President Obama's comment in one of the debates where he lauded the self-reliance of Americans? That one made me cough up part of my Diet Coke.

But the point is that for those conservatives who lament that we have just re-elected the most liberal president in history, so we therefore must now be a liberal country, we have the consolation of knowing that President Obama was re-elected using moderate, not liberal, rhetoric.

And speaking of the fiscal cliff negotiations, if the total expiration of the Bush tax cuts is what ultimately happens, we have the silver lining of knowing that some lower-income people will now have to pay taxes again. This will end a major problem I had with the Bush tax cuts when they were originally enacted: a whole swath of lower-income people were totally kicked *off* the tax rolls. Their tax rates were effectively cut 100%. And from that point on, that group of lower-income people had no problem in voting for more government benefits – after all, someone else would be paying for it. Now, with this part of the Bush tax cuts repealed, that group of people has some "skin in the game." This deficit is now their problem too.

Another silver lining is the great energy boom that our country is now experiencing, and the government's inability to stop it. Thanks to the hydraulic fracturing, or "fracking" method of getting oil and natural gas out of the ground, whole areas of the country are boom-towns. Parts of south Texas, western Pennsylvania, the entire state of North

Dakota and a few other areas of the country that have engaged in fracking have almost non-existent unemployment.

So far, the Environmental Protection Agency has been the government's weapon of choice against the fracking industry. But just a few days ago, EPA Administrator Lisa Jackson resigned after being discovered that she had a secret e-mail account, so as not to reveal her e-mail communications. The leader-less EPA will buy some more time for the fracking industry to maintain its growth.

When President Obama appoints a replacement EPA Administrator, the appointee will need to be approved by the US Senate, which now includes my final silver lining, Texas Senator-elect Ted Cruz. Cruz earned his conservative credentials as Solicitor General of Texas, where he won some monumental Supreme Court cases, like the 2008 decision *District of Columbia v. Heller*.[1] *Heller* held that the 2nd Amendment defines individual rights to gun ownership, not some "collective right" for a state-run militia, so a constitutional amendment will now be needed if the government tries to outlaw guns.

Texas Senator-elect Ted Cruz is smart and aggressive, and he is young, so he could be in the US Senate for another 30 years, making the conservative case to the country on all issues high and low. Barack Obama may have won the election to be our president for another four years, but Ted Cruz won the election to be the next senator from Texas, and this is quite a consolation.

Yes, it will be a long four years for the United States, but there are a number of good things, or silver linings, behind the clouds overhead. Things aren't all that bad.

December 31, 2012

A CALL FOR FULL DISCLOSURE IN THE GUN CONTROL DEBATE

It used to be that a person who managed a mutual fund, hedge fund, endowment or personal account could go onto CNBC and recommend that viewers buy or sell a certain stock, and the person being interviewed would give their reasons. Then, at some point in the late 1990's or early 2000's, CNBC began insisting that their on-air guests actually disclose their own position in the stocks they discuss.

In other words, an investor who advocated buying Intel, for example, would have to admit that they had just sold off their shares of Intel and they did not own any Intel stock. So why do they feel the rest of us should buy Intel?

Or, if the CNBC guest touts a stock that they already own, the viewer can figure that that makes sense. The person touting the stock also owns the stock and also feels it would be a good stock for everyone else to own. The disclosure of the personal holding would be another factor, besides the other reasons given, for the viewer to consider before deciding whether to buy that stock.

The "full disclosure" of holdings rule was a way to cut through the "abstract" recommendation and get down to the rubber-meets-the-road element of the person being interviewed. *We know how you think our viewers should treat this stock for their portfolios, but how have you personally treated this stock in your own portfolio?* the disclosure rule seemed to say. The rule is fair and illuminating.

Now that we have another tragic school mass murder that involves guns, it is a time for politicians far and wide to advocate gun control, as if more rules against law-abiding people getting guns will keep guns out of the hands of criminals who want to commit mass murder. It is almost an American tradition: gun violence begets calls for gun control. What is missing in every gun-control discussion is a "full disclosure" of which politician has a concealed weapons permit, any guns in their own home, or is protected by armed security guards. Just like the CNBC disclosure regarding touting stocks and the personal holdings of the person touting the stock, we need a "full disclosure" rule regarding armed protection of the politicians who advocate gun control.

Here is how it would work: New York Senator Charles Schumer recently complained[1] to CBS' *Face The Nation* that "mass shootings are becoming 'a new normal'" and proposes new gun control legislation[2], saying that the recent school shooting in Newtown, Connecticut may be the 'tipping point,' inspiring legislators to finally do something about gun control. Shortly before the end of a hypothetical interview, the interviewer will say, "and as a matter of full disclosure, Senator Schumer, you have your own concealed carry weapon permit and you have armed security guards, is that correct?" "Yes, I do[3]," he will say if he is honest.

That clarifies things. It says that Senator Schumer is touting a position for the rest of us that he personally does not follow. It would indicate that Senator Schumer feels that his personal safety requires that he have a concealed weapon on him and that he has armed guards to use for protection if the need arises, even though he feels the rest of us should not be similarly protected.

Granted, it is possible that a politician who has a concealed weapon permit advocating no weapons for the rest of us could make some good points. But it would be more information for the rest of us to use in making our decision in this debate.

Likewise, if President Obama enters the debate on gun control with specific gun control proposals, he should also be obligated to disclose his armed protection.

In this discussion it would actually be possible for a politician to advocate strict gun control laws and actually *not* have a concealed weapon permit, any guns at home, or protected by armed guards. If such a politician emerges in this debate, they will have more credibility and a lot of us would probably pay more attention to them. In this situation a "full disclosure" rule would help the gun control side more than it would the anti-gun control side.

In the coming days we will all have some important gun control decisions to make, aided by the politicians who will make arguments pro and con. Just like the investment decisions we all make as we watch investment advisors on CNBC tout certain stocks and then they have to disclose their holdings in that stock, the decisions we citizens have to make on gun control should be made using the advice of politicians who fully disclose their own personal involvement with guns: do they have a concealed weapons permit? Do they have guns in their home? Are they protected by armed guards? The public has a right to know before following their advice on gun control.

December 18, 2012

ABOUT THOSE ABSENTEE POLITICIANS

Great news! The outgoing Congress has passed the fewest number of laws since any Congress in the last 70 years. The Founding Fathers would be proud, and as a conservative I am pretty impressed. Instead of raising our taxes, increasing regulations, making life more difficult for citizens and businesses everywhere, the current Congress has done its part by sitting on its collective hands and passing as few laws as possible, specifically 196 at last count. This is great — let freedom ring!

Of course, you would never know of this great accomplishment by reading the NBC News *First Read* website. Bemoaning the low congressional approval rates, Kyle Inskeep of NBC News recently wrote[1] that the current Congress is the "least productive Congress since the 1940's" because it has passed so few laws. We can't have that. The next-least productive Congress, which lasted from 1995-1996, enacted a mere 333 laws.

According to Inskeep, an active Congress passing as many laws as possible is a good Congress. Even out-going Republican Senator Olympia Snowe got into the act, complaining that "I do find it frustrating, however, that an atmosphere of polarization and 'my way or the highway' ideologies have become pervasive in campaigns and in our governing institutions."

I hope no one on our side is falling for this. When Congress makes laws, money is taken away from someone, business is made more difficult, the fiscal hole our country is in gets dug even deeper. And when fewer laws are made, less of our freedoms are taken away and less money is blown. A Beltway reporter like Inskeep or a politician like Senator Snowe might not see it this way, but people outside of Washington DC are better off when fewer laws are passed.

Kind of reminds me of some conservatives who complain about all the vacations taken by the Obama family, or the fact that President Obama plays so much golf. A few days after the election there was a blog entry[2] at Weekly Standard, reporting with disgust that right after the election President Obama headed to the golf course. In the past, President Obama has also been sneeringly referred[3] to as the "Golfer in Chief."

People, let's be clear: the more President Obama plays golf, the less damage he can do from the Oval Office. Yes, our country is much better off when President Obama is on the golf course. For a few precious hours, we can know that things will not get worse.

Take for example President Obama's trip to a global nuclear summit last March in South Korea. President Obama was actually caught[4] on an open microphone telling the Russians that "after the election I will have more flexibility," then he looked around guiltily, hoping no one else had heard what he just said.

At that point there were a number of small countries that were put on notice: *you may be invaded by the Russians just like ex-Soviet Georgia was in 2008.* Would American or NATO soldiers rush onto a battlefield because the Russians invaded some friend of ours? Possibly.

But the point is, wouldn't we all have rather President Obama spent a nice, relaxing weekend on a golf course somewhere instead of going to South Korea that weekend? And this is just in foreign affairs. Instead of passing Dodd-Frank, Obamacare or the $800 billion stimulus, wouldn't it have been preferable to have President Obama spend some quality time golfing somewhere?

As far as I am concerned we should sign President Obama up for the PGA Tour. The more time he spends on the golf course the less time he will be in the Oval Office doing damage to our country. Or maybe we can all pass around the hat and buy President Obama a membership at Pebble Beach.

Here's an idea: let President Obama endorse golf stuff. Where is it written that a sitting president cannot endorse golf balls, shoes or clothing? In fact, "the Barry Putter" has a nice ring to it. (Well, let's face it, a wedge might be more appropriate.) And who knows? Rush Limbaugh might even be willing to interview President Obama on his show to promote the new Obama putter.

A few years ago it was the liberals who complained whenever President George W. Bush went to his ranch in Crawford, Texas, to clear brush with his chainsaw.

And chainsaws are dangerous. With all the best-selling books, movies, plays and liberal comedians waxing so eloquently about President Bush dying or somehow getting assassinated, you would think that liberals would want President Bush out of the Oval Office and on his ranch, wrestling with his chainsaw. He could have been seriously injured by that chainsaw. But no, the liberals who hated President Bush so much actually complained when he went to his ranch in Texas! It made no sense at all.

We conservatives need to be consistent here, and we need to keep our eyes on the prize: it is a good thing when Congress passes very few laws, and it is a very good thing when President Obama takes the afternoon off to go to the golf course. In fact, President Obama needs to stay on the golf course as much as possible.

December 12, 2012

THE ONE WARREN BUFFETT TAX HIKE PROPOSAL YOU WILL NEVER SEE

Billionaire investor Warren Buffett is out again with another proposed tax hike. In the *New York Times*[1] a few days ago Buffett noted with disgust that there are certain higher-income people among us who can find enough loopholes in the tax code so that they pay low tax rates or in some cases, no taxes at all. His solution: a super alternative minimum tax that will sock these legal tax scofflaws, so that no matter what loopholes are used, these millionaires will never pay less than 30% of their income in federal taxes.

This is the third time in recent memory Mr. Buffett has conspicuously proposed a tax hike on various high earning tax payers. Such proposals have made him the toast of liberal salons from Cambridge to Santa Monica, ensuring that his name is constantly invoked by liberals in tax discussions and loaning his prestige to liberals in just about any tax hike discussion.

But there is one particular tax hike on the rich that Mr. Buffett will never propose. No one will remember this, but for about five minutes during the first Bush presidency a tax increase was straight-facedly proposed to impute a capital gains tax on appreciated but still-unsold stock. In other words, it didn't matter that the tax-payer still held onto his stocks without selling them, under this proposal the net increase in value of the unsold stock would still be subject to a capital gains tax. Kind of an unrealized capital gains tax.

This was truly a bone-headed tax idea for several reasons, and thankfully it headed to the ash-heap of bad tax ideas only a few minutes after it was seriously considered.

But this is the tax hike that Buffett will never propose. And for good reason. Buying and holding onto appreciating stocks is how Buffett increases his net worth. To this day he makes relatively little in salary, which is taxable, and just about all of his wealth is in the form of appreciated, unsold stock. If he ever sells the stock then he will have to declare a capital gain, and be subject to a capital gains tax.

You know, if this is the case, one could conclude that Warren Buffett proclaiming far and wide the virtues of raising taxes on rich people would be a little hypocritical. Maybe even deceptive. Buffett is in fact not one of the type of rich people — salaried rich people — on whom he seeks to raise taxes. He makes his money on appreciated stocks, which are not part of his tax hike proposals.

There is kind of a "three-card monte" element to this. With all the attention heaped on raising the taxes on salaried rich people, less attention will be paid on those wealthy people who, like Buffett, are sitting on millions of dollars worth of appreciated but unsold stocks.

On the other hand, out-spoken liberals are probably very enamored with Warren Buffett. He is, after all, a billionaire and one of the richest people on Earth, and he proposes many tax hikes. Maybe there is a deeper method to Buffett's madness.

This could be some kind of rhetorical protection racket. Buffett could be figuring that if he proposes all sort of other tax hikes, then he and his unrealized capital gains will be left alone by the barbarians at the gate of today's tax debates. Kind of cynical for my taste, but hey, if this is what he is up to, more power to him. Stock investors will be protected, while the taxes of other Americans will go up as always.

If that is what is going on, let's just hope this never backfires.

December 4, 2012

SOME FAIR REASSURANCE

Whining is unbecoming. Granted, last week's elections were a disaster for conservatives, but must we whine about it? The reasons for the losses are legion, but do any of them really make any sense?

OK, Gov. Mitt Romney may not have been the perfect candidate, but give him a break. No one is. And the months of unanswered negative charges in swing states, like the "Stage[1]" ad in Ohio, did untold damage. And yes, the Republicans are earning a reputation of giving away at least a couple of easy Senate seats per election. That is annoying.

The day after the election, radio talk show host Rush Limbaugh made a pretty good case that President Obama's winning strategy for re-election was to act like Santa Claus handing out "free stuff." And I read somewhere that "the takers" now outnumber "the makers," which would explain why Americans would re-elect such a liberal president.

My personal favorite gripe is that Gov. Romney wasted a lot of time in Democratic strongholds, like Philadelphia, Pennsylvania, and Cuyahoga County, Ohio, both of which had 70+% victory margins for President Obama. If past election campaigns have taught us anything, it is to leave alone your opposition's strongholds. You certainly don't want to remind them to go out and vote.

As cathartic as it is to complain, it seems as if there is no single gripe that really explains our losses. You know, it sure would be nice if there was some mathematical formula to predict the outcomes of an election. Something in which we could input a few numbers, press enter, and have a prediction handed back to us. Something that would take away the emotion of it all. If only...

Well, there is. While there have been several formulaic electoral predictors in the past, the most accurate through the years has been a formula developed by Yale professor Ray Fair. The "Fair Formula" predicts the re-election of the president or his successor depending on recent quarterly GDP growth and inflation numbers since inauguration, with an added figure of how many quarters during the incumbent's term that the real GDP rate has increased over 3.2%. Input these numbers into his equation, and you get a pretty accurate prediction of the success of a president's re-election, or the re-election of the candidate from the president's party of the president isn't running for re-election.

Picture Robby the Robot, from the 1956 movie *Forbidden Planet,* and a few other appearances like the TV show *Lost In Space.* Robby doesn't care what the candidates do or say. Just input a few numbers and Robby will spit out an answer, with less than 3% margin of error. Kind of takes the fun out of it all, but it works. This formula has correctly predicted all presidential elections since 1916 with the exceptions of 1992 and 2000. (The 1992 election featured Ross Perot, the spoiler, and 2000 was a squeaker, decided on only a handful of votes in Florida, so to be fair to Prof. Fair, we can't criticize his formula for those years.)

Professor Fair even has a website[2] where you can input your own numbers, so I gave it a try. I inputted the numbers from 1988, strong economic and low inflation numbers, with several quarters of real growth above 3.2%, and — voila! – the incumbent party candidate, George H.W. Bush was predicted to win re-election by 53.9%, almost exactly the actual popular vote victory of 53.4%. I then inputted the numbers from 1980, which were weak economic and high inflation numbers, and – danger, Will Robinson! – Jimmy Carter, lost re-election in a landslide, just as predicted by the formula.

For 2012, the numbers entered yielded[3] a very close result, 49.5% of the total popular vote for President Obama, when the ultimate result was 50.6%. That means that for all the ridiculous economic policies of the last four years, the wasted stimulus, Cash For Clunkers, four record-high annual budget deficits, Obamacare, Dodd-Frank, wacky energy policy, all the Solyndras, everything, there was just barely enough recent economic growth and low inflation to make the final call entirely within the margin of error as to whether President Obama would win re-election.

Of course, the economy four years from now could become a disaster. Deficits like this cannot last forever, even with the Federal

Reserve's printing presses running at full capacity like they are. Interest rates will rise, and once the world notices how many excess dollars are spoken for we are bound to face a pretty scary inflation. I am sure that in 2016 the Fair Formula will predict this, but only time will tell for sure. And remember that it will be the most recent economic and inflation numbers that will predict the outcome of the 2016 election.

So cheer up, conservatives. We can change minor things in the campaign, but anything we do can only tinker with the margin of error. The American people will basically vote for whomever improves the economy, specifically their after-inflation take-home pay. So stop whining, just be ready for the next election. Forward! Er, well, maybe some other expression for looking ahead. You know what I mean.

November 12, 2012

BIDEN HELPS THE SUPPLY-SIDE CAUSE

Of all the exchanges at the mostly-unwatchable Vice Presidential debate[1] last week, this one stands out:

REP. RYAN: You can cut tax rates by 20 percent and still preserve these important preferences for middle-class taxpayers —
VICE PRESIDENT BIDEN: Not mathematically possible.
REP. RYAN: It is mathematically possible. It's been done before. It's precisely what we're proposing.
VICE PRESIDENT BIDEN: (Chuckles.) It has never been done before.
REP. RYAN: It's been done a couple of times, actually.
VICE PRESIDENT BIDEN: It has never been done before.
REP. RYAN: Jack Kennedy lowered tax rates, increased growth. Ronald Reagan —
VICE PRESIDENT BIDEN: Oh, now you're Jack Kennedy.

Wait a minute! (Insert screeching record sound[2] here.) President Jack Kennedy, the darling of liberals everywhere, was a tax-cutter? And he justified his tax cuts as a way to increase revenue? That's crazy talk! Someone please change the subject – and fast!

If you asked the average man or woman on the street today whether the great President Kennedy proposed tax cuts, or whether he even tolerated talk of enacting "tax cuts for the wealthy," you would be scoffed at. No one believes that.

But President Kennedy made his case for cutting taxes to raise revenues very eloquently in a speech[3] from the Oval Office on August 13, 1962. On his radio show a couple days ago, Rush Limbaugh played audio of a similar speech[4] President Kennedy made at the Economic Club in New York in December, 1962. The thrust of both Kennedy speeches was un-mistakenly supply-side, that is, tax cuts of 20% across the board will incentivize businesses to expand and consumers to buy, generating more tax revenue for the government.

Kennedy had trouble getting his tax cuts passed, but only a few months into his administration, President Johnson got the Kennedy tax cuts adopted by Congress, and the 1960's American economy blasted off. Quarterly GDP gains of annual rates over 7% were commonplace, unemployment bottomed out at 3.8% in 1966, and total employment in the US rose[5] 24% (14 million workers) from 1964 to 1969.

But this all happened before raising taxes, especially against despicable rich people, was a standard Democrat proposal, and cutting taxes to raise revenue became an argument associated with the dastardly Ronald Reagan. At one point in 2001 some Republicans tried to remind everyone that the tax cuts proposed by then-President Bush were similar to those proposed by President Kennedy 40 years earlier. The late president's brother, Senator Ted Kennedy, sprang into action, calling[6] the comparison "intellectually dishonest and politically irresponsible." Since then the media has split hairs on why the comparison is off, or has avoided the subject altogether.

Of course, it does make sense to cut taxes and flatten the tax rates to raise revenue, no matter which party proposes it. When a small business owner contemplates hiring new employees or expanding their business, first and foremost on the business owner's mind is whether the new employee of business expansion will make money.

Lower tax rates will increase the likelihood of making more money for the business, especially if there is a class of consumers with more disposable money to buy the business's products. The combination of expanding businesses with more employees, and more customers buying the business's products all result in more tax revenue for the government. Before such thinking was labeled "Republican" or "Democrat," not many people disputed this. After all, the Kennedy proposed tax cuts were passed by 80% of both houses of Congress in 1964.

Nowadays it is common to mis-attribute economic gains. In his speech at the Democratic National Convention last summer, President Clinton suggested[7] that since 1961, there have been more jobs created under Democratic presidents than Republican presidents.

Clinton failed to specify the policies enacted by the presidents in question. If he had, he would have recounted how it is lower taxes and flatter tax rates that generate more economic activity and higher employment, not the party that holds the White House. Simply put, a Republican president is just as able to raise taxes as a Democratic president is able to lower them. It is not the party of the president, it is the tax policy pursued by the president that creates jobs and generates economic activity.

This is a secret that is more and more coming out of the closet.

Vice President Joe Biden has a reputation of making gaffes, and his performance in the October 11 debate with Congressman Paul Ryan has been called overbearing and disrespectful. But Biden's comparison of Romney's tax cut proposals to President Kennedy's tax cuts may be the dark-horse gaffe of the 2012 campaign. Slowly but surely the knowledge is becoming more commonplace that tax cuts, and flatter tax rates, generate economic growth and low unemployment, and President Kennedy showed how it was done in the 1960's.

October 18, 2012

NO ON NAPA COUNTY'S MEASURE U

Owning property in California can be a hassle. There are property taxes, upkeep and insurance costs, just to name a few.

Fortunately you can always do something with your property to make the hassle worth it, right? Try telling that to Pacific Union College (PUC), which owns 2,000 acres of land in unincorporated Angwin, California, and now faces a Napa County ballot measure to strip away most of its property rights for its most valuable parcels.

Measure U[1] is on the November 6 ballot for Napa County voters, and it is the culmination of an antagonistic history between the College and its Angwin neighbors over PUC's dreams of developing some vacant land. The measure needs to be defeated.

It all started a few years ago when PUC proposed developing small parts of its land into shops, restaurants, professional offices, a sheriff sub-station, retirement home, hotel, some open space for farmer's markets, and 800-1000 houses.

Anticipating objections, PUC called the development "Ecovillage," and filled a website[2] with pastoral drawings and descriptions that contained every politically-correct, green sustaino-babble cliche in the book. Picture a cross between Yountville and a 60's hippie commune. PUC even agreed to declare other parts of its land off-limits to any future development.

Who could object to something called an ecovillage? Sections of PUC land were going to be locally-farmed and 15% of the houses built would be reserved for low-income families. And instead of having to drive 25 miles to Whole Foods in Napa, local Angwin people could overpay for their produce right there in town.

The locals were having none of it. The group Save Rural Angwin[3] began its role of loyal opposition, speaking out at meetings and writing letters to the editor.

PUC reduced the number of proposed houses to 380, then to 215, but the opposition only grew. In October, 2010, PUC threw in the hemp towel and called off the whole proposal. But reportedly some of the land in question is still zoned residential and PUC still has a permit[4] application before the Planning Commission to build 191 houses, and 600 acres are for sale[5].

Measure U is being marketed as an attempt to "preserve agricultural land," but the measure is really a proposal to take away PUC's property rights by re-zoning several of its parcels as agricultural and to disallow the subdivision of educational lands in all unincorporated parts of Napa County. Of course, property tax and other expenses would stay with Pacific Union College.

If it seems strange to have a county-wide ballot measure targeting the lands owned by a single land-owner, it is. "Down-zoning" decisions are made by the County Board of Supervisors all the time, giving both sides a chance to make their case with the supervisors. Not so with Measure U.

Besides the unfairness, and the tyranny-of-the-majority of the measure, there are issues for some locals like me who would like some commercial development in Angwin. We in Pope Valley would love to shop locally, and are tired of having to drive to Lake County to overpay for produce or buy highly-sugared coffee drinks.

And what about the students of Pacific Union College? Shopping is great stress-reliever, you know. Who can forget the soothing background music in the movie *Clueless*[6] when Alicia Silverstone's character found sanctuary in the local shopping mall?

Napa County also stands to make some sales and property tax money from developments at PUC. Right now our roads need repair, and county employees have waited years for a cost of living adjustment, getting one this year of only 1.5%.

The only part of Measure U that doesn't specifically target Pacific Union College is the part that prohibits schools in unincorporated Napa County from subdividing their land. But is that even an issue outside of Angwin? What if another school in unincorporated Napa County wanted to subdivide? If Measure U passes, that will be illegal.

For example, take Napa Valley College (NVC), which currently has its own fully-bonded winery[7], under the fearless leadership of Dr. Steve

Krebs. If the NVC Winery ever wanted to buy some unincorporated land nearby to subdivide and expand, that would be illegal, and Dr. Krebs would be conducting his office hours from behind bars.

Has prohibiting schools from subdividing ever worked in any other county? I could find no precedent for this, but I did find that Napa County's impartial analysis[8] of Measure U said that this part of the measure "likely conflicts with state law." This part of Measure U will probably need to be cleaned up by some other ballot measure years from now.

We need to vote "no" on Measure U. Instead of spending money on getting signatures and campaigning for this measure, its backers should try instead to just buy the land from PUC.

October 9, 2012

WHEN SOMETHING IS DESCRIBED AS "COMPLICATED"

There is a part of President Obama's post-convention stump-speech in which he approvingly refers to a call to make former President Clinton his "secretary of explaining things." After last Friday's dismal jobs report, President Clinton has not sought to explain it. The closest Clinton came to explaining the dismal Obama economy was in his convention speech when he attempted to answer the question as to whether the average American is better off now than before President Obama was sworn in: "The answer is yes," President Clinton explained[1], "but too many people are not yet feeling it." Maybe their well-being is too complicated for the average American to realize.

Some in the media have mentioned the jobs report and its reduction in the unemployment rate only because hundreds of thousands unemployed people have just given up looking for a job. Other more Obama-friendly media have referred to the jobs situation as "complicated." A

Google search of "jobs report" and "complicated" shows many attempts by the media to state that the jobs report is just too complicated to accept at face value. One analysis in the *The New York Times*[2] reported that "on Friday Mr. Obama found himself making the complicated argument that the flagging recovery, while not good enough, is at least persistent enough to show that he has put the country on the right path."

In other words, what would to simple-minded citizens seem like a job report that exposes the current sorry state of the economy that is either hopelessly mediocre and possibly even slipping back into recession, things are more complicated than that. Smarter people can easily see that the country is on the right path even though it may look like we are entering another recession, or even a period of very slow growth. There is some fine print somewhere to recommend more of the same Obama policies in the future. We really are better off than we were before President Obama, and smart people realize that.

When I hear anyone explain that some policy is too complicated my mind goes back to my college years at the University of California, Santa Barbara, in the mid-1980's, when I considered taking a class on Marxism/Communism as part of my political science degree. I was close to graduating and had heard from other political science students that there was this fascinating class on Marxism/Communism, taught by a brilliant professor who had a reputation for being very difficult and giving out only low grades.

The class was especially attractive because college students never like to admit they care about grades, and if they rave about a low-grading professor long enough then that must mean that the student doing the raving has high grades. Kind of like GPA-bragging by implication.

I attended the first day of class to check it out. The professor was an angry-looking leftist who emphasized how beneficial Marxist theory was, but how so few people in the world appreciated it. Very complicated, indeed. He repeatedly used the word "complicated" throughout his introduction to Marxist theory and its application in communist countries.

By that time in my college years I was starting to wonder about the empty store shelves I had heard about in communist countries, and how Russian dissidents coming to the United States talked about how awful things were in the Soviet Union they had just left. But no matter. Communism was too complicated to be judged on such trivial matters as economic well-being and freedom.

At that time in my college years I had become quite a grade whore so I did not enroll in the class for fear that I might get less than an A. But I came away from that first and only day of class realizing how complicated communism was, and how simplistic my earlier opinions were. What a fool I had been! Silly me — I had always thought that communism was a system in which the government owns the means of production. There is a lot more to it than that!

It wasn't until a few years later that I realized that communism was not so complicated after all, that in fact it really is pretty simple. Communism is a disaster for everyone involved, except for a few people at the top. Sure, there might be some details about communism to be tested on, but the end result is that it produces a very low standard of living and very limited freedoms for its citizens. Pretty simple.

So too with the job of President Obama after his first and hopefully last four years in office: have his policies made the economy improve? Or, as President Reagan put it after addressing an economy even worse than the economy that welcomed President Obama, are we better off now than we were four years ago? Of course not. Pretty simple.

If the only way to get the still-high unemployment rate down is to get hundreds of thousands of people to give up on their job searches, this is a lousy job market, the fruition of policies of a person who has been president for almost four years. And if President Obama is reelected there is every reason to believe the same results will dog us all for another four years. Not very complicated. In fact, it is very simple, with no need for anyone to explain it to us. "Four more years"? Now *that* would be a complicated argument!

September 10, 2012

COLORADO DEMOCRAT REDISTRICTING MAY HAVE LEFT OPENING FOR REPUBLICAN UNDERDOG

Democrats in Colorado celebrated a hard-fought victory[1] in late 2011 when a state judge sided with the re-districting map of the recently-won Democratic majority statehouse. Congressional districts that were safely Republican were less-so, and competitive Democratic districts became safer.

When the smoke cleared, one congressional district, Colorado's 2nd congressional district, went from being safely Democratic to almost evenly-split between Republican and Democratic voters, with a slight edge to Democrats. Now the incumbent Democrat Congressman from the 2nd congressional district, Jared Polis, has a race on his hands with underdog Republican Kevin Lundberg.

And the differences in the positions taken by the two candidates are just as evenly-split as the district they hope to represent. According to his campaign website[2], Republican Kevin Lundberg calls for cutting federal taxes and fees, limiting the size and scope of government, repealing Obamacare, enacting tax credits for families who home-school, overhauling the EPA, encouraging domestic energy exploration, and restricting abortion. In fact, the Kevin Lundberg campaign website lists positions Lundberg has taken, not only as a state senator but also as a local state representative, as far back as 2003.

Incumbent Democrat Congressman Jared Polis has a campaign website that curiously has no campaign issues in it at all besides vague generalities. "Like many Americans, I am frustrated with the partisanship and posturing of our leaders in Washington D.C." he says on his website[3]. Well sure, I guess not taking any campaign positions is a good step towards ending the "partisanship and posturing of our leaders in Washington," but shouldn't a candidate for Congress tell the voters the candidate's positions before trying to get re-elected by the voters? Maybe this is what the Republicans are talking about when they keep referring to an "empty chair" in the debate of ideas.

We do know from the *Washington Post*[4] that in the last two years Congressman Polis has voted with the Democratic Party 88% of the time, and for the same timeframe the National Federation of Independent Business has ranked[5] Polis' support for small businesses at 0%. Polis rarely seems to make any news, except when issues of gay marriage come up.

Jared Polis was one of the only openly-gay congressional candidates to have ever been elected to Congress, when in 2008 he was elected to represent the then-safe Democrat 2nd district. In 2010, Polis won re-election by a disappointing margin against a poorly-funded and unknown Republican challenger. Now that there are more Republicans in his district one can almost understand deleting his positions from his campaign website.

Other positions that Polis has taken in office include rules supporting Obamacare, limiting "fracking" in oil drilling, favoring cap and trade, gun control, loosening rules against illegal immigration, legalizing marijuana, and subsidizing "green" energy. Truly, Polis and his challenger Lundberg are polar opposites on almost every issue.

Lundberg Campaign Manager Debbie Healy told me that after a recent candidate forum she asked a voter in the audience his impression of the forum, and the voter told her that "I just cannot believe there are two candidates with views so opposite. One candidate wants to have government control everything and the other one wants government to back off and give people their freedom."

To be fair to Polis, before being elected to Congress he had an impressive private sector experience, making hundreds of millions of dollars in Internet start-ups. A recent Open Secrets[6] article estimated that based on recent financial disclosures, Polis has a net worth of up to $228 million, making him the fourth richest member of Congress. Polis has set up an educational foundation that gives grants of computers to schools and has set up two charter schools.

Kevin Lundberg has also had a lot to do with education. Since the 1980's Kevin Lundberg and his wife Sandy have home-schooled their three kids, and in 1990 Kevin Lundberg founded the Christian Home

Educators of Colorado (CHEC)[7], which advises home-schooling parents with teaching curricula, compliance and legal requirements. Lundberg tempers his enthusiasm for tax credits for home-schoolers with the concern that "this should not become a back-door for government meddling in home-schooling."

As could be expected, Jared Polis has an impressive campaign war-chest, much of it self-funded, and as of the latest federal disclosure statements[8], Polis has more than a 10-to-1 funding advantage over Republican Kevin Lundberg. Still, Lundberg told me that he has had this much of a financial disadvantage in other elections and he has won. "I have been outspent in every election I have ever been in," he said.

A recent internal poll conducted by the Lundberg campaign was encouraging. The poll conducted in early August showed Lundberg was only 8% behind Polis in the district. The same poll showed that incumbent Polis had a name recognition lead of 80% to 45% over Lundberg. Lundberg told me that this shows that "getting the names and issues out there is critical in this campaign." My own suspicion is that some of Lundberg's name recognition stems from the fact that his name sounds a lot like "Bill Lumbergh," the name of the bad-guy in the movie *Office Space.*

Anyone wanting to contribute to the Kevin Lundberg for Congress campaign may do so here[9]. The Lundberg website is also a good place to sign up for other ways to help the campaign, like phone-calling potential voters. Lundberg Campaign Manager Debbie Healy told me that thanks to the numbers and enthusiasm of the local grass-roots supporters, including local Tea Partiers, "it's game on."

September 9, 2012

BRACE YOURSELF FOR THE PAUL RYAN SMEARS

I was cleaning out the Ryan family refrigerator and freezer. I looked into the back of the freezer and there was this round thing covered with newspaper. Slowly I pulled back the newspaper and ... it was a frozen head! With a scary expression on its face! As far as I knew I was alone in the kitchen but I turned around and Paul Ryan was standing there, sharpening a butcher knife, looking at me like he was possessed!

(Cue the music from *The Shining*)

I screamed and ran out of the house. As I ran away I heard Paul Ryan make this evil-sounding laugh, just like Vincent Price at the end of the Michael Jackson song, "Thriller." I still have nightmares with that laugh.

I do not think Paul Ryan realizes what he's done to anyone, and furthermore I do not think Paul Ryan is concerned. But I'm sure glad I made it out of that house alive and begged the employment agency for a different assignment. I doubt that head re-attachment surgery would have been covered by my health insurance. (Former cleaning lady at the Ryan residence)

This might look like a big joke but it is only a matter of time before a commercial like this lands in your television set. Last Saturday, Mitt Romney picked Paul Ryan as his running mate, and until then Romney had been called an outsourcer, a prep-school bully, a dog-abuser, a felon, a serial tax cheat, a suspect[1] in the murder of Jon-Benet Ramsey (well, OK, that was from *The Onion*), and now, a person responsible for the cancer death of a former steel-worker's wife. Clearly Mitt Romney is the lowest form of human debris ever to run for president! Has Romney no shame at all? Pretty soon the voters will prefer a team of Jeffrey Dahmer and Jack The Ripper over Mitt Romney and Paul Ryan. And it is still only August!

And the fact that the attacks on Ryan will be factually untrue and misleading will not be a stumbling block for Team Obama, as it would be for normal, honest people. Take for example the recent ad[2] that connects Mitt Romney with the death of the wife of a laid-off steel worker. Because Romney's Bain Capital had laid off the steel worker, the steel worker's family lost its health insurance and the wife died of cancer.

Right off the bat, you see that the timing is a little off. Actually that is not true; right off the bat, the viewer is outraged that Romney would do such a despicable thing. *Then,* when you cool down and think about it a while, you notice the timing is a little off.

Mitt Romney stopped managing Bain Capital in 1999. Remember? That is why he is a felon[3]. He left Bain in 1999 to run the Olympics, but his name still appeared in SEC filings for a few more months, which is a felony! (He probably wasn't even paying taxes at the time, the scoundrel.)

So when that steel-worker was laid off in 2001, Romney was long-gone. But no matter. The steel-worker's wife died of cancer in 2006 and it was Romney's fault.

But hang on: since the ad's release it has been revealed that when the steel-worker was laid off in 2001 he was offered but declined[4] health insurance[5] at his new job. And his wife had her own health insurance until 2003. And the wife wasn't even diagnosed[6] with cancer until 2006. Wouldn't those facts be relevant to whether the wife's 2006 death can be blamed on Romney? One would think so. The *Washington Post* thought[7] so, and awarded the ad "4 Pinocchios."

Since these and other revelations have made it to the news the Obama campaign team has been distancing itself from the Romney-cancer ad. Obama deputy campaign manager Stephanie Cutter has even denied[8] knowing anything about the steel-worker's story even though she had hosted a conference call[9] about it back in May. Now Cutter's career has been diagnosed with imminent mortality and news-watchers are on a death-watch.

Others in the media have compared[10] the Romney-cancer-ad to the "swift-boating" that happened to John Kerry in 2004. But I don't remember anyone blaming John Kerry for someone's wife dying of cancer. I do remember John Kerry being compared to Lurch in *The Addams Family,* but Lurch never killed anyone, he only answered the front door and scared people who came by.

You can't really blame the Obama campaign for trying to distract voters. What else are they supposed to campaign on, the economy? After almost four years under President Obama, it definitely does not look like Reagan's Morning in America.

So in the 2012 campaign we can expect some over-the-top campaign ads from President Obama and his supporters. Even Romney contributors can expect a little static coming their way. Recently Sheldon Adelson, billionaire CEO of the Las Vegas Sands Corp. and major Republican contributor, didn't appreciate essentially being called a pimp in a Democratic campaign pitch. So he got an apology from the Democratic Congressional Campaign Committee, and is suing[11] the National Jewish Democratic Council for $60 million. Good for him! Maybe this is what is needed.

Yes, Paul Ryan can expect all sorts of dirty ads coming his way. What could possibly come next?

NEWS FLASH: This just in, evidence has now been uncovered that suggests Paul Ryan, allegedly only 42, was in Dallas, Texas, on November 22, 1963, and may have been the second gunman on the Grassy Knoll. Stay tuned for more developments.

August 13, 2012

MIA LOVE: THE GOP'S RISING STAR IN UTAH'S 4TH CONGRESSIONAL DISTRICT

The Republican Party has a rising star in Utah's newly-created 4th congressional district: Tea Partier and former Saratoga Springs, Utah, mayor Mia Love. If elected, the 36-year old mother of three will be the GOP's first black woman member of Congress.

As with other Tea Party candidates, Love is not enamored with the out-of-control spending and economic mismanagement of the Obama administration. "I am laser-focused on getting our fiscal house in order and getting people back to work," she told me in a recent e-mail exchange. "My pet issues are attacking the debt, reducing spending and fixing the economy."

Love's website[1] is filled with strong conservative positions. "Washington does not have a revenue problem; it has a spending problem. Balancing the budget is only part of the solution. We must cut federal spending to begin to restore America's economic strength and citizen liberties."

If elected, Love plans on opposing the regulations of the Environment Protection Agency, known[2] for its recent rules that will shut down much of the coal industry and throw millions out of work. The Departments of Energy and Education are also on her opposition list. "We must reign in some regulatory agencies and eliminate others," she added.

Love has also pledged[3] that if elected to Congress, she will join fellow-black Republican Allen West as member of the Congressional Black Caucus, which she hopes to "change from the inside out." She recently stated on ABC News, "I told[4] Congressman West to hang in there, reinforcements are coming."

"I believe fiscal discipline, limited government and personal responsibility are vital to a stronger America," Love said[5]. "Nowhere is this message more important than among the lawmakers who profit from promoting an unsustainable entitlement system rife with failed poverty programs that perpetuates the culture of government dependency and discourages self-reliance among black Americans. This is the antithesis of Dr. Martin Luther King's dream."

Wisconsin Representative Paul Ryan recently appeared in Utah to campaign for Love. He told a local newspaper[6], "we need people who are sincere reformers who will do what it takes to get the country back on track. I see that kind of person in Mia — a real leader with natural leadership skills, who's not afraid to make tough calls and do what needs to be done to save the country from a debt crisis."

Love would know about managing public money and making tough decisions. Her website recounts how as councilmember and later mayor of Saratoga Springs, Utah, Love oversaw extreme growth followed by economic retrenchment that meant having to cut city services. After examining the city's needs, Love and the city council made the necessary cuts to keep essential city services, and keep taxes low. Following her election as mayor, one of Love's first acts as mayor was to reduce the property tax. She points out that while many cities saw their credit ratings cut, the City of Saratoga Springs, Utah, was one of the few municipalities that weathered the financial crisis and kept its highest-possible rating with Standard and Poor's.

Love is the proud daughter of Haitian immigrants who came to the United States with only $10, hoping to achieve the American dream. While her mother cleaned houses and worked at a nursing home, her father worked for a painting company and drove school buses and cleaned toilets for a local school.

"I am a product of that hard work," she told[7] Yahoo News, "a product of the American dream."

President Obama's recent comments about successful people not succeeding on their own struck a nerve with her. "Entrepreneurs are the backbone of the US economy," Love told me. "Obama basically said that success is not about individual effort and that is ridiculous. My dad scrubbed toilets. He did it himself. Obama didn't scrub toilets for him."

Recently Love was campaigning and she came across an owner of a bar-be-que restaurant who was also incensed about Obama's comments. "He told me that this election is not political for him; it is completely personal. His small business affects everything in his life. He told me, 'having you walk into my business and ask how I am doing and what we can do to make it better is important to me.'"

Understandably, liberals are getting nervous. In a recent analysis of the race, The Daily Kos[8] called Mia Love a "token black Republican," and said that she was "one of the two African Americans in Utah not playing for the Jazz [basketball team]."

Liberals will need more than insults to defeat Mia Love. Utah's 4th congressional district is a new district so it will have no true incumbent. The closest to an incumbent is the sitting congressman from Utah's 2nd district, Democrat Jim Matheson. Matheson won re-election in 2010 by a margin of less than 5% of the vote. His opponent that year was a relatively unknown, poorly-funded Republican.

Since his 2010 re-election Matheson has switched his votes several times on repealing Obamacare, which Love says is consistently and unequivocally opposed by the people of Utah.

"In early 2011, Matheson showed his true colors and voted against repealing Obamacare when the political ramifications were minimal. On July 10th, he voted against the rule that allowed July 11th's repeal vote to occur. He stuck his finger in the wind and voted 'aye' in a desperate attempt to save face and save his job in November," Love said.

Unlike his last election, in this election Matheson might not be facing an unknown in Mia Love, and he probably won't be facing a poorly-financed candidate either. According to recent FEC filings[9], Love has raised almost $500,000 to Matheson's $1.6 million, and she is closing in fast.

The Cook Political Report rates[10] this race as a toss-up. Anyone wishing to donate to Mia Love's campaign for Congress may do so here[11].

August 6, 2012

CHIK-FIL-A AND DOUBLE STANDARDS

We are very much supportive of the family – the biblical definition of the family unit. We are a family-owned business, a
family-led business, and we are married to our first wives. We
give God thanks for that. We operate as a family business ...
our restaurants are typically led by families – some are single.
We want to do anything we possibly can to strengthen families.
We are very much committed to that ... We intend to stay the
course. We know that it might not be popular with everyone,
but thank the Lord, we live in a country where we can share our
values and operate on biblical principles. (Dan Cathy, President
of Chik-Fil-A, *Baptist Press*[1], July 16, 2012)

Some people have a lot of nerve. Have you ever heard such hate
speech? Shocking.

In all seriousness, the food at Chik-fil-A might be a little bland, but
its politics are hot and spicy, with an extra helping of political incor-
rectness. And the Chik-fil-A president's opinions on marriage have a
lot of people's feathers in a ruffle, and they are starting to squawk.

Two mayors, one from Chicago and the other from Boston, have
criticized the political opinions held by Chik-fil-A's president. No longer will Chik-fil-A be allowed to open a restaurant in Chicago, and forget about Boston. No word yet on other traditional-marriage advocates
that have already made it into Boston and Chicago, like Catholic or
Baptist churches, or Muslim mosques.

Michael Graham of the *Boston Herald* had a great scoop[2], when he
pointed out that Boston's mayor took time out from his anti-Chik-fil-A
ranting to help dedicate a Bostonian mosque. According to Graham,
when the City of Boston sold the land to the mosque at below-market
cost, the mosque followed an imam who advocated the execution of
gays. The imam just couldn't decide whether gays should be thrown
from a high place or burned.

The imam eventually settled on stoning gays to death. But yet the mayor of Boston reserves his ire for Christians like Chik-fil-A president Dan Cathy, advocate of traditional marriage.

Honestly, what is it with liberals and Christianity? It seems as if Muslim countries can advocate and actually do any kind of torture or killing of gays and women and the average liberal will ignore it and instead find a Christian to hate. And of course it is the Christian who is branded the "hater."

This Chik-fil-A tempest reminds me of my own Facebook battle a few weeks ago with several liberals who attributed much of anti-gay actions in the world to Christians. Most of the time I ignore political posts like this, but when a liberal friend of mine posted a citation[3] to an article about a Ugandan church that debated imprisoning or executing gays, I had to respond.

"It is horrible that gays are mistreated anywhere, whether by a proposal in Uganda by a few rogue bishops, or by much of the Muslim world, where gays are routinely tortured or executed," I ventured. Immediately, others in the discussion referred me to other notable Christians and their views on gays, as an explanation as to why Christians "have blood on their hands."

I responded that whatever the level of gay-hatred from people claiming to be Christian, it is not even close to what really happens to gays in Muslim countries. "Enough hate to go around," came the reply.

I provided links to websites that chronicle Muslim torturing of women and gays, including one website that had a photo, front and center, of two gays in Iran about to be hanged. A few minutes after the photo was taken, those gays were dead. That photo had to make an impression.

It didn't. Instead, my opponents provided citations to a story of one Christian pastor who complained that the government won't kill gays, and to another pastor who advocated quarantining gays.

After some back and forth on glass houses and moral equivalences, I finally got an admission that Christianity is "graded on a curve."

As anyone who has been to sixth grade can tell you, "grading on a curve" means a double-standard in favor of lower-performing students. Bad students get help with their grades while good students get grade reductions.

And this is what is happening not only in the Chik-fil-A controversy but to Christianity in general. Christianity, and any organization like Chik-fil-A that advocates Christian positions, is "graded on a curve," or given a lower grade than the grade given to Islam and the murderous imam associated with the Boston mosque. That explains it.

And that might be the silver lining to this whole Chik-fil-A controversy: the double-standard exposed for all to see.

Meanwhile, anyone like me who supports Chik-fil-A is expected to participate in this week's "buy-cott" of Chik-fil-A's bland food, so I will dutifully join in. My only question is this: what will it take for a chain of Thai restaurants, or maybe a group of Szechuan Chinese restaurants to take the same position so that we can eat at their restaurants? Why is it that the only restaurant chain that defends traditional marriage also happens to be the purveyor of the most boring food around?

July 30, 2012

I did my part

PRESIDENT OBAMA CHANNELS DON RICKLES

A lot has already been written about President Obama's July 13th speech in Roanoke, Virginia. But none of the commentary explains the real anger that entrepreneurs feel after watching the speech. Sure, there is much to be argued about whether small businesses and entrepreneurs are mooching from the government to which they pay taxes, and how small business success, if any, is the result of the federal government's generosity. Similar arguments have been made in the past.

But the video of the speech has a certain Kennedy-vs.-Nixon-Debate quality to it: those who read the transcript have different reactions to those who actually saw the video.

On occasion, President Obama goes off-prompter and lapses into a schtick where he thinks he is a comedian and he is getting laughs at some improv stage somewhere. That is what he was doing that day, being the comedian-in-chief. Problem is, comedy isn't always nice. Many times a comedian will belittle or mock a person picked out of the audience. That is the type of comedian he was being that day, the insult comedian. Kind of like channeling a mean comedian like Don Rickles, known sarcastically as "Mr. Warmth" and whose best-selling album was titled "Hello Dummy."

The July 13th speech[1] in Roanoke, Virginia, lasted 42 minutes and the part of the speech where President Obama discussed small businesses and entrepreneurs can be found at 33:32, and lasts about a minute. If you watch a video of that part of the speech without sound, the first thing you notice is that there is no smile, only a determined, forced smile from time to time. President Obama looks angry, as if he is barely containing his foul tempter about the subject, even though he is speaking to a bunch of adoring fans.

And a real transcript of that part of the speech would really read like this:

PRESIDENT OBAMA: And you know there are a lot of wealthy, successful Americans who agree with me — because they want to give something back.

They know they didn't — if, if (stammer) you've been successful, you don't, you didn't get there on your own. (Pause)

AUDIENCE: No! That's right! That's right! That's right!

PRESIDENT OBAMA: You, you didn't get there on your own. I'm always struck by people who think, 'well, it must be because I was, just so smart.' There are a lot of smart people out there.

AUDIENCE: Yes...

PRESIDENT OBAMA: 'It must be because I worked harder than everybody else.' Let me tell you something — there are a whole bunch of hardworking people out there. (Pause)

AUDIENCE: YES! YES! (clapping)

PRESIDENT OBAMA: If you were successful, somebody along the line gave you some help.

AUDIENCE: YES!

PRESIDENT OBAMA: There was a great teacher somewhere in your life.

AUDIENCE: YES!

PRESIDENT OBAMA: Somebody helped to create this unbelievable American system that we have that allowed you to thrive. Somebody invested in roads and bridges. If you've got a business — that (stammer) — you didn't build that.

AUDIENCE: That's right...

PRESIDENT OBAMA: Somebody else made that happen.

AUDIENCE: Yes...

When he stammers like he did, he places himself in the role of an average person watching someone else make a false argument. This is the straw man of the day: the entrepreneur who stupidly thinks they are smart and have worked hard. Then President Obama straightens up and speaks authoritatively to remind the entrepreneur that "there are a lot of smart people out there," and "there are a whole bunch of hardworking people out there." The audience eats it up with laughter and clapping.

Of course, lost in all the laughter and applause is the fact that President Obama is talking about a whole group of Americans, small business people and entrepreneurs, who do most of the hiring, and whose companies create most of the new, innovative products in this country. Yet, he is mocking them. Making fun of them. According to President Obama, those entrepreneurs falsely think that they are smart and have worked hard. What a bunch of idiots!

And that is what is so infuriating about this speech. It was the mocking of it all; the ridicule.

At least Don Rickles confines his ridicule to a single person called out from the audience. Actually that isn't entirely true. Don Rickles manages to offend people wherever he goes. He just isn't asking those he offends to vote for him for president.

July 23, 2012

ELENA KAGAN: THE OBAMACARE RECUSAL THAT WASN'T

Later this month the U.S. Supreme Court will release its decision on the fate of the Patient Protection and Affordable Care Act, also known as Obamacare. Although there are many issues involved in the Obamacare appeal, possibly the Achilles' heel of the law involves the so-called "individual mandate," which mandates that people buy health insurance or pay a fine that, in turn, goes to purchase a government-provided health insurance policy.

In constitutional terms, this issue involves the Constitution's limitation of government action to interstate commerce, and whether citizens can be forced *into* interstate commerce so that their engagement in the commerce mandated can then be regulated. One would think that this approach would expand the government's presence into commerce to such a point that any vestige of the Commerce Clause's limiting ability is now gone. Indeed, this is the issue that during the oral arguments left Solicitor General Don Verrilli[1] almost resembling Austin Pendleton's trial performance in the movie *My Cousin Vinny*[2].

But can you blame Verrilli? He was an attorney sent in to court to defend the indefensible. I have heard of attorneys in the exact same situation. I wonder what that feels like.

Anyway, the more relevant question in the Obamacare decision is why Justice Elena Kagan has not recused herself. The relevant rule[3] requires that a Supreme Court justice recuse himself or herself if in their previous capacity they served as "counselor or advisor" concerning a current matter before the Court, or if there is anything about the proceeding that the justice's impartiality can reasonably be called into question.

E-mails[4] released to Judicial Watch[5] revealed that when in 2010 Obamacare passed and Ms. Kagan was Solicitor General, Ms. Kagan viewed[6] the passage as "simply amazing" and that she assigned[7] a deputy in her office to help prepare legal defenses to any challenges to Obamacare. When in another e-mail she was asked for her opinion on a meeting to discuss legal defenses to Obamacare, Ms. Kagan replied "what is your phone number?," indicating either that she had too long-winded a response or that she foresaw a possibility that her e-mails might force her to recuse herself if she sat in review of the law, or both. At any rate, she had in fact participated as "counselor or advisor" of the law when she was solicitor general, and she is clearly not impartial about the fate of Obamacare, so she should recuse herself in this case.

But she won't. The problem is that recusal of a Supreme Court justice is self-executing. That is, the Supreme Court justice has to do it herself.

There are many other examples, but the most instructive example that I could find of justices recusing themselves was in the tragic case of the appeal of the killer of Michael Luttig's father. J. Michael Luttig was an appellate judge in the 4th Federal Circuit Court of Appeals, and at one time was himself on a short list of possible appointments to the Supreme Court.

But earlier in his life, Luttig had clerked for Justice Scalia before Scalia was appointed to the Supreme Court, and Luttig had also worked in the George H.W. Bush administration, where Luttig advised nominees David Souter and Clarence Thomas on their Supreme Court confirmations in the Senate.

In 1994, Luttig's father was shot and killed in a carjacking in Texas, and the perpetrator was arrested, tried, convicted and sentenced to die. The appeal worked its way up to the U.S. Supreme Court, where three of the nine justices on the Supreme Court, Justices Scalia, Souter and Thomas, decided to recuse[8] themselves from hearing the case. Apparently those justices felt that their professional relationships with the victim's *son* brought their impartiality into question. No one had ever alleged that the recusing justices had ever known or even met the victim in this case, but the fact that the victim's *son* had clerked for one of the justices, and had advised two of the justices on their conformations in the Senate, convinced the justices that they should recuse themselves from the case.

Clearly a different standard is being used in Justice Kagan's decision to stay in this case. Not only had she e-mailed her excitement of Obamacare's passage but has shared in the Obama administration's strategizing on the legal defenses for Obamacare. As sitting Supreme Court justice, Elana Kagan could very well be deciding on responses to arguments that she herself had helped formulate when she was solicitor general.

If Obamacare survives its Supreme Court challenge with Justice Kagan's help, her refusal to recuse herself could become one of several rallying cries for conservatives who will try to repeal Obamacare. Let's hope it won't come to that.

June 18, 2012

WHY THE ELIZABETH WARREN CONTROVERSY CONTINUES

Recently there has been a steady drumbeat of not only new revelations in the affirmative action controversy involving Massachusetts Senate candidate Elizabeth Warren, but also the quest for columnists to publish Native American puns while covering it. And some of the puns have been pretty good. As a columnist, I can vouch that a pun-rich story is catnip for opinion-writers. Indeed, using humor as a way to keep the reader's attention is one of the arrows in my personal literary quiver.

Sorry, I couldn't resist. But there is a lot more than humor that is keeping this story going. Granted, the campaign of incumbent Senator Scott Brown loves to generate buzz on the issue every day. And it is fair to say that the *Boston Herald,* the newspaper that broke the story in late April, has a conservative bent.

An argument can also be made that this controversy shows the bankruptcy of affirmative action. Ms. Warren has never been on the receiving end of any racial discrimination because of her claimed Native American heritage, and if she had, the racism would have exhibited even more stupidity than usual. Her features are almost the exact opposite of Native American features: fair skin, blond hair, blue eyes. She has even been compared[1] to the members of the late 70's Scandinavian rock band, ABBA.

Yet the claim that she was part Cherokee was out there when she was hired at Harvard Law School, and later when she was granted tenure there. And it is generally accepted that at the time Harvard Law School was promoting racial diversity in its faculty.

But all this was known within a couple weeks of the birth of this story. Nevertheless, the media keeps referring to it. And not just the conservative media – even the *New York Times*[2] and the *Washington Post*[3] have recently discussed the controversy. So what is it that keeps the story going?

I have a theory, and here goes. As anyone who has pondered the idea of applying for affirmative action help can attest, the temptation is great to "check the box," whereby you claim some kind of minority ancestry.

There is this guy I know – not me; some other guy — who, even though his parents were paying his bills, got alarmed at how much his tuition and housing cost as he progressed from college into law school. He looked into minority-based scholarships, and considered "checking the box," but there was a problem: he had the same physical features as Ms. Warren: fair skin, blond hair, and blue eyes. He also had a quick wit, muscular build and extreme intelligence, but that is beside the point.

But this guy did feel the temptation to apply. There must be thousands Caucasian students who face the same temptation all the time, or so I have heard. But to do so would be wrong, not playing by the rules.

Similarly, the temptation to apply for an affirmative action scholarship was probably a lot like the temptation felt by a lot of people who signed up for mortgages that they couldn't afford, requiring no down payment. Although it may have been legal, when applicants took advantage of programs that eased mortgage requirements, they stepped in front of others who followed the traditional route to home ownership: save up for a down payment and get a mortgage only for a house you can afford.

When the bottom fell out of the housing market and the Obama administration tried to bail out those who shouldn't have gotten easy mortgages in the first place, voters were outraged. They were angry that people who had not followed the rules were getting a free ride, an unfair advantage.

The Elizabeth Warren website taps into the anger felt by the public about those who have not played by the rules. "I believe we must be a country with a level playing field," she says on her website[4], "where everyone willing to work hard has a chance to get ahead."

It may be a stretch, but I would argue that the same outrage is at play in Elizabeth Warren's affirmative action scandal. Instead of working hard and waiting her turn for employment and tenure, she "checked the box" and claimed phony Native American ancestry. Now that she has been found out, the public is being told to give her a pass and let it go.

We live in a country with a recent history of un-even playing fields. And even worse, those who have enjoyed an unfair advantage, whether by applying for mortgages they cannot afford and haven't earned, or by claiming phony minority status, want their advantage paid for or excused by the rest of us. It simply isn't fair.

As I read the smoke signals of this controversy, this common outrage is why the story continues to resonate.

June 4, 2012

HEY CALIFORNIANS: GO TO TAHOE!

A few weeks ago my family and I went to Lake Tahoe for a little snow skiing. We had a great time, except for some obvious "grade deflation" that occurred with the ski slopes. I skied some intermediate slopes and fell many times, indicating that the slopes were probably really expert slopes. Either that or the laughably-improbable alternative that I am not in as good shape as I was only a few years ago. No, it had to be the mis-graded slopes.

But during the trip we drove across the state border from California to Nevada and back several times. Except for the different colored-license plates and the fact that smoking is still allowed in restaurants in Nevada, we would have never known the difference between the two states we drove through. The roads were just the same, the restaurants were just as overpriced, and the scenery was the same, and the ski slopes were just as incorrectly graded. Yet, the times when we drove from California into Nevada we drove from the highest-taxes state to one of the lowest-taxed states.

In fact, California currently has the third-highest state income tax in the nation, and the nation's highest sales and gasoline taxes. Meanwhile, Nevada has no state income tax, a much lower gasoline tax and a lower state sales tax of 6.85%.

With such a difference in state taxes you would think that leaving California and entering Nevada would at least entail a huge change in scenery, like gold-plated roads with pampered, uniformly-wealthy people on the California side and huddled masses living underneath highway overpasses, asking for hand-outs on the Nevada side. But no, things were pretty much the same.

So what gives? What accounts for the difference in taxes and indifference in the states? Essentially, a lack of leadership, and the lack of political will to make difficult choices. While Nevada makes do with its lower income, sales and other taxes, California is mired in a huge budget deficit and has been for some time. Just this last week, California Governor Jerry Brown announced that California is in the hole not

$9 billion as reported earlier, but closer to $16 billion[1]. Of course, only $4 billion of this additional red ink was because of un-materialized revenues from state taxes while the rest was increases in spending this year and next, but no matter. The governor is proposing a tax increase[2] on November's ballot, and it is expected to raise $7 billion per year, raising the state's sales tax even higher, and its top income tax bracket to 13.3%, the nation's highest.

Another proposal[3] facing California voters this fall will be the "Molly Munger's California State Income Tax Increase to Support Education Initiative," named after Molly Munger, daughter of Berkshire Hathaway billionaire Charlie Munger. (Question: what is it with Berkshire Hathaway? First Warren Buffet and now his partner's daughter are pushing huge tax increases. Maybe there is something in the water at the Berkshire headquarters in Omaha.) If passed, the Munger initiative would raise an estimated $10 billion per year by raising taxes on all but the poorest Californians, with the windfall earmarked for education.

Other tax hikes for Californians are being proposed, making this November's ballot an orgy of tax hike proposals for Californians. Cumulatively, the proposed tax hikes could cost Californians almost $25 billion more per year, including an increased tax on out-of-state businesses, which will undoubtedly be passed along to California consumers. In one of the already highest-taxed[4] states with an anual economy[5] of $1.9 trillion, these new tax hikes could take a pretty big chunk out of the state's fragile economy.

Obviously, Californians need to reject these tax hikes and force the politicians in Sacramento to concentrate on cutting spending. This is what normal people do when faced with a short-fall in their income.

To any Californian who might be tempted to vote in favor of any of these tax hikes because of whatever state service or group of workers who are in jeopardy, let me just give this simple advice: go to Lake Tahoe and just drive across the border into Nevada. As you drive into Nevada you will notice a very similar state except much lower taxes. No other difference. There is no reason why California needs such higher taxes when Nevada doesn't. Californians should vote "no" on all its proposed tax hikes and demand that the state government get its act together and cut spending.

May 21, 2012

TED CRUZ, THE TEA PARTY'S BUNKER-BUSTER

Here is how it works: a federal agency re-interprets its job to encompass whole new areas of the economy. For example, the EPA says that the Clean Air Act allows it to create a whole new cap-and-trade system[1], or to outlaw the lead[2] in bullets. Never mind that such ideas weren't even hinted at in the Clean Air Act or in any of the laws that created the EPA.

Or the Fish and Wildlife Service decides that a lizard[3] that lives in an area that perfectly matches the Texas Permian Basin oil fields is endangered, thus turning the west Texas oil business into a paperwork chaos. Or the Department of Health and Human Services mandates[4] that some catholic hospitals have to begin dispensing contraceptives or abortion pills. Or the National Labor Relations Board decides to sue[5] if a company moves its manufacturing plant to a location the NLRB doesn't like.

At that point, any Republican office-holder who gets elected, hoping to be there and vote against stuff like this when it happens will have already lost. There won't be any vote. Federal bureaucrats, like people secure in their bunkers, need not worry about any vote on what they are doing.

Enter the Texas Tea Party's favorite GOP senate candidate and bunker-buster, Ted Cruz. "These bureaucracies," Cruz recently e-mailed me, "must be reined in. Instead of allowing the people to participate in the democratic process, the bureaucrats create the rule and then declare that it will benefit society, sidestepping the constitutional legislative process. That's why we must re-establish the proper role of the federal government. To do that, we need new leadership in the U.S. Senate."

Pass the popcorn — it will probably be a good show when Ted Cruz gets onto those Senate oversight committees, shaking things up. He probably can't wait for the oversight of these bureaucracies.

Ted Cruz has a history of shaking things up in a big way. As the author of 70 Supreme Court briefs as Texas Solicitor General, Cruz was instrumental in several U.S. Supreme Court decisions, including *District of Columbia v. Heller*[6], which held that the 2nd Amendment defines an individual right to gun ownership, as opposed to a "collective right" for a state-run militia. That was a huge win for gun owners.

Also, in *Medellin*[7] *v. Texas,* Cruz led the defense of Texas against not only the Bush administration but the World Court, the United Nations and 90 other nations when they attempted to pressure Texas against executing a rapist/murderer who was tried and convicted in Texas.

Recently Cruz has been stirring things up on the Justice Department's "Fast and Furious" scandal[8], calling for impeachment and possible prosecution of Attorney General Eric Holder. Not exactly your average go-along and get-along politician. In fact, it sounds pretty obnoxious.

But I say that as a compliment. See, we conservatives need all the obnoxious representatives we can get. How many times does a candidate promise to get tough, only to succumb to the usual big-money Washington politics? Someone always seems to be scratching someone else's back, contributions are made and the stupid people who follow the rules, we citizens, get stuck with the bill. That is what brought about the Tea Party movement in the first place. Early in the big-spending days of the Obama presidency, watching bail-outs, rescues and give-aways from "Obama's stash[9]," our limit was reached. Enough is enough. Time for a correction.

My personal favorite Ted Cruz campaign issue is his approach to Obamacare, which has become a mantra[10] of his campaign: "I will work to repeal every word and every syllable of Obamacare." Sounds kind of like a Matthew 24, not-one-stone-left-upon-another approach, which is exactly what will be needed for the Obamacare monstrosity.

Cruz' main opponent in the Republican nomination battle will be current lieutenant governor and establishment GOP favorite David Dewhurst, who also pledges to repeal[11] Obamacare. But in a recent filing[12] with the Federal Elections Commission, Dewhurst was shown to have accepted donations from Pfizer, Humana, Harden Healthcare, the American Hospital Association, and AstraZeneca, so he probably cannot be taken seriously on that issue.

And although Dewhurst was recently endorsed by Texas Governor Rick Perry, Dewhurst's website lists endorsements[13] of many lobbyists and political action committees that have had dealings with the Texas government, which also doesn't look good. Not exactly a stranger to the type of political back-scratching that happens with lobbyists.

One recent controversy in the campaign was whether in 2005 Dewhurst proposed a "wage tax," as opposed to an income tax, which is outlawed by the Texas constitution. Allegedly such a tax would have raised a small amount of money for Texas schools.

Cruz said[14] that Dewhurst did in fact make such a proposal, and Dewhurst denied[15] it. As evidence, the Cruz website presented a *Wall Street Journal* editorial[16] published at the time, and an interviewer[17] who heard Lt. Gov. Dewhurst actually make the proposal back then. To be fair to Dewhurst, he sure isn't proposing any tax hikes in Washington now. No sane Republican candidate in Texas would. (Oh, be still my beating Californian heart – these Texas guys are arguing over who might fudge a zero state income tax while the knuckleheads in Sacramento are battling over whether to raise[18] California's top rate to 11% or to 13%!)

But every argument like this means a lot to Texas conservatives in this heated Senate nomination race. FEC filings[19] show an uphill battle for Cruz, but things can change. While Dewhurst has raised more than twice what Cruz has raised, almost $12 million to about $5 million, the current cash on hand figure, about $3 million, is about the same for both candidates. And a recent poll[20] shows Ted Cruz inching closer to David Dewhurst for the May 29 Texas primary. With national conservative supporters[21], including not only Tea Party Senators Pat Toomey, Mike Lee, Jim DeMint, and Rand Paul, but also endorsements from the Club For Growth, FreedomWorks, and the Eagle Forum, things are looking up for what could be the Senate's next conservative senator and Tea Party bunker-buster.

April 23, 2012

THE PLAGUE OF FINANCIAL RUIN

There is a scene in the 1947 book *The Plague* by Albert Camus in which the citizens of the sequestered city of Oran, Algeria go to an opera to take their minds off of the bubonic plague that has beset their city. Instead of entertainment and diversion, the viewers of the opera watch in horror as the main actor in the opera collapses on stage from symptoms of the bubonic plague.

After having to read this book in high school, I did my best to forget it and all of its various metaphors. And I was doing fine until last weekend when I opened the local newspaper and read[1] about how an acquaintance, educated, middle class, and, until recently, successful, had declared bankruptcy and is about to have his family's house foreclosed. The article described the possible situations that could influence his future living situation, and, ominously, admitted that homelessness is a very real possibility for this man's future, unless he and his wife and kids can find either low income housing or some family or friends to move in with. Just like the citizens in *The Plague* who craved diversion from the plague around them, my attempt to read about the local happenings around town didn't bring distraction but instead highlighted the fact that a person close to my circle of friends had succumb to the epidemic of financial ruin and possible homelessness that has been attacking the rest of the country.

What is particularly distressing about this case is the fact that the family didn't take particularly irresponsible financial risks to get where they are. The article details the family business, a golfing store, that the family began in 2005, and by 2007 the business was so good that the family leveraged their home to expand. Then in 2008 the economy soured and revenues plummeted. All things having to do with golf were suddenly seen as luxuries and not necessary. Then in 2009 the store experienced an inventory theft and denial of insurance coverage, and finally closed in mid 2009, and the family filed for bankruptcy. Sure, his job wasn't a standard 9-to-5 job working for the government or big company, but it wasn't anything very unstable either.

In my corner of the world I am noticing more and more cases like this, where a family makes the kind of business decisions that are not irresponsible, and after several unfortunate events the family faces ruin and possible homelessness. A family whose future once looked promising is now talking to in-laws or parents, asking if they can move in, or "double-up," as it is known.

And "doubling-up" is becoming more common. According to a recent study[2] by the National Alliance to End Homelessness, while the number of homeless in the United States from 2009 to 2010 has held steady, the number of people "doubling up," defined as people who live with friends, family or other non-relatives for economic reasons, increased a whopping 13 percent. The number of those doubling-up has increased 50% between 2005 and 2010. A recent Census study[3] echoes this trend and reports that in the spring of 2011, 18.3% of all American households were doubled-up. That is a lot of people like my friend who just cannot afford their own home and look to family or friends to loan them a couch for a while.

But this is not just an issue of housing statistics and bankruptcy filings. There is a human element there. It has to be completely demoralizing to have to declare bankruptcy and lose your home. When someone declares bankruptcy and leaves their house for their parents' couch or someone's spare bedroom, how is a person like that ever supposed to bounce back? How can they ever hope to have the self-confidence needed to start their own business or send out resumes? It has to be pretty hard on the confidence and self-worth of the families who are going through this. Depressing, in fact.

Meanwhile, my friend's wife has started a blog[4] where she gives all the details on where to file for unemployment insurance, food stamps, low-income housing, veteran's benefits, and so on. In a recent blog post she discussed the expiration of her unemployment insurance, and she wondered what her family will do after that income source is gone.

Yes, this recession is a nasty one. We are under attack by a plague of financial ruin. And just like in *The Plague,* our epidemic will some-day run its course and things will get better. Until then, we need to help those among us who are now or who may someday face the prospect of homelessness. Money can definitely help, but more importantly, they need our compassion and understanding.

April 2, 2012

THE PERILS OF A LIVE MICROPHONE

Towards the end of a 90-minute Monday meeting with Russian President Dmitry Medvedev, President Barack Obama, apparently unaware, was recorded by a live microphone saying[1] "On all these issues, but particularly missile defense, this can be solved but it's important for him to give me space," then, "this is my last election. After my election I have more flexibility," to which Mr. Medvedev responded, "I understand. I will transmit this information to Vladimir [Putin]."

So what did this mean? Obviously what is being referred to is something that the American people might not want, otherwise it could be mentioned in public before the election. And why does Obama have to ask the Russians for any cooperation on this issue at all? That doesn't sound like a strong negotiation approach to me, assuming it is a real negotiation and not just a big giveaway.

President Obama's body language is also very unsettling, leaning forward and then patting Medvedev's hand like he did. Then he sat back and looked around to make sure no one heard what he just said. President Obama *really* wants cooperation, or "space," from the Russians until after the election.

Besides the physical closeness, the closeness of positions of President Obama and the Russian leaders is unsettling. This is definitely not a negotiation between adversaries. In fact, the only adversaries in this equation are these world leaders and the American people. This scene is more reminiscent of Jimmy Carter's kiss[2] of Leonid Brezhnev than any negotiating President Reagan had with the Soviets in the 1980s.

And what is the "space" that President Obama says he needs? It probably means that he wants the Russians to hold off on some action they would be inclined to do otherwise–actions that would remind the American people that the Russians are still adversaries.

If there is some aggressive action the Russians want to take somewhere, like helping Assad in Syria quell the revolution there or supplying the Iranians with their nuclear equipment, then the American people would be wondering why the US is disarming in the face of this.

Implicit in President Obama's comments Monday is that the Russians can resume their actions after the elections–assuming the incumbent Democrat wins.

Here are some ideas as to what is going on: we have had reductions in warheads before. The New START treaty signed last year was already pretty lopsided against[3] the United States. In exchange for reductions in American long-range nuclear missiles and missile defenses in Western Europe, the Russians agreed to limit the numbers of their mobile missile launchers, while shorter-range missiles in which the Russians have at least a 5:1 numbers advantage were left alone.

Maybe what is on Obama's mind is even more of a lopsided arsenal and missile defense deal, or even a huge unilateral giveaway, like the total elimination of American and NATO nuclear warheads in Europe. Or it could be a huge reduction in warheads or abandonment of what little European missile defense still exists. The administration's proposed budget[4] already cuts back on SM-3 interceptor missiles[5] that are the backbone of our missile defense.

Or President Obama may have in mind something that doesn't need Senate ratification, like sharing[6] missile defense secrets such as hit-to-kill technology and velocity at burnout information. He may be referring to divulging strategic secrets of allies, like his administration did[7] last year. Whatever President Obama has in mind, we will all have to wait until after the election to find out what it is. But none of the theories look good for world peace.

To me, this exchange also highlights the lack of judgment possessed by President Obama, possessor of the most overrated intellect we have seen in a long time. Why even mention an election in the middle of a discussion on arms control anyway? Not too smart. Some observers will inevitably charge President Obama with signaling a request for some kind of help in his presidential campaign, or at least running the risk that the Russians might get that impression. After all, Obama did imply to the Russians that they will be better off if he wins the election.

That's definitely a cynical interpretation, but stranger things have happened in past elections. Remember how Chinese military money kept finding its way into President Clinton's re-election campaign[8]? That coincided with the relaxation of export controls for missile technology, which allowed the Chinese to greatly advance their ICBM guidance capabilities. Or recall the time when the late Senator Ted Kennedy offered[9] to meet with Soviet leader Yuri Andropov to coordinate their efforts to defeat President Reagan's re-election.

On his radio show Monday, Hugh Hewitt said "this sounds like a bad *Rocky and Bullwinkle* episode." Let's all hope that this is one of those quirky, slightly-funny news items that will become a footnote in history, nothing more. With international bullies like the Russians, you never know.

March 26, 2012

NEWT'S APOLLO 13 CANDIDACY

Between his angry Iowa concession speech[1] and his anti-capitalist talk[2] in the days before the New Hampshire primary, Newt Gingrich cemented several major problems with his campaign: an out-of-control temper, an unreliable ideological rudder, and plentiful baggage. These are problems that people who have been paying attention, including me[3], have pointed out. Newt's candidacy was like the Apollo 13 capsule and command module that had just experienced several explosions and was shooting into space without much power, and losing oxygen. Somehow, gravity from the Moon and the Earth combined to pull the Gingrich candidacy back and resulted in a victory in Saturday's South Carolina primary.

Fox News Analyst Juan Williams had a lot to do with Gingrich's return. One doesn't normally see a standing ovation at a presidential debate, and in fact the only time I have ever been tempted to stand up and cheer at a debate was when someone announced that the debate was over. But in last Monday's debate, Juan Williams asked[4] the questions that provided Speaker Gingrich with the slow pitch, right above the plate. With his answers, Gingrich hit the ball right over center field stands and got a standing ovation.

Here is how it happened: Williams asked whether Gingrich's previous comments about black Americans and food stamps and whether poor kids should work as janitors would be offensive to black Americans. If Gov. Romney had been asked a similar question, he could probably have been counted on to artfully dodge the question, or at least diplomatically disagree with Williams. Instead, Gingrich explained[5] that

> you could take one janitor and hire 30-some kids to work in the school for the price of one janitor, and those 30 kids would be a lot less likely to drop out. They would actually have money in their pocket. They'd learn to show up for work. They could do light janitorial duty. They could work in the cafeteria. They could work in the front office. They could work in the library. They'd be getting money, which is a good thing if you're poor. Only the elites despise earning money.

Williams pressed further, only to be told that "the fact is that more people have been put on food stamps by Barack Obama than any president in American history... I know among the politically correct, you're not supposed to use facts that are uncomfortable." Then, after referring to the unemployment along the I-73 corridor as not having been improved in three years, Gingrich concluded: "every American of every background has been endowed by their Creator with the right to pursue happiness. And if that makes liberals unhappy, I'm going to continue to find ways to help poor people learn how to get a job, learn how to get a better job, and learn some day to own the job." The crowd went wild.

In my own legal practice, I occasionally represent someone who is wrongfully accused. After many pre-trial hearings and court settings, where in front of the defendant the prosecutor explains to the court his version of the case and the ultimate guilt of the defendant, my client will get tired of hearing the wrong version of the case mentioned time and again. It gets old, and the client yearns for the truth to be spoken out loud in court. When we finally get the case in front of a jury and the truth of the case is finally heard out loud, it is so welcomed that sometimes you can see tears coming down the defendant's face. Someone is finally speaking the truth in open court!

So too with American conservatives. For over three years we have heard a president describe the short-comings of the American system, how racist and unfair America is, how unequal the country is and how unfortunate it is that in a our system while some people succeed, other people will fail, and how that is bad.

This narrative dovetails the constant drumbeat from academia and Hollywood, and it echoed President Obama's angry anti-capitalist speech[6] in Kansas a few weeks ago. The message heard by American conservatives has been: "we elites don't like you or your way of life." Gingrich's answer in Monday's debate was a full-throated defense of American capitalism, with a little Horatio Alger thrown in for good measure. Gingrich basically said that America is a great country with a great capitalist system, and he is here to defend it! Finally, somebody gets it!

Even Juan Williams said[7] that Gingrich won the debate, and most South Carolinians agreed[8]. And it isn't that the other candidates did anything wrong, but Gingrich spoke the words and had the attitude that American conservatives so desperately want to hear.

His South Carolina victory has put Newt Gingrich back in the race, much like the crew of the Apollo 13 spacecraft carefully made their way back to Earth after gravity pulled them back following some near-catastrophic explosions.

The Gingrich candidacy truly is the Apollo 13 Candidacy. It remains to be seen whether Gingrich's candidacy will skip off the Earth's atmosphere and fly back into space or whether his candidacy will make a successful re-entry into Earth's atmosphere and have a safe landing. But as the Tom Hanks character said at this stage of the

Apollo 13 movie, "we have good gimbles," whatever gimbles are. Get some popcorn, folks, the rest of this nomination contest might be interesting, and for a change someone might show up to defend America.

January 23, 2012

THE OLD NEWT IS BACK

Newt Gingrich's angry concession speech[1] in Iowa a few days ago brought him back to his ill-tempered persona from the 1990's. No longer is he the elder statesman he pretended to be only a few weeks ago. It would appear that despite his occasional forced-smiles, Newt Gingrich has spent the last several weeks an angry man. The cameras didn't show Gingrich's hands while he made this speech, but if they had, I wouldn't be surprised if he was rolling in his hands several Chinese Health balls, a la Captain Queeg[2], in the 1954 movie *Mutiny on the Bounty,* accusing people of hiding stolen strawberries.

And it is too bad, because as recently as November, Speaker Gingrich had so much promise. Talk about a bad six weeks!

The end of November saw Speaker Gingrich vault to the lead[3] of the GOP field. Everyone noticed his great debate performances, answering questions with well-thought-out positions and the occasional barb directed at the moderator. Not only did he win the September 7 debate[4] at the Reagan Library, it is fair to say that he *owned* it. He also did very well in the November 12 debate[5], in which he complimented other

Like Richard Nixon without the charm

Republican candidates. Everyone thought that a new even-tempered Newt was upon us.

In early December, Gingrich declared that it was inevitable that he would win[6] the GOP nomination. And he might have if only he had kept his tempter in check.

Other candidates, especially Mitt Romney, countered with negative campaign ads. Gingrich criticized Romney, charging that while at Bain Capital, Romney laid off employees. Here in California, Senator Barbara Boxer made the same argument[7] in 2010 when she was challenged for re-election from former Hewlett-Packard CEO Carly Fiorina. It didn't sit well with California conservatives then and doesn't sit well with American conservatives now. Businesses hire and lay off employees all the time.

By late-December, Romney made a very mild criticism, which should have been laughed at by Gingrich. Romney compared the Gingrich campaign organization to the *I Love Lucy* episode where Lucy frantically packaged chocolates. "I'd love to have him say that to my face," Gingrich angrily replied. Apparently, the constant negative ads in Iowa were getting under Gingrich's skin. Voters noticed, and Gingrich's poll numbers plummeted.

Pundits began remarking at how obsessed Gingrich was with criticizing Romney. Jonah Goldberg's pre-New Hampshire debate tweet[8] was typical: "Gingrich's opening line to Romney tomorrow? 'Hello. My name is Newton Gingrich. You killed my presidential campaign. Prepare to die.'" Actually comparing the *Princess Bride* character Inigo Montoya to the current Newt Gingrich might make poor Inigo look bad.

And Gingrich didn't disappoint in last Saturday's New Hampshire debate. Visibly irritated at Romney, he called for Romney to drop the "pious baloney" regarding not being a career politician.

On the stump, Gingrich repeated his earlier criticism of Romney's work at Bain Capital, when employees got laid off by companies being turned around by Bain. This has actually put Romney in the position of defending capitalism, which is a real gift in a Republican nomination contest.

But Gingrich didn't care. The possibility of damaging Romney's campaign seemed to be all that interested Gingrich. Columnist Charles Krauthammer compared[9] Newt's pursuit of Romney with Captain Ahab of the movie *Moby Dick*: "Ahab is loose in New Hampshire, stalking his great white Mitt."

On the day of the New Hampshire primary, Speaker Gingrich appeared on the *Today Show*[10], and agreed with an ad that described Romney as "a greedy, ruthless, corporate raider who slashed jobs for profit." According to Gingrich, this ad was "based upon historical fact."

The Club For Growth called[11] these attacks "disgusting." On his radio show[12] Tuesday, Rush Limbaugh said that Gingrich's candidacy is no longer a real campaign, but "payback time" for Romney's negative ads in Iowa.

Bottom line: Newt Gingrich is not a presidential candidate who makes you smile. He has become someone you would not want in your living room by the TV news each night, as the old saying goes. In my case, I have a young child in our house and Newt Gingrich and his sour-puss expressions would probably frighten her.

Inevitably, Gingrich won a mere 9% of Tuesday's vote in New Hampshire, but a recent *New York Times* blog[13] put his chances of winning the up-coming South Carolina primary at 9%, not far from ahead of the percentage[14] of Americans who believe the moon landings were faked.

In a November column[15] I referred to Gingrich as "Dick Cheney without the Darth Vader music." Now I think he is more accurately described as "Richard Nixon without the charm." He truly has come full circle. The old Newt Gingrich is back.

January 9, 2012

DON'T MESS WITH WEST TEXAS OR EASTERN NEW MEXICO

I just sent a comment to the US Fish and Wildlife Service (FWS) regarding its proposal to list the Dunes Sagebrush Lizard (DSL) on the "endangered" list of the Endangered Species Act, and I feel great about it. Absolutely great! After I pressed the "enter" button on my computer and sent this comment to the FWS, I celebrated by eating a third of a roll of raw Christmas cookie dough[1] instead of baking these cookies for an up-coming Christmas party. My friends at the party will understand – this was done in the name of something big!

My comment to the FWS can be found at this link here[2]. I encourage everyone in west Texas and eastern New Mexico to submit a similar comment (either e-mail or snail-mail) to the FWS at the address listed. Your jobs and economy are at stake. All comments are due early next month.

In fact, you don't even need to live in west Texas or eastern New Mexico to submit a comment to the FWS. You can write as an American who will be affected by such a ruling. And believe me, if this little lizard is listed as "endangered," we will all be affected in a big way.

Here is how it works: some critter somewhere gets listed as endangered, and the US government springs into action. To stop everyone else's actions.

In this case, this lizard hangs out in a small bush called the shinnery oak tree and sleeps in the sands nearby. This lizard seems to live only in an oil-rich part of the country (oil exploration companies, take note), specifically the Permian Basin area of west Texas and eastern New Mexico. There have been previous efforts to list this lizard as endangered, and last year a formal proposal[3] was made to do just that. The proposal was originally to be acted on by this month, but Senators Cornyn and Inhofe wrote a letter[4] to the Interior Department, which prompted new deadlines for this proposal, including the new comment deadline.

An endangered listing for the DSL would ruin the oil drilling industry in the Permian Basin, that area of west Texas and eastern New Mexico that currently produces about 20%[5] of all the oil from the lower 48 states and 5%[6] of total oil produced in the US. The oil produced there also constitutes 68%[7] of all oil produced in the state of Texas.

The FWS proposal itself, found here[8], contemplates not only denying all new oil-drilling permits, but curtailing current oil drilling, seismic testing and even operating oil pipelines in the area. All these activities supposedly disrupt the DSL, possibly leading to its extinction.

"But wouldn't that be economically disastrous?" you might ask. Of course it would, but don't think it won't happen anyway. Anyone who has driven along Interstate 5 in California has seen the results of the efforts to save the obscure Delta Smelt fish, a small, 4-inch long fish that can't swim very well and gets sucked into pumping stations of the California Aqueduct. In 2007 a federal judge ordered the aqueduct water pumps to be seasonally shut off[9] to protect this fish. The result: dead farms as far as the eye can see along I-5. Up to 1 million dried[10] up acres of Central California farmland, tens of thousands of unemployed farm workers, billions of dollars in losses, unemployment rates[11] as high as 35% in some farming communities, and higher food prices across the US. But look at the bright side: while the population of this fish may not have rebounded[12] to its pre-Aqueduct numbers, it at least has a little more respect in the animal kingdom.

Not only should everyone write a comment to the FWS, but we should also get all local congressmen and senators to get involved. In the 1970's there was a small fish called the snail darter[13] found in the area of an almost-completed dam in Tennessee. When the snail darter was listed as endangered, construction of the dam was halted. Senator Howard Baker got involved and doggedly pursued an amendment to the ESA law, and the dam was allowed to be completed once the fish was transplanted. There is no reason why today's Washington representatives from Texas and New Mexico could not raise a similar stink over the DSL issue.

Another victory of sorts for industry happened recently when a solar farm encroached on the habitat of a threatened tortoise[14] in the Mojave Desert near Needles, California. After the company involved, BrightSource Energy, agreed to a cordoned-off area for the tortoise the project was given the go-ahead by the FWS. Of course, it doesn't hurt that the chairman[15] of BrightSource has been a long-time contributor to Democrats and that BrightSource has a guaranteed government loan[16] ($1.6 billion) even bigger than the loan guarantee given to Solyndra.

But the complaint[17] from a BrightSource detractor was telling. "I don't even know why we have an Endangered Species Act at this point. The directive has come down from the very top of the Interior Department that we're building these projects regardless of their impact on the environment," said Chris Clarke, co-founder Solar Done Right. "To say that killing hundreds, perhaps thousands of tortoises on this site won't jeopardize the species is absolutely crazy."

Call me cynical, but I suspect that the standard applied to the Permian Basin oil-well drillers will be different from the standard applied to the Brightsource solar developers. Maybe the Permian Basin folks should consider installing some solar panels near their oil wells.

So dear reader, won't you send your own comment to the FWS? You might not be able to refer to the movie *Giant,* and vineyards in medieval Norway, like my letter did, but send something off today! If you don't send a comment, don't be surprised to find your name on the naughty list, deserving lumps of coal.

December 12, 2011

NEWT IS NO GECKO

Former House Speaker Newt Gingrich is an interesting candidate because he has been around so long and is only now topping a recent Gallup poll[1] for the Republican nomination, and yet as a candidate he comes pre-packaged with his own dirt. No need for investigative reporting here. Usually a candidate has to top a poll or two before some dirt comes out about them.

And some of the dirt is pretty ugly. When his first wife was recovering from surgery, he showed up to discuss[2] terms of their divorce (an episode attempted[3] to be revised by Newt's daughter Jackie). And during the late 90's Clinton-Lewinski scandals, Speaker Gingrich admitted to his own extra-marital affair while married to his second wife. This affair and others may be included in the "moments of regret" he has confessed[4] to in his personal life. Then when he left the House in 1999, he faced[5] a $300,000 fine from the House Ethics Committee for various ethics charges. There are other skeletons but you get the picture. Nothing too huge, but fairly obnoxious.

But as the nomination process enters the critical next few months, the most talked-about skeletons will probably be the most recent ones, including the almost $2 million in consulting fees he got[6] from Freddie Mac, which he says was for consulting, not lobbying; and the climate change commercial[7] with Nancy Pelosi, which Newt now admits[8] to be "one of the dumbest single things I have done in years." And my personal most loathsome recent Gingrich mistake was his criticism[9] last May of Paul Ryan's proposal to reign in government spending. Incidentally, Ryan's plan is now incorporated[10] into Newt's own 21st Century Contract With America, so maybe Newt was just kidding.

But there is a lot to say for the Gingrich candidacy. He has been around in Washington longer than any of the other Republican candidates, 1979 to 1999. He was part of the 1994 Republican take-over of Congress, and as Speaker he worked with President Clinton to reform welfare, pass a balanced budget, and cut capital gains taxes. He has taught history classes, published both fictional and policy-oriented books and served as president of GOPAC. Kind of like Dick Cheney without the Darth Vader music.

Whatever reptilian qualities he has, Newt is no gecko. Since the beginning of his career he has held steady positions on taxes, government spending, foreign policy, abortion, gun control and social issues. You have to give him credit for not changing his colors.

Of the leading candidates for the Republican nomination, it is former Massachusetts governor Mitt Romney who has been the chameleon. Romney has an ambivalence to tax cutting[11] and is late to the idea of entitlement reform[12]. Romney has also had previous opposite positions on abortion[13], gun control[14], global warming[15], even ethanol[16] subsidies. He recently wimped[17] out on taking a position in the recent Ohio union benefits fight. And as governor of Massachusetts, Romney passed Romneycare[18], which has similar[19] provisions to Obamacare, which Republicans can't wait to repeal.

Romney has been a good debater, but Newt has been the candidate who lectures or scoffs at the moderator's simplistic or gotcha questions[20]. Recently he scoffed[21] at a question from Maria Bartiromo when she asked Newt to spell out his philosophy on healthcare in 30 seconds. In a recent debate Newt lectured[22] moderator Scott Pelley on why an enemy combatant does not get the protections of the US legal system when the citizen is at war with the US. As one of many conservative viewers who is tired of debate moderators and their snarky questions, I was gratified by his response. And it happened so quickly, I am not sure Pelley even knew that he had been corrected.

And what Republican doesn't love Newt's recent comments about the Occupy movement: they "should[23] go get a job right after they take a bath"? And arguing[24] with reporters on lack of real economic perspective on the economy? Love it! It all took a bit of obnoxiousness, but obnoxiousness might be what the country needs right now.

See, we conservatives know the routine, whether it is a long-term discussion about budget priorities, a committee hearing on Medicaid or veteran's benefits, a debate about prescription drugs, farm subsidies, whatever. Here is how it works: first, a conservative makes a sensible proposal; second, one or more hard-luck cases are presented (cue the violins), pleading for more money to save someone's life or end their misery, or whatever; third, the conservative folds; and fourth, the budget remains hopelessly out of balance and getting worse, inevitably leading for calls of higher taxes. In the end, only a jerk would follow the ridiculous original conservative proposal. What was he/she thinking?

But we conservatives are getting really tired of this. We might be ready for that jerk who will make the proposals we need, get slammed by the media, ridiculed, but not fold and continue fighting. Newt may be that candidate.

In a recent debate[25], moderator Wolf Blitzer peppered candidate Ron Paul with questions of a hypothetical uninsured person who contracts a terminal disease, and eventually Blitzer interjected "should society just let him die?" Someone in the audience yelled out "yes!" and the crowd cheered. Translation: we are tired of having to pay these huge government bills to make sure that the .0001% of hard-luck stories never happens. Whoever proposes any kind of spending restraint, like Wisconsin Representative Paul Ryan or Newt Gingrich, needs to stick to their guns and not recoil from this kind of questioning and hard-luck stories.

Painted as obnoxious? For Newt Gingrich, been there, done that. Newt is no gecko, and we need a non-gecko for our next president.

November 21, 2011

MITT ROMNEY: 2012'S GERALD FORD

Glenn Reynolds of Instapundit[1] has written[2] that comparing President Obama to Jimmy Carter would be a *best*-case scenario for President Obama. But President Obama may be in the process of getting a lucky break.

This next election might not be an exact replay of 1980, with President Obama playing the part of Jimmy Carter. Imagine if, instead of nominating Ronald Reagan for president, the Republicans had dusted off Gerald Ford and run him against Jimmy Carter in 1980. That is a good analogy of what is probably going to happen in a Mitt Romney nomination in 2012. Mitt Romney now leads in most of the polls of the first four states, Iowa[3], New Hampshire[4], South Carolina[5], and Florida[6], and after winning most of these states Romney will probably have the momentum needed to cross the finish line for the GOP nomination for president in order to run against President Obama in November. This is a reality conservatives will have to accept. And it will constitute a replay of 1980 except with President Obama playing the part of Jimmy Carter, and Mitt Romney playing the part of Gerald Ford, had Ford run again.

And what did we get from the Ford presidency? One can make an argument that Gerald Ford's elevation to president after President Nixon's resignation gave force to the 25th Amendment[7], healing the country after Watergate, blah, blah, blah, but I personally think the best thing about President Ford — and this is just me — was the amusing falls he had walking down or up stairs.

Do a Google image or YouTube search of "President Ford" and "fall" or "falling down" and you can see what I'm talking about. When I was a budding young middle school student, barely paying attention, I actually learned to notice when President Ford was shown walking down the stairway from Air Force One. He would get about half-way down the stairway, miss a step or two, let go of the handrail, and then… splat! Head first! How he managed to get up after these falls was quite amazing, but we have to remember that Ford played football in college, so he had special training for his time as president.

I was able to find one time when President Ford was seen tripping while climbing up some stairs, and this was not as funny a pratfall, but the brown plaid jacket he was wearing was so tacky that he was asking for trouble even being seen in public in it. I know these were the 1970's, when fashion lost all sense of civility, but still.

And slapstick is funny, even when unintentional. So when NBC began a new comedy show named *Saturday Night Live* during the Ford administration, actor Chevy Chase began every episode acting like President Ford, falling down and stumbling[8], then announcing the opening of the show. No offense to Mr. Chase, but all NBC had to do was roll the films its news division had of President Ford's latest falling down. The real thing was much funnier than Chevy Chase's falls. It might be true what they say: a Chevy imitating a Ford is just not that funny...

But as amusing as he was, Gerald Ford was not only a tacky dresser but a milquetoast Republican. Vietnam was formally lost under President Ford. Helsinki Accords and the SALT Treaties were signed and they were roundly criticized as favoring the Soviet Union. Ford also gave a conditional amnesty for draft-dodgers from the Vietnam War. Conservatives saw all this as a limp-wristed foreign policy.

And President Ford proved to be pretty moderate in domestic policy as well. The US economy experienced a bout of inflation, so President Ford had what he called[9] a bold initiative: wearing WIN buttons ("Whip Inflation Now") as a fashion accessory, asking people for unenforced pledges not to raise prices on whatever they sold. It was all kind of comical. Predictably, nothing came from the WIN buttons, because businesses charge whatever the market will bear. Then inflation became less a priority to Ford than addressing the next problems of recession and unemployment. President Ford tried to cut federal spending and raised taxes, then later proposed a tax cut.

And as his sole Supreme Court appointment, we can blame President Ford for Justice John Paul Stevens, a pretty consistent liberal justice, who more than once was seen wearing a bow-tie. Striped.

Mitt Romney comes with several "moderate" problems that might remind conservatives of President Ford, most notably the fact that Romney has an ambivalence to tax cutting[10] and entitlement reform[11]. Romney has also had previous opposite positions on abortion[12], gun control[13], global warming[14], even ethanol[15] subsidies. And when Mitt Romney was governor or Massachusetts, he passed Romneycare[16], which has many similar[17] provisions to Obamacare. This doesn't sit too well with conservatives, who have repealing Obamacare as a rallying cry. Conservatives will definitely not be too happy and maybe even hostile to a Romney candidacy. It has been said[18] that if Romney gets the GOP nomination, a possibility exists that there will be a third-party conservative challenger.

Will Mitt Romney fall down stairways as did Gerald Ford? Will he be seen in public with a tacky brown plaid jacket? Who knows. We might not get a solid conservative contrast to President Obama with a President Romney, but we conservatives should look at the bright side of a Romney presidency: we might get another new comedy show out of it!

November 7, 2011

WHERE IS THE URGENCY?

Right about the date of Republican debate last week it started to rain pretty heavily here in Napa County. Rains like this are rare for early October. A rainfall right before the grapes are picked can form a fungus on the grapes called Botrytis, which can distort the fermentation of the grapes when the winemakers try to ferment the grape juice into wine. Within a few hours, grapes in Napa and Sonoma Counties, at least the most vulnerable chardonnay and sauvignon blanc grapes, were being picked before the fungus could set in. Traffic here was pretty bad, with those flat-bed trucks hauling the grape bin-thingies driving pretty slowly. There was urgency in the wine country!

You sure can't say the same for the Republican candidates for president, not for grape fungus but for the country's financial fungus of deficits and debt. Our country is in the process of spending itself into bankruptcy and the Republican candidates are treating this like any other election. If the deficits are not ended pretty soon a certain economic fungus will set in, and it won't be pretty.

In the last Republican debate[1], only Representative Michele Bachmann referred in detail to our high annual deficits. For the rest of the debate the deficits and total national debt was barely mentioned. I would give these candidates a score of 72, about the same score that the wine Two-buck Chuck[2] gets! So there!

Here is how we got here, and like a fine wine that ages with time, we have to dust off these facts: after a few years of political stalemate-inspired surpluses during the Clinton years, the George W. Bush years had an average[3] annual deficit of $412 billion per year. Conservatives were pretty miffed, and for good reason. All these deficits mean that of each subsequent fiscal year, a larger and larger amount has to be spent on interest *before* any spending takes place on other national priorities.

But with the election of President Barack Obama, deficit spending entered into a whole new dimension. Instead of the approximately $200 to $500 billion per year deficits, we were treated to $1.3 *trillion* annual deficits or more. In the first year of the Obama presidency, 2009,

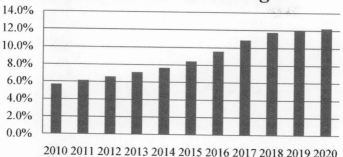

Interest Payment As Percent Of Entire Federal Budget

Source: Congressional Budget Office, *Budget and Economic Ourtlook, An Update*, August 2011

much of that deficit can be blamed on the $787 billion stimulus[4] bill, which was designed to be a Keynesian boost to the economy. But for the years 2010 and 2011, President Obama piled on another $1.3 trillion annual deficit[5] per year. According to the Congressional Budget Office, United States total debt[6] currently stands at $14.9 trillion, and the interest on that debt takes up approximately 6%[7] of our annual spending. By 2018, 12%[8] of our annual spending will be for interest on the debt, before spending any money on anything else. (Notice how the CBO numbers assume a sudden burst of responsibility in the years 2019 and 2020. Consider me skeptical.)

This explains why a few weeks ago people were urging Wisconsin Representative Paul Ryan to join the presidential contest. After marinating himself in the reality of our out-of-control entitlement spending, as chair of the House Budget committee, Ryan made the only serious proposal to reign in entitlement spending. Granted, his proposal[9] wasn't perfect, but it addressed the main budget-busters, Medicaid and Medicare, and limited federal spending overall. So it was a good start, and the seriousness of the plan led to serious people urging Ryan to run for president. After a vacation in Colorado, and no doubt reading my column[10] urging him *not* to run, Representative Ryan decided to gave it a pass.

Now I am not so sure that was such a great idea. While any sensible Republican felt let down with President Bush's overspending, Representative Ryan appears to have been one of the few who has noticed and been alarmed by the total debt that has accumulated under President Obama. His detractors — and their media supporters — seem not to notice what a mess our national finances are. In fact, America's impending bankruptcy is probably one of the most ignored stories of the press.

Well, that isn't entirely true. While they might not be capitalist-inclined, at least *Pravda* has noticed the out of control spending. Check out what a *Pravda*[11] columnist had to say only a few months into the Obama administration in April, 2009:

> The final collapse [of American capitalism] has come with the election of Barack Obama. His speed in the past three months has been truly impressive. His spending and money printing has been a record-setting, not just in America's short history but in the world. If this keeps up for more than another year, and there is no sign that it will not, America at best will resemble the Wiemar Republic and at worst Zimbabwe. (Hat tip: Ace of Spades)[12]

This week there will be yet another Republican candidate debate[13], and let's hope the candidates spend at least a little time on the America's deficit and cumulative debt. Show some urgency, guys! We don't have much time left!

October 17, 2011

GOVERNOR PERDUE DOES STAND-UP

Wouldn't it be hilarious if a governor suggested postponing congressional elections for a couple years? Recently, Democratic North Carolina Governor Bev Perdue did just that[1] in a speech before a local Rotary Club. Her reasoning was that if elections were postponed then politicians who don't have to worry about re-election will be better able to handle the current economic crisis in our country. When I first saw the headline on this suggestion I missed the name of the person suggesting it and I assumed it was some kind of Obama straw-man argument. They usually go like this: "some say [insert awful idea here], but I say [insert reasonable idea here]."

But no, it was the North Carolina governor making the suggestion, and she appeared to be totally serious! She really developed the idea. Among the explanations given by her spokesman was that Gov. Perdue was just joking – you do have a sense of humor don't you? — but that didn't sound like a real knee-slapper of a joke to me. Maybe I just didn't get her schtick.

In fact, I listened to the audio[2] on this speech, and either the governor was totally serious or she has the driest sense of humor of any politician I have ever heard. Reportedly she didn't even make this proposal and do anything silly like roll her eyes or pause for a punch-line. Nothing! Not even a rimshot[3] by a drummer nearby or a comment like "thank you – you've been a great audience," followed by a reminder to tip your waitress. If she had said something like that while making this proposal, the Rotarian audience would have at least given her a sympathy chuckle and the press secretary would have had something to point to in arguing that it was just a joke.

No, while it may not have been a serious proposal, it definitely was not a joke. It was probably a stream of consciousness idea based upon the lousy chances the North Carolina Democratic House delegation has going into the 2012 elections.

See, as it stands now North Carolina will not have a senatorial election in 2012, but all 13 House Representatives will be up for re-election, and currently 6 of 13 of North Carolina's representatives are Democrats. Of those 6 Democratic congressmen, 4 are having their districts brutally re-drawn[4] by a Republican state house, and those 4 are going to have a very tough[5] re-election. After the 2012 elections, North Carolina's House delegation could very well go from 6 Democrats and 7 Republicans to 2 Democrats and 11 Republicans, a net loss of 4 Democratic congressmen. Between now and 2012 I would not be surprised to hear of at least one retirement (David Price from moderate the 4th congressional district is 71 years old) and a possible party-change (Heath Shuler, from conservative district 11, who challenged Nancy Pelosi for the Democratic leadership post after the 2010 elections).

Also, let's not forget the punishment voters in special elections have been giving Democrats even after the 2010 mid-term elections. Just a couple weeks ago voters in Nevada elected[6] a Republican in Nevada's 2nd congressional district, and voters in New York's 9th congressional district actually elected[7] a Republican to replace the disgraced but well-endowed former congressman Anthony Weiner. With all this doom heading towards Democrat Congressmen, not only nationally but in North Carolina, can you blame Gov. Perdue for thinking aloud about putting off those pesky elections for a couple years? It would have been difficult to joke about that, but every once in a while "gallows humor" can get a laugh.

And she wouldn't be the first Democrat office-holder to be a comedian. Remember Al Franken, senator from Minnesota, who may not be funny but you have to give him credit for trying.

Reportedly, on his deathbed, the actor Edmund Gwinn said[8], "dying is easy. Comedy is hard." He sure had that right! Before dying he should have talked with North Carolina Governor Bev Perdue.

October 3, 2011

WINNING IDEAS FROM LOSING CANDIDATES

Why do we always totally discard the ideas from candidates who lose presidential elections? Many times a perfectly good idea gets chained around the unsuccessful neck of a losing candidate, and the winner shies away. Granted, we don't want winners of elections morphing and changing their colors like some kind of a reptile. Americans usually want their presidents to be mammals, not reptiles. But what is wrong with a little discretion in picking over the rubble of a lost presidential candidacy? Kind of like a garage sale of ideas. Haven't you ever gotten something perfectly good at a garage sale? Be honest.

Case in point: Ross Perot, and his use of pie charts and bar graphs. Remember him? 1992 and 1996's Reform Party spoiler candidate for president, always there to ensure a splitting of the Republican vote, until he suffered a self-inflicted flame-out of credibility. Something about government spies sabotaging his daughter's wedding.

But he had a great way of making points with pie charts and bar graphs. They were a great way of getting his points across. In fact, in any given television appearance, usually on CNN's Larry King show, there was a 33% chance Perot would present a pie chart, 20% he would present a bar graph, a 39% chance he would use both a pie chart *and* a bar graph, and only a 8% chance he would appear without any visual aids at all. Oh, I feel my own pie chart coming on...

Ross Perot's Use Of Visual Aids On CNN

■ Use a pie chart   33%

■ Use a bar graph   20%

■ Use a pie chart and a bar graph
   39%

■ Use no visual aids   8%

OK, it is pretty easy to get carried away with pie charts and bar graphs. But the point is that Ross Perot used visual aids a lot. And he may have lost the 1992 and 1996 elections, but Perot's pie charts and bar graphs should be dusted off and re-used in the today's debate on fiscal policy. They put things into perspective pretty quickly.

What we are used to in today's arguments over President Obama's deficits is a situation in which the conservative tries to argue that the current fiscal deficits are huge and have lost all sense of proportion, and the liberal concluding that the conservative is just racist because criticism of President Obama is involved. Deadlock. Contrast that conversation with this hypothetical conversation, using a Perot-style chart:

Conservative: "Boy, those Obama deficits are ridiculous."

Liberal: "Bush also did deficit spending. You are just being racist."

Conservative: "But just look at this bar chart from the Napa Whine Country website, showing the deficits and surpluses from 1990 to today. These huge red bars to the downside on the right are the Obama deficits."

Liberal: "No kidding, I see what you mean. I apologize for calling you a racist. These Obama deficits are really crazy."

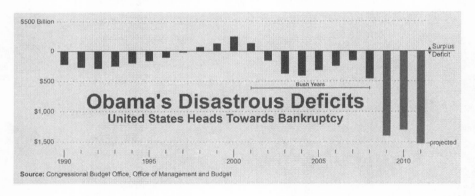

Remember this is just a hypothetical discussion.

While the annual deficit chart is important, an even more important chart is the percent of the annual budget that goes to pay for interest on the debt, because this underscores the urgency of getting our fiscal house in order. Just like a person, the federal government could over-spend so much that the interest on the debt crowds out spending on everything else. With a human being this situation is called *bankruptcy*. For a country that prints its own money, this might not lead to bankruptcy but will lead to hyperinflation, as so many more dollars are printed to pay for debt, and people who hold dollars realize how worthless it is. That is why precious metals like gold and silver are getting more and more expensive. They are substitutes for the dollar, and many people envision the dollar being inflated away.

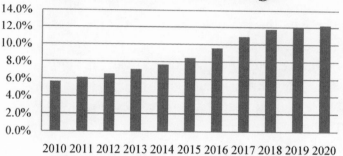

Interest Payment As Percent Of Entire Federal Budget

Source: Congressional Budget Office, *Budget and Economic Ourtlook, An Update, August 2011*

This week President Obama will present another jobs plan, and Congress may pass it or modify it, or reject it altogether. But one theme desperately missing in the recent discussion about debt, debt ceilings, jobs and everything else is economic growth. It is economic growth that gets more people employed and paying taxes. Whether we can get the economy growing again by raising taxes and spending (the Obama approach) or by cutting taxes and slowing the growth of spending (the House Republican approach), there needs to be a discussion on what government can do, or stop doing, to get the economy growing again.

If things aren't straightened out — and soon — the stampede of people out of the American dollar and economy will cause a giant sucking sound. Hey, where have I heard that expression before?

September 5, 2011

THE LIFE ALERT PRESIDENT

"Help! I've fallen and I can't get up." So said the commercial that was the bane of late-night cable TV for much of the 1990's, advertising Life Alert ®'s medical alert for at-risk seniors living alone. After about its 150-th viewing, the commercial made you want to burst out laughing, but your laughter was tempered by the shame of realizing you are about to laugh at an elderly person who had just fallen down and needed help. The commercial claimed to be based on a true story, you know.

But that phrase had legs, excuse the pun. From cell-phone ringtones to the punch-lines of many late-night comedians, even a chorus in at least a couple of rap songs, it was impossible to go through life in the 90's without hearing "I've fallen and I can't get up."

Nowadays the phrase could easily apply to President Barack Obama, whose poll numbers have fallen and no matter what he does, those poll numbers cannot "get up." According to Gallup[1], Obama's approve/disapprove numbers went from 47% to 45% last December to a 38% to 55% today. Scary enough, but Rasmussen has a poll that measures "strongly approve" (apparently there still are some) vs. "strongly disapprove." In the Rasmussen poll[2], 23% strongly approve of the president's job performance, while 40% strongly disapprove. This figure may matter more than the Gallup number because when a percentage of the country feels "strongly" about something they are more likely to vote that way.

Here's a wild guess to explain the numbers: the economy, specifically the over 9%[3] unemployment rate. According to another recent Gallup poll[4], 77% of Americans think the economy is getting worse. But not to worry, President Obama is about to give a speech to address the economy and jobs now that Hurricane Irene has cut short his vacation in Martha's Vineyard. Let's hope that preparing the speech didn't ruin his concentration on his golf game.

You can almost understand Obama's reliance on making speeches. While campaigning in 2008 against then-Senator Obama for the

Democratic nomination, Sen. Hillary Clinton pointed out that Obama's main claim to fame on the international stage thus far was making speeches[5]. But she was way off: besides giving great speeches, by the age of 47, Obama had already written two autobiographies.

And why did Obama have to go on vacation at Martha's Vineyard anyway? Could he possibly have found a more elitist place to vacation? Not good for polls. The least the White House could do is send out some talking points, something like "Martha's Vineyard is the blue-collar version of Davos, Switzerland," or at least that the Obama rented compound there was on "the inexpensive side of the island." And why golf all the time? Isn't there a bowling alley anywhere on Martha's Vineyard? And can't we re-name the place "Martha's Orchard," at least while the Obama family is there?

A Martha's Vineyard vacation is the last thing President Obama needed after a disastrous bus tour through the mid-west, the highlight of which was an exchange with a farmer[6] in Atkinson, Illinois, who begged the president not to "challenge us any more with more rules and regulations from Washington DC." When Obama pressed the farmer for details, the farmer mentioned that he had heard that farmers were about to be hit with "noise pollution, dust and water run-off regulations." A better politician, say Bill Clinton in 1996, would have said "those sound like stupid regulations, and I haven't heard about them, but I happen to have the head of the USDA right here and maybe we can hear from him..." Then any farmer within earshot would feel very relieved. But instead President Obama urged[7] the farmer not to "don't always believe what you hear" and added a very lawyerly "a lot of times we are going to be applying common sense," and then urged the farmer to do something simple, like "contact USDA. Talk to them directly." And he wasn't kidding.

See, if a president called the USDA directly, he would probably get straight answers in about two minutes. But as we all know, a citizen calling the USDA, or any federal bureaucracy for answers is a huge waste of time. This was proven just the next day by reporter M.J. Lee at Politico[8], who tried to get the answers the farmer wanted. But the reporter spent all day getting the run-around at USDA. After four hours of phoning and getting put on hold and getting referred to other offices, the reporter finally got referred to the EPA, and the next day the reporter repeated his runaround with the EPA, where he spent two hours phoning around and finally got an e-mail[9] denying new noise or dust regulations.

So let's face it, it is elitist missteps like the bus-tour followed by the Martha's Vineyard vacation during a time of over 9% unemployment that has President Obama's poll numbers fallen to the ground, and a mere speech will probably not be able to get those poll numbers back up. If President Obama starred in a present-day version of that famous commercial, he would say something like "Help! Let me be clear! I've fallen and I can't get up. And, make no mistake — it's all President Bush's fault!"

August 29, 2011

PAUL RYAN: PLEASE DON'T RUN

The beltway punditocracy is buzzing with speculation that Wisconsin Republican Representative Paul Ryan might sign up for the presidential slugfest, reversing his previous admonitions of wanting to stay at home with his kids. Maybe that was all tongue-in-cheek anyway, as politicians usually claim to want to be around their kids when the politician gets into some kind of trouble, not when they are signing up for a troublesome job.

The speculators of a Ryan candidacy include such well-known conservatives as Stephen Hayes of The Weekly Standard and Salem talk-show host and former Education Secretary Bill Bennett. As a conservative, I admit being tempted to support someone who came out with a serious, adult-like plan to restrain entitlements and grow the economy with a 25% top tax rate. And what conservative doesn't have at least some secret admiration for Paul Ryan because of the glare

President Obama gave Ryan at that healthcare round-table last year, when Ryan made such a great case as to why Obamacare was such a loser? Or what about the time when President Obama invited Ryan to the front row to hear a speech wherein President Obama demagogued the Ryan Plan as cutting healthcare for children with autism or Down syndrome? I mean, really – to have the president reduce himself to such cheap demagoguery in opposing a plan *you* came up with? Paul Ryan should have been honored, and is probably admired by many on the right, who have to settle for mere opposition to their ideas.

Well I have a plea for Representative Ryan: don't run for president. For several reasons. First and foremost, your plan is the only responsible plan anyone has come up with to reign in entitlements before they swallow up the entire federal budget. Currently 40% of the federal budget, at current rates of growth, Medicare, Medicaid and Social Security will swallow up the entire federal budget by the year 2049. Medicare is going to be broke by 2029, while Social Security will be broke by 2037. And yet, no one in Washington wants tobe caught anywhere near a proposal to do anything about it. At this rate of entitlement growth even a 100% marginal tax rate in 2020 still won't be high enough to pay all of our bills.

OK, I might have exaggerated, but the point is that unless something is done by a serious adult in Washington, we are all doomed. The Ryan Plan would cap federal Medicaid contributions to the rate of inflation and send block grants to the states, who will then develop different approaches to spend within their means. For Medicare, the Ryan Plan would end the open-ended entitlement feature and subsidize private insurance for retirees.

With an entrant into the race with such a signature plan, it will be too tempting for the other Republican candidates to criticize this plan, and we certainly don't want that. While it isn't perfect, the Ryan Plan offers solutions to inter-generational problems that have been looming for decades, and now we are close to actually solving them.

And another reason: the field is too crowded already. Did you notice how close Libertarian Ron Paul came to actually winning the

Iowa straw poll? 153 votes! The last time we had heard from Ron Paul, he was advocating silly things like legalizing heroin and abolishing Social Security. The mathematical reason for Ron Paul's near-win is pretty simple: all the sensible candidates split the sensible vote. With yet another sane candidate there to further split the sensible vote, Ron Paul will be that much closer to actually winning a state primary or two. Scary.

And here is a possibly-silly reason for Paul Ryan not to run, but someone has to say it: your name sounds too much like Ron Paul. Which voter will not be confused with a ballot that has two names that sound so similar?

But the main reason not to run for president is to stay exactly where you are now, as House Budget Chairman, doing your best to get as much of your plan enacted into law as possible. Let the Ryan Plan be to a President Perry or Romney what Kemp-Roth was for President Reagan.

Workable and realistic plans for economic growth are so rare nowadays. The left still wants to raise taxes, and lynch anyone who has even come close to being on a corporate jet. Oh, and don't forget an infrastructure bank – all those new roads and bridges we constantly need. Infrastructure spending was the reason why 2009 was such a roaring success. And did I mention raising taxes? All more of the same.

Maybe the most original idea of growth to come from the left was from liberal economic columnist Paul Krugman, who with a totally straight face speculated that an extraterrestrial invasion would generate economic growth, kind of like what World War II did for the Great Depression. And lest you think he was joking, just remember that outspoken liberals generally don't have a sense of humor and they definitely aren't funny even if they think they are. Just look at Al Franken.

So my plea to Representative Ryan remains: don't run for president. Hey, think about your kids!

August 22, 2011

CHAPTER 2

STRONG OPINIONS ABOUT TRIVIAL SUBJECTS

Of course it is trivial, but most things are.
—John Malkovich

FOOTBALL PLAYER SHOOTS OFF MOUTH, UNITES PREVIOUSLY-AMBIVALENT FANS BEHIND OPPOSING TEAM

There I was, minding my own business, watching the after-game show on TV after the Seattle Seahawks had just narrowly defeated my team, the San Francisco 49'ers, in the playoffs. Now I had to decide which team to root for in the Super Bowl, the Seattle Seahawks or the Denver Broncos.

There were pros and cons to each team. I have close family living near both Denver and Seattle. On political matters, Colorado voters had recently recalled some of their legislators who had passed some gun control laws, and this made me like Colorado. But Washington state is one of the few states without a state income tax. I like that.

Regarding the mascots of the two teams, the "Bronco" is the same mascot as my law school, so this doesn't sit well with me, but the "Seahawk" is a fictional creature. No such thing exists in nature. Maybe I am a stickler for details, but I have a hard time rooting for a team with a totally fictional mascot. True, I once advocated[1] voting for a fictional person, George Bailey, for president, but this is important. Which Super Bowl team to root for is a very important issue for the average American guy.

The mascots, the cities, the players, the local political issues; all were important considerations, but no single issue had yet made up my mind as to which team to root for. Then I saw the following interview[2] between *Fox Sports* reporter Erin Andrews and Richard Sherman, a pass defender for the Seattle Seahawks:

Andrews: Alright, Richard, let me ask you the final play, take me through it.

Sherman: Well I'm the best corner in the game! When you try me with a sorry receiver like Crabtree, that's the result you're gonna get! Don't you ever talk about me!

Andrews: Who was talking about you?

Sherman: Crabtree. Don't you open your mouth about the best, or I'm gonna shut it for you real quick! L.O.B.!

Andrews: Alright before ... and ... Joe, back over to you!

Richard Sherman sounded like a total thug; a graceless winner! What an incredible jerk! True, football is an aggressive, physical game, but when a player is interviewed, especially after a close win like this, they are supposed to thank their teammates and show a little sportsmanship. For a moment there Sherman even looked like he was a danger to anyone nearby, especially the unfortunate reporter who quickly ended the interview.

What is it with celebrities nowadays? Why is there so little class and respectability among those famous sports players and entertainers? It's pretty frustrating.

Even more frustrating is the way some people are defending Sherman's thuggish rant.

One commentator said, "Sherman was in the zone, give him a break."

But the game was already over. If that was Sherman's mindset, he needs to learn to shut it off after the game is over, so that he can act like a normal person and not a thug.

Then there was this: "Sherman graduated from Stanford, you know."

Like I care! Stanford, like any other university is perfectly capable of graduating jerks.

Kids nowadays look up to sports figures like Richard Sherman. Any time a sport figure or celebrity accomplishes anything immediately tangible, like a football game, they gain the admiration of countless American kids. It would be nice if a celebrity in the spotlight would realize this and act accordingly.

Instead we are treated with television spectacles of Sherman's rant, or basketball star Dennis Rodman yucking it up with North Korean dictator Kim Jong-un, or formerly-wholesome Mylie Cyrus sexually-dancing, or "twerking" with other singers on a stage. I could go on.

Of course there have been exceptions. Not every American celebrity is a jerk. Steve Garvey, Cal Ripken, Jr., Tim Tebow, and Joe DiMaggio are some names that come to mind.

I once met a celebrity with class. A few years ago, through a series of family connections and events, I found myself having lunch with country-western singer Brad Paisley. Just a few handlers, friends, Brad Paisley and me. Paisley's career had just begun, but you could already tell that he had class.

I relayed to him that I had recently seen a movie about the rock group R.E.M., and the lead singer refused a fan's request for an autograph. The R.E.M. singer just couldn't be bothered.

Paisley couldn't believe it. "Ah reckon ah will always give an autograph to anyone who asks f'r it," he said. He might not have used the word 'reckon,' but he did have a country accent. Paisley also said that signing autographs was important.

But the point is that despite his success, Paisley showed respect for someone besides himself. Maybe not DiMaggio-esque, but good enough. We fans don't expect perfection, just some respect for the fans and a semblance of humility.

And we fans certainly don't like it when what should be a pretty routine interview turns into a thuggish proclamation of superiority over some rival, a threat of "shutting your mouth real quick," and a reporter who feels unsafe standing nearby.

Yes, for this Super Bowl I am now officially a Broncos fan. And I am sure there are many formerly-ambivalent fans, just like me, now rooting for the Broncos.

And I hope that the Broncos score the winning touchdown by a pass that is caught in spite of Richard Sherman's pass defense! That would be nice.

January 23, 2014

TIPS FOR THE WEDDING SPEAKER

"Here," the wedding planner handed me a 3×5 card at my little sister's wedding. "Read this into the microphone after the head bride's maid is finished with her speech." What was handed to me was my "wedding reading," in this case a short drivel filled with unicorns, puppies and beaches. Well, maybe not exactly, but you get the picture. It might as well have been. So overly-sweet and corny that anyone hearing it would have immediately become a diabetic. I would have none of it.

A quick re-write later, and this is what made it into the wedding video:

"May you embrace one another, but not encircle one another, or become obsessed with each other and certainly not stalk each other."

It is June, the month of weddings, and countless other brothers, sisters and relatives of all kind will be handed similar overly-sweet and corny things to read in a wedding. Or be told to participate somehow in a wedding with pre-planned, pre-approved comments. Everyone has been through it. The whole family is there, even people who have lost touch with everyone else. Cousins and in-laws you haven't seen for decades will be there. What you figured will be 20 to 30 people will be more like 100.

The only suspense is whether anyone will mess up their lines and how badly they reveal their nervousness. "Can they see me shaking?" countless people will be asking themselves as they speak into a microphone.

And the words usually spoken don't really matter. People expect to hear trite, well-worn empty phrases at a wedding. To the person *not* asked to participate in the wedding, the spectator, it usually becomes a blur of predictable wedding phrases and words, easily interchanged and rearranged from one wedding to the next. Nothing original or memorable.

Don't do it. Don't read that assigned boring, statement you are supposed to read, or speak that scripted comment. Spice it up. Rewrite in an awkward comment or two, blend it in with other wedding-like comments, and make it funny. Don't overplay the humor, and remember this is someone else's wedding, not yours. Don't take too long, just make your comments or read your speech a little different from what you were handed, and a little funnier. People will think you are really reading your lines as assigned.

When I re-wrote that brief speech and read it, there were no smirks or smiles, and certainly no laughs that I could hear. As I read my amended speech I didn't laugh or present it like it was anything out of the ordinary. For a few seconds after my speech, I thought no one had really heard what I said. The wedding proceeded as if nothing unusual had happened.

But at the reception it was the only subject people wanted to discuss with me. And when the wedding video was mailed to everyone, surprisingly very little of the wedding itself was in the video except for my strange speech. Success! And I am not normally a funny guy! Well, not intentionally funny.

Every occasion when people are asked to make a comment at the podium, everyone in the audience is nervous and everyone knows that the person at the podium is nervous. Very few people at these occasions do these ceremonies all the time. The nervousness transmits itself from the podium to the audience, and then back again. So bring in some humor. People will appreciate it. In fact, even slight attempts at humor will go over very well. You will be surprised.

Of course there are limits. After all, you are at a ceremony celebrating real love for two people, and this is their show, not yours. So don't stray too far in your humor. Sexual jokes and crude comments will not work; they will just embarrass.

But if you keep it funny and not crude, an unexpected rewritten speech with some comedy in it will go over very well.

It has been five years and two adorable baby girls born since my little sister's wedding, and while it was otherwise a beautiful wedding, what family members still remind me of was my wedding reading and how unexpected and funny it was. And I know that 10, 20, 30 or more years from now, people will still be talking about that slightly-changed wedding reading and its unexpected humor.

So just do it. Years from now this will be a great memory, and you will be glad you did it.

June 3, 2013

THE SANCTIMONY TAX

Glenn Reynolds of *Instapundit*[1] has a great rallying cry of "ending the Hollywood tax cuts[2]," as a way of raising the taxes on the Hollywood wealthy. And it is tempting, because if higher taxes on the rich is what the wealthy in Hollywood really want, then this is what they should get. On themselves. To hear the Hollywood rich tell[3] it, rich people like them "don't need tax breaks," so it would only be fair to raise taxes on them.

But the issue is not only wealthy actors and producers who call for higher taxes. There are also wealthy academics, journalists, politicians, racial grievance hustlers, former presidents – the list goes on and on — of people who are wealthy, calling for higher taxes of wealthy people, and identifying with wealth of those whose taxes are to be raised. The added identification with those whose taxes should be raised is a cheap, easily-virtuous element in an argument that adds credibility and virtue at the same time, thus advancing the argument. Those of us who oppose it would correctly define this tactic as sanctimonious malarkey.

There is also an element of a bluff when a rich person calls for higher taxes on rich people like them. A person making such a call knows that there is no way the tax code could be changed to specifically target their own individual tax rate, so it is a cheap and inexpensive feel-good proposal. They know that their bluff will never be called.

Well I say it is high time we call their bluff. I hereby propose the Sanctimony Tax. This is a new tax that even Grover Norquist could support. Or if he opposes it, he would seriously consider it for a few minutes before opposing it.

Here is how the Sanctimony Tax would work: anyone who openly calls for a higher tax rate for people in the top tax bracket, and then also identifies with the top tax bracket, will be subject to a surcharge on their current calendar year's federal income taxes. The specific surcharge rate could be decided on by Congress, but I would suggest an additional 10%, at the least.

One example of the Sanctimony Tax in action would be a wealthy Hollywood actor who calls for higher taxes on rich people, then holds himself out to be rich so we should take his word for it. This rich person would see his federal tax rate go from 36% to 46%, in addition to the now-higher California state income taxes. Or take the Princeton University professor who also has a well-paying gig writing columns for the New York Times. If that winner of life's lottery calls for higher taxes on the wealthy like himself, his federal tax rate would go from 36% to 46% — still not the ideal 91% tax rate Prof. Krugman wrote[4] so longingly of a few weeks ago, but still.

The Sanctinomy Tax would not apply to people who call for taxes on rich people in the abstract. Also, a poor or middle-income person could call for higher taxes on rich people and they would not be subject to the added tax. It is only the wealthy person who openly calls for higher taxes on wealthy people, and then identifies themselves as a wealthy person whose taxes would go up under the proposal. When a wealthy person suggests higher taxes on the wealthy, the phrases to watch for are "people like me," "those in my situation," "take it from me," or, my favorite, "my secretary pays a higher tax rate than I do..."

That person would be subject to the Sanctimony Tax, the reason being that with their cheap sanctimony they have poisoned the public debate on the subject of taxes, so the general public should be recompensed.

There are some other features of the proposed Sanctimony Tax that will help its adoption. Rewards could be offered for people who successfully report others who call for higher taxes on wealthy people like themselves but don't voluntarily pay the Sanctimony Tax. And the government could even earmark Sanctimony Tax revenue to go to children's programs (which would allow the funds already going to children's programs to be diverted to pay for other essential government services). How could anyone oppose that?

And if you think this would be a violation of the taxpayer's free-speech rights, because they will get a higher tax rate based upon the content of their speech, save your breath. This is a tax, which attracts minimal scrutiny from the Supreme Court. Just last summer the Supreme Court held that forcing citizens into a contract so that the contract could be regulated was not a violation of the Contracts Clause.

The Sanctimony Tax, being a tax, would receive the same pretzel logic, end-results lack of scrutiny from the Supreme Court. Chief Justice John Roberts would want to steer the Supreme Court clear of this controversial issue, so the constitutionality of the Sanctimony Tax is in the bag!

Now that we have that settled, we need to look into enacting a corporate Hypocrisy Tax for corporations like Apple or Google, that closely align themselves with tax-raising candidates and then hide their corporate profits off-shore. A corporate Hypocrisy Tax would also be applied to entertainment companies made up of liberals who film their movies in Canada because Canadian taxes are lower. And that brings us back to Hollywood, which, Glenn Reynolds is right, really needs to have its taxes raised.

December 28, 2012

CONFESSIONS OF A SHOPKICK DETRACTOR

A few weeks ago some friends and I got together for dinner in a restaurant that had a Target store nearby. Just before dinner one of my friends said "I have to get a couple things at Target" and with some extra time to kill, we all walked towards the Target store. At the very threshold of the store, out came a couple of iPhones, fingers dashed on screens, and some kind of credit was given as we walked into the Target store.

"What is that?" I asked, and the Shopkick application[1] was explained to me. It is pretty simple: when you turn on the Shopkick app, you get credit for walking into some stores and scanning certain items in that store or other stores. The credit, or "kicks," add up to discount shopping cards, free iTune downloads, whatever you choose. Marketing people have calculated what advertising money has been spent getting a sale of anything, and they figured that it was worth it to just give money to the shopper for walking into a store or scanning some item for sale.

How cool is that? This was a few days before the election, and I actually felt original in talking about the "free stuff," that was sure to come my way. So I took the bait and installed the Shopkick app. on my iPhone.

It seemed too easy! I walked back out of the Target store, activated the Shopkick app., walked back into the same store, and got some kicks! Then, I found my way to some Eveready batteries for a new AA-size charger, scanned the bar code, and got some more kicks! Way cool.

I figured that if I kept this up, in a month or so I would get a reward item, and in my case I chose the $5 Starbucks gift card. I could already taste the Frappuccino with chocolate chips. The fact that it would be free seemed to make that future Frappuccino taste even better!

I quickly figured the time spent per benefit received, and it was about equal to a minimum wage job. That's OK. I have worked minimum wage jobs before. But this was not really work, this was free stuff!

Even forgetting about the rewards part it all, there was a certain "scavenger hunt" quality to it. If you find yourself in a store like Macy's, Lane Bryant, Petco, Foot Zone, or others, the Shopkick app. tells you which items to find and scan to get some more kicks. How fun!

Despite the initial excitement, a few days went by, and I had forgotten the Shopkick app. on my phone. Then one day on my way to do some shopping in another store, I walked by a Wet Seal store. "You idiot!" I chastised myself, "turn on that Shopkick app, walk in and then leave and get some kicks!" Hopefully no one would see me walk into a store that sells clothing for teenage girls.

But why the inactivity with Shopkick? It had been several days since I had used the app., and I had been into several stores that were part of the program. Was I just being shallow and fickle, or was there something else going on?

After some soul-searching, it dawned on me. Far from being a fun thing, this Shopkick app. had become a burden. An obligation. It was officially not fun anymore, and I had only earned 230 kicks!

But there was something else going on. Something that you could only see by looking down from 30,000 feet, as they say. See, I am not a typical shopper. I have a stressful job. I am an attorney, and my workday usually involves getting yelled at by judges or other attorneys, sometimes yelling back, and in general dealing with people who are stressed out. I knew this going in to the job, so I am not complaining.

But when I go shopping, it is not just a trip to a store to buy something. It is a de-stressing event. I walk the aisles of some store and try to absorb the mindlessness of other shoppers. Being around other people whose top concern is finding some item on their buy-list really appeals to me. Walking around, with part of my brain on hold, is a highlight of my day. I know where they get the term "retail therapy," except for me there is more therapy than retail.

It's the same thing with lunchtime at Costco. Everyone talks about how there is no need to pay for lunch, just go to a Costco store and eat

Free samples at Costco. The trick is to get a free
sample, circle an aisle or two, then go back and
get a second free sample. At least that is what I
have heard.

all the free samples that are handed out at lunchtime. And it is true:
if you are totally cheap it is a great way to get a free lunch. Chicken
burgers, pot stickers, pita bread smeared with humus, Chinese chicken
salad, sausage made with small bits of apple, all of this and more is
freely handed out to Costco customers everyday at lunchtime. The only
price is a salesperson hovering, telling you how tasty the sample is,
how easy it is to fix and clean up afterwards. Stuff like that.

But for me it is just a hassle. I like being left alone when I shop and
when I eat. If they were to just hand me food and leave me alone that
would be fine. But when someone is talking to me and I feel obligated
to answer and sound impressed or even interested, the thrill is gone.

So I am un-installing that Shopkick app from my iPhone. There
really is no free lunch, or in my case a free $5 Starbucks card. I look

forward to returning to the oasis of mindlessness that is present-day shopping, reward-less. And for the few moments when I am in a Target, Macy's or Old Navy, I will once again be alone with my thoughts, de-stressing and enjoying myself.

November 29, 2012

"BUS BEAT-DOWN" VIDEOS

Has anyone besides me noticed the number of "bus beat-down" videos making the rounds on the Internet lately? It is almost as if getting on a bus is getting a front-row seat to some fight, where getting from Point A to Point B is beside the point. Buses have now become a *Jerry Springer Show* on wheels.

Just last week there was a video[1] (warning: explicit language) of a Cleveland bus-driver who apparently had had enough of the taunts of one passenger, so he stopped the bus and gave the passenger an unexpected uppercut. All caught on video.

It has gotten so bad that the word "bus" has been used in at least one common expression. Whenever a politician gets in trouble, the question becomes which underling will take the fall, or "be thrown under the bus." It is a fitting expression: merely getting thrown *off* a bus would be a good thing, because buses are dangerous places, but getting thrown under a bus is even worse.

I first read about the Cleveland bus attack while getting gas at a local gas station. While filling up my car, a video monitor on the gas pump broadcast a number of news items like the Cleveland bus assault, and standard celebrity news like celebrities divorcing, getting arrested or going to rehab.

But the bus beat-down videos stuck with me, and I did some research. Did you know that if you do a YouTube search with the term "bus beating" you could spend all day watching people getting beaten up on buses? No wonder school kids are often disheveled by the time they get to first period.

Why are people so fascinated with videos of "bus beat-downs?" It is a pretty sad commentary of our society that if someone is getting picked on, the first instinct of people nearby is to pull out their I-phones and videotape the incident instead of helping the victim. And then there is the possibility that your video will "go viral," which would be exciting to some. Meanwhile the victim is battered and bruised, and will henceforth be walking or bumming car rides to their destinations.

The "bus beat-down" videos are all pretty scary. Granted, it usually starts with someone complaining about something, but sometimes there is no warning at all. A kid on a school bus sits down and another kid nearby starts punching[2] him. That happened a couple years ago in

YouTube screen grab

Although this bus confrontation in Oakland in 2010 worked out OK — the aggressor got his butt kicked — the question remains: how many people on that bus would rather not have been there?

Belleville, Illinois, when one kid sat down and was immediately beaten by another kid. A crowd cheered, and another kid broke it up and made the news.

As you watch these bus assault videos, there are always several of the same players, like actors in a play. Besides the attacker, the victim, and the person filming the event, there are also by-standers, some cheering, and others who try to distance themselves from the assault. Occasionally there is the peace-maker, but this person doesn't usually succeed in stopping anything, and often gets punched a few times for his or her efforts.

While there are other factors involved, the common denominator of all the parties to the assault, except the victim, is boredom.

So what can we do to stop bus violence?

One possible answer is to lower the price of gas. If gas were cheaper, more of these lower-income people would drive themselves to work in the safety of their own cars instead on taking a chance on the local bus. But who are we kidding? Trying to lower gas prices to get people off of buses and into their own cars is a non-starter.

We could also pay for police officers to ride buses, but that would be expensive. Or we could have a volunteer monitor ride the school buses and break up fights, but sometimes the monitor would become the victim of violence, as happened to the grandmother[3] who volunteered to break up bus fights in Greece, New York, last summer.

Here is another idea: cover the inside of buses with video advertisements. These would be different from the print ads that are already there. If video ads can be cheaply put on gas pumps, like the one that distracted me during my recent fill-up, they can also be placed inside buses. Video ads would be distracting, and who knows, the bus company or school district might even make some money.

Another use of technology could be the placement of several cameras inside the bus, catching everything that happens on a central hard drive. That would make it easier to prosecute the bullies.

States could also enact laws that provide for greater sentences for those convicted of assaulting others on buses or other public transportation. As opposed to other assaults, bus assaults occur with a captive audience whose members may not have any choice but to ride the bus.

But whatever is done, something needs to be done to make riding the bus safer. It is sad to see these "bus beat-down" videos making the rounds on the Internet. If people want *The Jerry Springer Show* they can always watch it on TV.

October 26, 2012

CHAPTER *3*

MOVIE AND EVENT REVIEWS

No good movie is too long and no bad movie is short enough.
—Roger Ebert

PERSECUTED MOVIE REVIEW:
THANKSGIVING TURKEY COMES EARLY

B ack when my wife and I would often go to movies with other couples, I would tell a joke that "if I were a movie producer, what I would do is read *Variety* and keep track of the next blockbuster movie being made. Then I would make a similar movie, with a similar name, but extremely low budget. That way, when the blockbuster movie comes out and the ticket-buyers circle the block for it, maybe some of them will settle for my movie instead of waiting in line for the blockbuster. Or maybe some people will just get confused and go to my movie instead of the blockbuster. Either way, this plan is a sure-fire moneymaker!"

Jurassic Plaza, Insomniac In Spokane, and *Supraman* were some names suggested. This joke usually got a few cynical laughs.

I have since retired that joke, but you would think that with the other Christian or religious-themed movies out there, this might have been what motivated the promoters of the movie *Persecuted*. After all, religious movies *Noah, Son Of God,* and *Heaven Is For Real,* have just recently appeared in the theaters, so one could easily confuse the movie *Persecuted* with being in the same genre as the others. But no.

And that is a shame, because there is so much actual Christian persecution going on in the world. Like the Christians being killed in Nigeria, Egypt and Iraq, Meriam Ibrahim and her children held in Sudan, Pastor Saeed Abedini imprisoned in Iran, and many, many others.

Or even the softer forms of Christian persecution going on everyday in the United States. For example, the Christian-run businesses like wedding cake-bakers or photographers who now must participate in gay weddings or shut down. Or the Mozilla CEO who was fired[1] because he had supported a ballot measure, California's Proposition 8, which passed with a majority of California voters in 2008.

Unfortunately, the movie *Persecuted* is a cheesy political thriller that involves a television evangelist pastor who opposes some legislation and gets framed for murder by the corrupt senator promoting the legislation. After faked photos turn up that show the drugged pastor and the girl later found murdered, the pastor goes on the run and becomes a fugitive. To clear his name, you know.

But the "persecution" for which the movie gets its name is not the widespread persecution of Christians. It refers to the persecution of an individual who happens to be Christian. Christianity is only tangentially related. The movie might have been more appropriately named "Frame-Up," except it wouldn't sell movie tickets to Christians like me, who want to see a movie addressing the issue of Christian persecution, and didn't fully research the movie before putting our money down.

So the title *Persecuted* is misleading.

The movie is not even a good political frame-up movie. Loose threads abound. At one point the pastor's wife was shown having a glass of champagne with her husband's replacement pastor. The two of them make comments that give the impression that they were both in on the plot to frame her husband. But yet the wife looked stressed and guilty, and when her fugitive husband called her on the phone, she fills him in on the evidence against him, and advised him to lay low.

And how did the fugitive pastor make a phone call to his wife without his cell phone being traced?

And why did the pastor, while on the run, begin carrying rosary beads? Someone should pull the movie director aside and explain to him that an evangelical pastor, like the protagonist here, would not carry rosary beads. Unless he converted to Catholicism while on the run.

And the fugitive pastor became less of a pastor and more like any other run of the mill fugitive when he carried a gun into his meetings with various players in the scheme. I'm pretty sure it is written in a pastor rule-book somewhere that you lose your moral authority as a pastor being framed when you bring a pistol to talk with someone.

And at another point in the movie the fugitive pastor calls a sympathetic priest "Dad." Excuse me? Not "Father," but "Dad." "Dad" is a pretty loaded nickname to call a priest. It requires some explanation.

What about the involvement of Jesus or Scripture in this film? A couple of Bible verses, like John 14:6, were recited, but not explained or made relevant. Almost window-dressing.

And while he was on the run, the fugitive pastor prayed to God, but nothing changed as a result of the prayer. The plot didn't change and the pastor didn't change any of his strategy. The pastor didn't even feel any more at peace.

What I would like to know is this: how did this movie get such a cast of respectable actors? Not Tom Cruise or Brad Pitt, mind you, but *Persecuted* include some experienced actors like James Remar, Dean Stockwell, and former senator Fred Thompson. I am sure each of them have had lousy scripts suggested to them before, so they probably know the difference between a good movie and a bad one.

I have a theory, and here goes: the script that got these actors on board was far from what survived the editing process. The final product may have taken four hours, but there were no loose ends and everything made sense. Who knows, maybe the fugitive pastor did convert to Catholicism while on the run, got confirmed and was handed some rosary beads. That's possible.

And then the film's editor went to work and shortened the movie to two hours.

And speaking of the production process, at times the sound effects in *Persecuted* were just too loud. It gave the movie the feeling of a Spaghetti Western from the 1970's. I almost expected a long list of Italians in the closing credits.

In the end, *Persecuted* is a flop of a movie — a real turkey — either as a movie of Christian persecution or as a political thriller. Save your money and wait for the movies *Exodus* or *Mary,* which come out later this year. Or with any luck the Kendrick brothers will come out with another movie soon.

July 22, 2014

MAN OF STEEL: CHOCK FULL OF CHRISTIAN DOG WHISTLES

As we walked into the *Man Of Steel* movie, my wife and I ran into two groups of friends who had just seen the movie and were leaving the theater. One group was Christian, the other group was not. Our Christian friends agreed with what we had heard, that there were several Christian themes and images in the movie. Our non-Christian friends told us that they had not noticed any Christian messages at all. This fits the definition of a dog whistle, a message broadcast to all but heard only by certain ears. And we Christians are the dogs.

But that's OK with this Christian. In fact, the movie was so chock-full of dog whistles for Christians, it almost felt intentional.

Christian images and themes were all over this movie, starting with the fact that Superman was a likable, humble servant, respectful of his parents, even having been born with the last name of "El," the Hebrew name for God. The bad guys from his old planet, led by General Zod, fit the part of fallen angels, pursuing and trying to kill the Christ-like Superman here on Earth.

Crucifixion poses by Superman exist throughout the movie, as are crosses themselves. Superman's mother wears a cross necklace, and a church is seen with a prominent cross on the side of the building. A cross is also seen formed from the i-beams of one of the collapsed buildings at the end of the movie.

At one point, a young Clark Kent is seen getting picked on by schoolyard bullies, and he is seen with out-stretched arms. As with Jesus on the cross, Superman could have easily fought back and killed those who were persecuting him. Whereas Jesus purposely offered himself a sacrifice for our sins, Superman didn't want to blow his cover as a person with superpowers. Later in the movie, Superman even allows himself to be handcuffed when he turns himself in to the American military to be interrogated.

In one scene of a younger, grade-school aged Clark Kent, as he is getting to know his super-powers, sees through the flesh of his class-mates and teacher, essentially seeing skeletons with eyeballs, talking to him. While the scene acquainted the viewer with the super-hero's x-ray vision, the images of skeletons with eyeballs was clearly more graphic than needed.

And this was unique to the young Superman. Other immigrants from Krypton also experienced x-ray visions, but their views were merely of their hand bones, not of entire skeletons.

These skeleton visions seen by the young Clark Kent may have been meant to evoke the image from the Old Testament book Ezekiel, known as the Valley of Dried Bones, in which the bones await God's breath to bring them to life. These visions may also have been meant to refer to the New Testament books Ephesians and Colossians, where non-believers are described as "dead in their trespasses and sins," until they would accept the savior Jesus Christ, who brings them eternal life.

There are other similarities between Superman and Jesus. Clark Kent is 33 years old when he is fully engaged with his powers and risks his life to save the world, the same age as Jesus when he went to Calvary.

Superman's Earthly father, played by Kevin Costner, filled the part of a blue-collar Joseph figure, having had a strong moral impact on his adopted son but having died several years before the epic battle.

There is even a parallel to the biblical scene of Jesus in the Garden at Gethsemane. When General Zod and his team begin their attack, Superman struggles with whether to submit himself to Zod in order to ransom Earth. Superman consults a priest in a church, and as he asks the priest whether he should engage General Zod, immediately behind Superman is seen a stained-glass depiction of Jesus in the Garden of Gethsemane. A Christian in the audience can almost hear Superman ask God to "take this cup from me."

Still, *Man of Steel* is not a coherent gospel message, and there are some serious differences between Superman and Jesus. For example, Superman is attractive, whereas Jesus, according to a passage in Isaiah, had an appearance that did not attract attention. And Jesus never disguised himself, unlike the casual suit and black-rimmed glasses that Clark Kent donned towards the end of the movie (and what a great disguise it was — those glasses never fail to throw everyone off!).

There may be other Christian themes in this movie, but what does it all mean? Is it all on purpose? I researched the director, all of the producers, the writers and the top actors in this movie, and none of them appear to have made any news proclaiming their Christian faith. If any of them are Christians and purposely injected Christian themes into this movie, it was done without any fanfare.

In fact, most of the *Man Of Steel* writers and producers have resumes filled with work on other superhero-type movies. A year or two from now, most of them will be rolling out the next *Batman, Captain America,* or *Spiderman* movie. Currently, a couple of them are putting the finishing touches on the movie *300: Rise Of An Empire.*

So what happened here? How did a group of apparently-secular Hollywood veterans produce a movie with so many Christian dog whistles? While there are some biblical undertones in the original *Superman* story, I would like to think that this may be a case of what is described in the book of Romans, that even a non-Christian has the law of God written on their heart. And in producing this movie, the hearts of the cast and crew led them to produce quite a Christian-themed but otherwise secular action movie.

It worked for me. Not every movie will remind us of the gospel message like *Passion Of The Christ[1]*, or *The Gospel of John[2]*, but I was still glad I saw *Man Of Steel.* And I would definitely recommend it to other Christians.

June 22, 2013

JULIE BOROWSKI INTERVIEW, PART 1

We all know the routine. You turn on the TV or radio to hear some comedy, and you might get a few laughs. Then the comedian turns to recent political events, and then he or she uses a few stereotypes or cli-chés about conservatives, how racist, sexist, homophobic they are, or just how un-kind they are. Boy, those racist tea-partiers! Those violent gun nuts! Then another joke. Then the comedian moves on to another subject.

The political arguments are never really made, just hinted at. But the viewer gets the impression, backed up by mockery, laughs and applause, that it sure is un-cool to be conservative, and that it is only sensible, kind, neighborly, and hip to be liberal.

Only recently has there been any attempt by conservatives to use humor to fight back. Unlike the leftist comedians, these conserva-tives, like Bill Whittle[1], Andrew Klavan, Kurt Schlichter and Steven Crowder[2], reason the arguments through, use facts, consider alterna-tives, and anticipate results. The conservative keeps the viewer hooked by using visual props and comedy. And it works!

One such conservative, who says she is more of a libertarian than conservative, is Julie Borowski. Julie Borowski's blog-videos, entitled *Token Libertarian Girl,* can be found at YouTube[3], and her personal blog[4] can be found at julieborowski.wordpress.com.

While some of her videos can be serious, like when she discussed[5] the Boston Marathon bombings, oftentimes Borowski dresses herself up, like when she discussed[6] minimum wage arguments, or when she criticized[7] make-up ads in women's magazines. Many of her videos are just so funny you watch them just for the humor, no matter what the message is.

And that is where she advances conservative and libertarian causes, because she keeps viewers engaged and entertained. And persuaded. The viewer can watch both the Comedy Channel and Julie Borowski's videos, and come away much more informed and persuaded by Borowski's videos.

Borowski agreed to an e-mail interview, and below is the transcript of the first of a two-part interview.

Question: Congratulations on the CPAC [Conservative Political Action Committee] award for "Best Video Blogger." Your YouTube videos are very entertaining and persuasive of conservative and libertarian ideas. What is your goal in producing these videos?

Answer: Thank you very much. My goal is to spread the message of liberty to as many people as possible. No one wants to watch boring videos. I can get a little unpredictable and downright goofy at times. But hey, if that's what it takes to get people to care about the decline of liberty in this nation... then I'll gladly do it. I have fun thinking of new weird things to do.

Q: Now that you are rich and famous, do you still make these videos by yourself at home? Who does the editing? Have you considered adding a laugh-track or sound effects?

A: Since starting to make videos, I've moved out my parents' house. So that's pretty cool. Ha, yes, I still make all my videos by myself in my bedroom: writing, filming, changing costumes, editing, etc. I go to the Party Depot frequently for new costumes so the cashiers probably think I'm a big time party animal... nope. Just being weird at home. I am trying to learn new editing techniques like laugh tracks and sound effects. Just one step at a time though...

Q: What else do you do? I noticed you work for FreedomWorks, and there are a few columns of yours at *Townhall*.

A: Yes. I do have a regular column at *Townhall* and my day job is working as a Policy Analyst for FreedomWorks. I've been there for over 3 years now. I just started making videos on the weekends, completely separate from my normal job.

Q: Growing up, did you always want to be a video blogger/columnist/trouble-maker?

A: When we were little, my older brother and I liked to make silly skit videos. I was the co-host of his *Late Night TV* show where he would interview guests such as Barney the dinosaur and Bob Dole. But it was just us dressed in crazy costumes. Somewhere there is a video of us doing a *Cops* parody show. My brother was the police officer and I was the drunken troublemaker resisting arrest. I was maybe 8 years old. I never thought I would be making a fool out of myself on camera when I became an adult, but here I am.

Q: Where did you get your humor? Did you have any favorite comedy acts or movies when you grew up? How about nowadays? What humor do you enjoy?

A: My family has a wacky sense of humor. I grew up watching Conan O'Brien, Adam Sandler and Will Ferrell movies, skit shows like *Saturday Night Live* and *All That* on Nickelodeon. I always liked to make people laugh. I love stand-up comedy. I always keep my humor on my YouTube videos clean. I get messages from parents thanking me for keeping it PG since their kids like to watch my videos. I don't want to lose their trust. I think it's incredible that 10 year olds watch my videos.

Q: Where did you get that facial expression? It looks like a mix between genuine surprise and "I'm trying to look strange." Maybe an homage to Jim Carrey?

A: I spent a lot of time alone as a kid so I practiced ridiculous faces in the mirror.

Q: Is that a southern accent you have? I thought you were raised in Maryland, land of no accents whatsoever. At least that is what it says on Maryland license plates.

A: Do people from Maryland not have accents? I don't live there anymore but it's funny to see people guess in the comments where I am from. Some think Boston. Some think Alabama. Others think my "accent" is fake. Nope, it's real. It's probably because neither of my parents is from Maryland. My mom once said something like: "you have a Yankee Polish father and a southern mother, you weren't meant to speak normally."

Q: Where did you get your political beliefs? Any family, school, work influences that led to your libertarian/conservative views?

A: The Internet made me a libertarian. My grandfather also had a lot to do with it. He is the most libertarian member of our family. I listened to him speak about politics and how dumb politicians were at the holiday dinner table growing up so that had a big effect on me.

Q: I read an April interview of you by Joseph Diedrich of the *Washington Times,* in which you mentioned toning down your political views in college so that you would get a good grade from your liberal professors. There is this guy I know who did that when he was in the political science program at UC Santa Barbara. Would you also advise today's college-age conservatives to tone down their political beliefs to get decent grades?

A: I don't know if I'm the right person to give that kind of advice. But yeah, I played the game most of the time. It worked. I wrote papers that I disagreed with but that helped me to understand the other side of arguments and their weaknesses. There was one liberal political science professor that I had for public policy class who was really interested in my libertarian views. He would always call me out during class to give the libertarian perspective on everything. It just really depends.

To be continued ...

May 27, 2013

JULIE BOROWSKI INTERVIEW, PART 2

Move over, political humorists like Bill Whittle[1], Andrew Klavan, Kurt Schlichter and Steven Crowder![2] Julie Borowswki has entered the public arena, and she is hilarious! Julie Borowski's blog-videos, entitled *Token Libertarian Girl,* can be found at YouTube[3], and her personal blog[4] can be found at julieborowski.wordpress.com.

The Conservative Political Action Committee (CPAC) recently awarded Borowski the "Best Video Blogger" award. And it is no wonder. While her videos can be very persuasive, like her videos on the Boston Marathon bombing[5] and the searches that followed, and the scandals[6] of the Obama administration, her videos can also be very funny, like when she ridiculed[7] Obama voters, and when she complained[8] of her recent treatment at the hands of the TSA.

In this second half of her interview, Borowski discusses her response the Lena Dunham political video[9] calling for young people to vote for President Obama's re-election, the clichés that liberals inject into political discussions, and the current collection of conservative political leaders.

Question: One of your videos[10] was an answer to that silly Lena Dunham video[11] that was made shortly before last fall's election, in which she advocated casting your very first vote for Obama, making it sound like a sexual thing. You must have made your video answer to that one in record time. Do you have any thoughts about the irrationality of today's younger generation voting to re-elect a president who has loaded that generation with so much debt?

Answer: Ha, yeah. That video was gross. I think the Democratic Party has done a much better job at marketing to young people than has the Republican Party. The Democrats have marketed themselves as the party of tolerance, peace, and freedom (sooo not true). The Republicans are seen as the party of intolerance, war, and old people. They are usually on the defensive and rarely on the offensive. The Republican Party needs to re-brand and re-think foreign policy and social issues. Big government foreign policy as promoted by the likes of John McCain and Lindsey Graham is the opposite of limited government, fiscal conservatism, and life. On social issues, the Republican Party needs to be more consistent. It's fine to have social conservative views (I definitely lean that way in my private life), but it's not fine to dictate moral values through the government. We should be advocating for limiting the size and scope of government in every aspect of people's lives. The government isn't the answer to a moral society.

Q: How huge of a mistake was it for the American people to re-elect President Obama? In one of your videos you seemed to agree with a fictional argument that an Obama re-election will doom the US.

A: Yes, it was a big mistake to re-elect Obama. I would have been disappointed no matter who won the general election though. Ha. I actually think Congress matters more than the President. All I have to say is that we have a lot of work to do.

Q: Have you read the book *Tyranny of Cliches*[12], by Jonah Goldberg? Actually neither have I. But I heard a great interview of Goldberg, in which he made the point that liberals like to win political arguments by using clichés instead of actual arguments. It has occurred to me that you do the opposite in your videos, you engage and argue conservative principles instead of using clichés. Seems kind of complicated!

Julie Borowski

Borowski mocks when mocking is needed, like when she mocked the silly Lena Dunham video that called on all cool 20-somethings to vote for President Obama's re-election

(Playing Devil's Advocate here): wouldn't it just be easier to throw out a cliché or stereotype of the opposition and win the argument without having to engage in actual arguing?

A: I haven't read that book. Sure. Going back to the college question, it is so easy to write papers supporting universal healthcare. Argument: everyone should get free health care because compassion, niceness, butterflies. You have to be a monster to argue with butterflies. But in all seriousness, libertarian arguments seem to be deeper than that.

Q: I saw by your website that you oppose the death penalty, proving that you aren't perfect. Are there any libertarian policies with which you disagree?

A: Yes, I oppose the death penalty. I used to be a big supporter of the death penalty so I understand the emotional arguments for the death penalty. I started to oppose the death penalty when I started to think about more than just "I want to get revenge." If you distrust and want to limit the government, then you shouldn't give the government the power to kill people especially if it cost more taxpayer money. Also, I got to experience the ridiculousness of the judicial system: guilty people are let free, innocent people are put in jail all the time. Now, I just can't trust the government with the power to end lives.

I don't know if there are any solid libertarian policies with which I disagree. There are a few policy issues where libertarians disagree with each other: most notably, immigration and abortion. I am pro-immigration and pro-life.

Q: As a libertarian, how do you feel about libertarian voters in 2012 throwing various elections to the Democrats? Mike Flynn of Breitbart wrote a great article[13] pointing out that two Senate races and six House races could have gone to the GOP if Libertarian voters had voted Republican.

A: I'm not a member of the Libertarian Party. Good liberty minded-candidates won't get elected by running on the LP ticket. They can get elected by running on the GOP ticket. See: Ron Paul, Rep. Justin Amash, Rep. Thomas Massie. We don't have 30 years to build up the Libertarian Party, especially when the system (unfortunately) is stacked against third party candidates. That being said, I have voted for the LP candidate when I couldn't stand the Republican or the Democrat on the ticket. I know the LP candidate stands no chance of winning but if someone wants my vote, they have to earn it.

Q: Speaking of humor, are you following or and impressed or unimpressed with any of the current crop of politicians?

A: There are a few good ones out there. But they are few and far in between.

Q: If Rand Paul were somehow out of the picture or decided not to run for president in 2016, whom would you consider supporting for president and why?

A: That's a tough one. Rand Paul is the most libertarian-leaning potential candidate with an actual chance of, you know, winning. I haven't been impressed with any of the other potential candidates the media is throwing around. Same old type of candidates they recycle every election.

Q: What is next for Julie Borowski?

A: People keep asking and I shrug my shoulders. I think I'll just keep doing what I'm doing and see where it leads.

Thanks for your time, Julie. Keep up the great work!

June 3, 2013

ADDICTS CAN LEARN NEW LESSONS FROM AN OLD MOVIE: *STUART SAVES HIS FAMILY*

A recent *Wall Street Journal* editorial[1] speculated that Minnesota Democratic Senator Al Franken may be unopposed by former senator Norm Coleman or any other serious contender in the 2014 election. If so, this follows a recent GOP tradition of putting its worst foot forward, sending candidates into Senate races where they step into all sorts of "gotcha" questions and lose what should have been an easy Republican pick-up.

One of many examples is Missouri Republican senatorial candidate Todd Akin and his wacky comment about female biology reacting differently if the woman was "legitimately" raped. That unforced-error in 2012 allowed the un-popular Democratic Senator Claire McCaskill to handily win re-election.

On the other hand, one advantage to a seriously unopposed Franken candidacy would be that we are free to review and glean the lessons from a movie Franken starred in long before he got involved in politics. If a serious challenge arises to Franken's re-election, please disregard anything positive I have to say about Al Franken or this movie.

The movie is a real under-noticed charmer. It is 1995's *Stuart Saves His Family,* one of several movies inspired by characters from the TV comedy show *Saturday Night Live.* This movie grossed less than $1 million, so the chances of a sequel are remote at best. But the DVD can still be bought on Amazon or Ebay, or rented at Netflix.

The Stuart Smalley character, played by Al Franken, holds himself out as a "caring nurturer, but not a licensed therapist" holding therapy sessions on his cable TV show and in person for people who, like himself, have all sorts of problems, mostly emotional. The effeminate, pastel-wearing Stuart Smalley encourages discussions of feelings, interjecting worn-out, twelve-step expressions to guide the conversation and resolution.

"Listen to me, I'm should'ing all over myself," he says after whining to a friend about his family situation. "I need to just let go and let God," he says at another point in the movie, realizing he cannot improve every bad situation with himself and his family.

It may be sadistic, but a repeated chuckle of this movie comes from the situation in which Stuart Smalley, being such an openly-vulnerable person, interacts with characters who have no time or inclination for discussing weaknesses, vulnerabilities or in fact any feelings at all. Smalley repeatedly gets smacked-down from his station manager at his public-access TV show, a customer at a restaurant, his parents, even the neighbor of his deceased aunt, where he was sent by his family to negotiate a better deal on an easement. Confronted with this honest, sincere, admittedly vulnerable person, all of these people coldly walk all over him, getting the best of him and leaving him miserable and seeking the nearest twelve-step program to recover.

Rarely, Smalley will have enough of the abuse, viciously shout back, and then calm down and offer "an amends" to the confused victim.

Al Franken's ever-so-slightly crossed eyes are a crack-up, as are the characters with their various problems. In the span of the movie, the viewer is introduced to all sorts of maladies that need group treatment, from overeaters to rage-aholics, compulsive gamblers to sex-addicts. At one point in the movie, Smalley's father tells him that he is addicted to 12-step programs. And he is probably right.

Smalley eventually does save his family, encouraging them to go to recovery programs for their various issues. It might seem silly and trite, but the film respects the problems of the characters enough to take them seriously.

And this is how the movie becomes helpful to those who watch the movie and may have problems that need addressing. There are whole groups of Americans with problems that are not quite criminal in and of themselves, but the problems lead to depression and unhappiness. These people carry on their lives as if they have no problems, yet they repeatedly turn to alcohol or drugs and never realize that they will never be able to satisfy their body's cravings. An arrest is usually the alcohol or drug addict's first introduction to the idea that they might have a problem.

In my law practice I have worked with alcoholics and drug addicts, many of whom initially appeared to be hopelessly addicted. I encourage them to go to Alcoholics[2] or Narcotics[3] Anonymous[4] meetings, even getting a sponsor, and oftentimes they clean themselves up.

My pitch always starts with persuading the addict that they in fact have a problem with alcohol or drugs, and that this problem is not a character flaw but rather a biological problem. Everyone knows that diabetes is a biological problem, and are diabetics ashamed of their diabetes? Diabetics, just like alcoholics or drug addicts, need help and they need to openly address their biological problems.

The first step is the most important one. From that point onward, if they want to recover, they will. *Stuart Saves His Family* is helpful by introducing the viewer to recovery groups, twelve-step programs, associating with sponsors, and unashamedly talking about battles with addiction with others, all of which are important steps to recovery. Even friends or family members of struggling alcohol or drug addicts can learn from the movie the importance of moral support in an ongoing struggle. After all, an addict must always be on their guard against relapse.

It is not only an entertaining movie, but *Stuart Saves His Family* is helpful to anyone who has addiction issues, or who is friends with or related to someone who is. Well done, Al Franken.

But like I said, all bets are off if Senator Franken has a serious Republican challenger for re-election. I like his movie, not his politics.

January 14, 2013

THREE CHRISTMAS MOVIES EVERY FAMILY SHOULD OWN

For our family the Christmas season begins right after Halloween. The decorations slowly go up and as November progresses into December the Christmas DVD's from our Christmas movie collection find their way into our DVD player to broadcast the Christmas message to our family for eight weeks straight. We love it!

Immediately preceding Christmas we watch the Christmas classics like *A Christmas Carol, The Bishop's Wife, The Nativity Story,* and *It's A Wonderful Life.* But before that time we watch lesser Christmas movies like *A Charlie Brown Christmas, Home Alone, A Christmas Story, The Santa Clause,* and a few others. It is to this class of Christmas movies that I would recommend every family add the following movies: *The Lemon Drop Kid, A Christmas Wish,* and *The Homecoming: A Christmas Story.*

The Lemon Drop Kid is a Bob Hope movie from 1951, in which Hope plays a racehorse promoter/con-man with a weakness for lemon drops. After getting into trouble by accidentally promoting the wrong horse to a mobster's wife, Hope then spends the rest of the movie trying to raise money to pay off the mobster. Eventually Hope gets a bunch of Santas to collect money in street-side kettles for a rest home for "old dolls," planning to skim some money to pay his debt.

Bob Hope's humorous quips and one-liners are a delight: discussing the horses at a race-track, Hope says "half these horses should be in wheel-chairs," and later, when encouraging a portly woman who is to stay in his rest home, Hope tells her to keep her "chins up."

Towards the end of the movie, Hope's loveable rogue character softens up and becomes good, and along the way the viewer gets to see some endearing mobster characters in action, including the one played by William Frawley, later known to TV viewers as *I Love Lucy's* Fred Mertz. Hope and his fiancé, played by Marilyn Maxwell, debut the Christmas song "Silver Bells" in this movie, and for a comedian Hope has a surprisingly nice singing voice.

Overall, while *The Lemon Drop Kid* has some good Christian themes like forgiveness and redemption, the movie has so much humor that it can be seen any time of the year, just for the laughs.

Anyone who has had a prayer answered in a quirky way can identify with *A Christmas Wish* (formerly known as *The Great Rupert*), a Jimmy Durante movie from 1950. The movie involves a rich family who rents a shack attached to their house to a poor family that includes the character played by Jimmy Durante, his wife and their daughter, Rosalinda. Rosalinda has grown out of her only pair of shoes and cannot walk without experiencing pain. The head of the rich family has just been notified that an investment he made in a gold mine just paid off big, and he would receive $1500 every week. The miserly man decides to hoard the money by hiding it behind the wall that adjoins the shack.

At the end of her rope, Durante's wife prays for some financial help from God, explaining that "Rosalinda needs shoes." Just at that moment the miserly man next door thinks he is hiding his $1500 behind the wall, but a squirrel that lives in that wall space sees the money coming into its lair, so it throws the money out. Surprised and shocked, Durante's wife sees hundred dollar bills coming down, and she figures the money is coming down from Heaven.

The poor wife and her miserly landlord keep up this routine for several weeks, allowing Durante's family to live quite comfortably. But they know they must stay in that shack and pray that "Rosalinda needs shoes" every Thursday afternoon. Eventually the poor family has bought several local businesses and live off the dividends. They begin to tithe some of their income to a charity that involves, fittingly, shoes for poor children.

As the movie ends, the landlord is notified that the gold mine is now out of gold and his house burns down. Jimmy Durante's character magnanimously decides to rebuild his landlord's house and the two families become good friends.

It is a great story that involves prayer and God's great sense of humor, and Jimmy Durante gets a few funny lines into the script. My only reservations with the movie are that it involves a prayer, not a "wish," and the "Christmas" portion of the movie is confined to the first third of the movie. Still, it's an enjoyable film, and Durante plays the piano and sings "Isn't It A Shame That Christmas Comes But Once A Year," which should have become a perennial Christmas song.

The Homecoming: A Christmas Story was the 1971 pilot for the successful TV show, *The Waltons*. The plot revolves around the Depression-era Walton family who is awaiting the return home of their father after they hear of a bus-crash in which he could have been involved. John-Boy takes off on a desperate search of the nearby area, familiarizing the viewer with his neighbors and the friendly and colorful characters who populate the later TV series. John-Boy also has some time for introspection regarding his father and his father's misplaced hope that John-Boy would someday become a successful hunter. Happily, the father arrives home safely and the Walton family has a poor but love-filled, family Christmas celebration.

Signaling the father's acceptance of John-Boy's plans to become a writer instead of a hunter, John-Boy's father gives John-Boy some writing tablets as a Christmas present. This movie has several prayers by various characters, and the birth of Jesus is recounted, a rarity in many Christmas films nowadays.

The Homecoming: A Christmas Story ends with the characteristic "goodnights" between all the Walton family members that also occurred at the end of *The Waltons* TV show. As we watched this movie with our home-schooled daughter, my wife and I devised a good word-math problem: if nine members of a family all say "goodnight" to each other, how many "goodnights" are there total? The correct answer was arrived at by realizing that each of the Walton family members only said goodnight to other family members, not to themselves. Hence nine times eight, or 72.

Our daughter did not get the answer right, so we will try again next year, probably around November 1.

December 24, 2012

JAMES BOND: SUPER SPY, LIFE COACH

A few weeks ago a minor scandal occurred in our household when my wife discovered our 7-year old daughter had taken a bath with a turned-on space heater nearby. Almost as disturbing was the fact that we didn't initially know how to explain electricity to a 7-year old.

I knew just what to do. I dusted off my *Goldfinger* DVD and showed my daughter the opening scene, where James Bond is in a fight that isn't going so well. Bond shoved the bad guy into a nearby bathtub, and when his foe reached for a gun, Bond kicked a nearby space heater into the bathtub, frying the guy instantly.

My daughter immediately understood the danger of having an electrical appliance near a bathtub.

Most of life's essential lessons can be learned by watching James Bond movies. Sure, the Bond franchise offers great action movies tailor-made for guys, but it is amazing how much smarter a viewer is after having seen a Bond film.

Ever get pushed out of an airplane at 20,000 feet without a parachute? No problem: find a guy with a parachute nearby and go get his chute. That happened in *Moonraker.*

If someone ever tries to kick you with a dagger-tipped shoe, grab the nearest chair and impale them on a wall nearby until you can do something else to defend yourself. That nugget can be found in *From Russia With Love,* and you never know when you will need to know that maneuver.

Thunderball revealed that a spear gun works just as well on land as it does underwater. Who knew? And if you come across anyone with a huge set of stainless-steel teeth in their mouth, as in *The Spy Who Loved Me* and *Moonraker,* be careful. Those choppers can probably be used to kill a human!

But at least such a guy like that would reveal himself to be a threat the second he opens his mouth even slightly. When a beautiful woman expresses a sudden interest in you, how do you really know that the feeling is the standard human physical attraction to your good looks, and not that the woman is following orders to seduce and kill you? Think Barbara Bach in *The Spy Who Loved Me.*

Here's a critical one: a bad guy's lair always blows up after his plans to destroy the world are foiled. So when you press that "abort" button, you better start running. Pretty standard. Espionage Studies 101, really. That happened in *Dr. No, Thunderball* and most other Bond films up to and including the 2008 movie *Quantum of Solace.*

That also occurred in the humorous Bond-like film, *Austin Powers.* Come to think of it, some Bond off-shoot films also have some of life's essential lessons in them.

Take for example the humorous spy movie *The In-Laws.* After watching that 1979 romp anyone would know the importance of "serpentining" if you ever find yourself running and getting shot at. Knowing that skill could save your life!

Fortunately, these and other of life's essential lessons can be learned now that the entire James Bond collection is available in a box set of Blu-ray disks, sold on Amazon for $150. Amazon[1] even has a trailer[2] of the Blu-ray disk release itself.

According to Amazon, the box will come with one disk that contains brand new bonus content on the Bond films, and nine of the Bond films will be released in Blu-ray for the first time. However the box will also contain an "empty slot" to be used for the disk of the forthcoming James Bond film, *Skyfall,* which will be released in theaters in the U.S. Nov. 9 three days after the elections, when Americans will be ready for some apolitical, action-packed entertainment.

This year marks the 50th anniversary of the Bond franchise, so the producers are spending $200 million on *Skyfall* to mark the occasion. That's still a hefty chunk of change for a film.

Skyfall will also be available in IMAX, giving theater viewers the opportunity to duck when bullets or knives fly their way. As with all Bond films, *Skyfall* is sure to have some eternal truths in it that will make the movie entertaining and educational.

September 30, 2012

AN IRREVERENT REVIEW OF THE MOVIE *2016: OBAMA'S AMERICA*

I just caught a matinee viewing of the Dinesh D'Souza movie *2016: Obama's America*, over the lunch hour in a Silicon Valley metroplex theater. At first I didn't notice, but after a few patrons in front of me it became pretty obvious: no one going into this movie wanted to be seen, ticket payments were primary by cash, and they were not receptive to the small-talk from the staff as they entered the theater. Not quite dark glasses and overcoats, but similar. For us patrons, watching this movie was to be a guilty – and secret – pleasure.

It is a great movie, answering many questions about the train-wreck that is the Obama presidency. D'Souza connects a lot of dots that have been unsettling for Obama detractors for a long time. Someday, assuming we are still around, our great-grand-kids will ask us "what was your generation thinking in 2008? Were you guys nuts?" If we remember this movie, we will have some answers.

I will leave the serious movie reviews to others, but I have some comments in no particular order.

First, what was it with the interviews with people on their cell phones? I saw that twice. D'Souza was on his cell phone interviewing someone else who was on his cell phone. Apparently the camera crew was in the interviewee's office, so why not have the guy being interviewed put down his cell phone and just talk directly to the camera? Or why not add a little humor and have D'Souza on his cell phone, interviewing someone also on his cell phone, but both of them in the same office?

And why force the audience to listen to so many Obama speeches and recordings? I caught this movie right after eating lunch, and it didn't sit too well in my stomach. If you must have the audience listen to so much of President Obama, at least add in a laugh track. I know this is a documentary, but still...

Think of the audience: conservatives. If D'Souza wants to refer to a specific part of President Obama's speech or audio book, why can't

D'Souza just read it himself, or paraphrase it? We promise to take your word for it.

And speaking of laugh tracks, I have seen that 2008 clip of the Tom Brokaw and Charlie Rose discussion several times. There *had* to have been some laughs by the camera crew that were edited out. You know, the type of barely audible laughs that Bill O'Reilly gets as he jokes at the end of his show.

Think of it, journalistic titan Tom Brokaw, interviewed just days before a presidential election and admitting he knew almost nothing of the guy who will soon be elected president. And seemingly not being embarrassed by his lack of curiosity. That had to elicit a cynical chuckle or two inside the studio. Chuckles that I believe were edited out, and you cannot convince me otherwise.

And why can't we on the right have unfair, "gotcha" interviews like in Michael Moore's documentaries? Remember that time in *Bowling For Columbine* when Michael Moore tried to ambush Dick Clark and blame him for a school shooting? After all, the single mother of the kid who did the shooting was busy working at a Dick Clark restaurant, so her un-supervised kid predictably grabbed his uncle's gun and went to school and shot a classmate.

Of course this was all very unfair to Dick Clark, and I was probably the only one in the audience cheering as Clark drove away. Why can't we on the right do something like that once in a while? If for no other reason, just to point out the unfairness of the other side? You know, our titular leader, radio talk-show host Rush Limbaugh, will occasionally "be absurd to illustrate absurdity." Why not do that in a documentary? Hmmm?

Of all the people interviewed in this movie, President Obama's brother George Obama, in Kenya, probably made the most sense with his anti-anti-colonial talk. I could be wrong but I am not convinced the guy was sober when he was interviewed. I have seen that look before: talking, then an eye-blink that takes a little longer than necessary and for a split second you wonder if the guy is falling asleep, then he comes back and resumes his comment.

And why was D'Souza asking him if he agreed with what he wrote in his book? "Well yeah, I agree with what I wrote in my book..." Was that the hoped-for response? Or maybe there was a possibility that George Obama had a ghost-writer who injected some incorrect ideas into the book.

On the other hand, the whole "white colonials should have stayed in Kenya longer" argument is something that would get George Obama placed in probation in most American universities, so maybe D'Souza was basically asking him "you did mean to write this, didn't you?"

At the end of the movie there was the spontaneous applause that I hear happens at the end of this movie, even a few approving whoops and right-ons. But when the lights in the theater came on, the cheering stopped abruptly. The people there must have realized that they could be spotted by someone who knew them, so everyone got quiet and tried to blend in with the exiting crowd for the *Diary Of A Wimpy Kid* film next door as they left the theater.

A few years ago an Academy Award was given to the song "It's Hard Out Here For A Pimp." Well, those pimps need to experience the difficulties of watching a great, conservative movie like this in deep-blue California. Now *that* is hard!

August 27, 2012

CAROLLA AND PRAGER: THE NEWEST ODD COUPLE CLICK ON STAGE

Much as I hate to admit it[1], there was one interesting idea from the 1981 movie *My Dinner With Andre*: the notion of just sitting down and spending two hours listening to an interesting conversation at a nearby dinner table.

Well, dinner may not have been served, but the mostly-unplanned conversation between Adam Carolla and Dennis Prager was delightfully entertaining for the mostly-sold-out crowd Saturday night in San Diego's Spreckels Theatre.

And the pair-up was truly eclectic: Prager, the politically conservative radio talk-show host[2], orthodox Jew who in his spare time teaches the Torah, and Carolla, the apolitical atheist comedian whose edgy podcasts[3] are the guilty pleasure for countless subscribers.

Prager appreciates Carolla's humor and spontaneity, while Carolla appreciates Prager's intelligence and judgment.

"There is a ton of wisdom in Prager," Carolla said in a recent podcast. "We have almost nothing in common."

But you have to wonder how they would interact together to produce an interesting conversation worth the price of admission for two hours.

Somehow it worked.

Prager pursued a dialogue of general topics, with freedom to stray from the subject, and Carolla interjected humor along the way. Carolla began discussing his son's recent T-ball prowess and then reminisced about his own days of school dodge-ball, a sport that is currently outlawed, along with many other fun sports.

"My kids will never know the joys of Smear The Queer," he said.

The subject of racism in America came up, and Prager reiterated a point he has made on his radio show that "the United States is the least racist country in the world."

To which Carolla replied, "1,400 white people are now applauding that comment."

Typical of the evening, when Prager referred to street riots, Carolla questioned whether "do you really need the word 'street' before 'riot'? Where else are you going to riot, in an entry way?"

Both Carolla and Prager described how when they grew up their parents would cover the upholstery of their couches with plastic or sheets. I have seen this and never understood the point of it – the only people getting to enjoy the couch would be the future owners, if any. But it was a pretty personal moment for both men, opening up this part of their childhoods for the crowd.

Carolla reflected that he "wasn't raised with low self-esteem. I was raised with no self-esteem." After more discussion on self-esteem in kids, the two agreed that the higher the self-esteem of the kid, the worse the resulting adult is, and vice versa.

Among the laughs there were some other ultimate truths: cohabitating before marriage leads to a marriage that ends in divorce, government care should be reserved for military amputees and disabled people, not freeloaders, and the bigger the government the smaller the citizen.

At one point Carolla asked Prager, "if it is so obvious that socialism, communism or the western European model has failed, why do liberals keep proposing it?"

Prager answered that leftism is a religion and facts rarely get in the way of any religion. Prager mentioned his recent non-profit project, Prager University[4], a collection of 5-minute online courses from notable authors and lecturers. At the mention of the word "university," Carolla interjected "I rushed a frat at Prager University but it didn't work out."

Both Carolla and Prager had books to sell, but they were clearly not there to promote them. Prager referred to his book, *Still The Best Hope,* only in passing, and Carolla never mentioned his upcoming book, *Not Taco Bell Material,* available for pre-order now before its June release.

They had a certain chemistry together, if for no other reason than the fact that they have so little in common and yet they respect and enjoy each other. One thing that could add to this great pairing would be more comedic interactions between the two, where one of them pokes fun at or criticizes the other, and the audience gets to see a resolution or impasse of the dispute. Sure, Prager isn't known for his own sense of humor, but he is able to follow along the arc of Carolla's gags. They could become a kind of Bob Hope and Bing Crosby, or at least Tony Randall and Jack Klugman.

On the other hand, this might be a show that is impossible to improve upon, as viewers will be able to see for themselves as this show progresses through the country.

May 7, 2012

PALIN'S PRIVILEGE

Former Alaska Governor Sarah Palin was on the *Today* show last week, and she did very well.[1] It was an enjoyable show and she handled the occasional barbs against her with class. But don't mention that in mixed company (liberals and conservatives), or anywhere online. There are prohibitions against foul language online, you know.

Palin's appearance on *Today* was met with an avalanche of criticism from the left. Websites like Democratic Underground and Huffington Post stewed in their hatred for Gov. Palin. Lefty mocker Jon Stewart[2] ridiculed her. Former *Today* host Bryant Gumbel even said he was "embarrassed by Palin's appearance on the show," and complained[3] that she lacked the capability of reporting or interviewing, or having "a degree of gravitas."

In their attacks against Gov. Palin the familiar refrain is that she is stupid, but that doesn't sound right to me. When liberals criticize Sarah Palin is being stupid, they have a real anger in their voice or urgency in their blog posts.

If they were really concerned about a public figure who is stupid they would focus on Vice President Joe Biden. To those who pay attention to the news, if they are honest, they would agree that Vice President Joe Biden is a real buffoon. His[4] recent rambling explanation regarding gasoline prices was yet another proof of his foolishness.

But it is Sarah Palin for whom liberals have a special hatred when they assert that she is stupid. Why is this?

The last time the Left in this country had such a full-throated denunciation of someone as stupid, it was of Ronald Reagan. I remember it so well because I too was a liberal during Reagan's first term as president. It was very frustrating to denounce someone a stupid as they win two landslide elections.

Even more frustrating, Reagan didn't seem to care when he was called an idiot. He just kept doing what he saw as his mandate: unleashing the American economy and defeating the thugs of the Soviet Union. At the time I remember feeling guilty in admiring the self-confidence of someone repeatedly called stupid but not seeming to care. It almost seemed a privilege to him to be called stupid by liberals.

Sure, President Reagan graduated from an unheard-of college, and he did not sound intellectual, but he did his job well. When he spoke directly to the people about a certain issue, he connected and persuaded.

Same for Sarah Palin. She got a bachelor's degree from University of Idaho after spending a lot of time in junior college. Yet when she discusses the issues, she has a certain connection with the people, and she persuades.

The formal education argument is a common one. "Why should we listen to someone who barely has any formal education?" liberals ask. It all feels so nouveau-intellectual because it is usually asked by someone with a wall full of college and post-graduate degrees, implying that *they* should be listened to, simply by virtue of their own formal education.

Smart people should take Gov. Sarah Palin seriously, just like one smart person took Ronald Reagan seriously. I recently bought a DVD of the William F. Buckley's *Firing Line* interview[5] with Ronald Reagan in 1980. Now *there* is a guy who had some high-brow credentials:

William F. Buckley Jr. graduated from Yale, used words in conversation that people had never heard before, started *National Review,* and even had some kind of impressive accent[6] that no one could really place.

Buckley took Ronald Reagan seriously because he knew that Reagan was a real conservative who could persuade the country to follow conservative principles. If Buckley had any intellectual insecurity, he easily could have sided with the better-educated but hapless Jimmy Carter.

And this shows the important part of the job of president or political leader, whether it was Reagan back in the 1980's or Sarah Palin today. We aren't choosing someone to be philosopher or pontificator-in-chief. We are choosing someone who will advance the cause of freedom and opportunity. The question is whether they believe in the American people, and do they have conservative values that they can advance.

I realize Sarah Palin isn't perfect. She resigned her only term of Alaska governor before the end of the term, giving conservatives false hope that she would run for president this year. And although it wasn't her fault, I was greatly disappointed in 2008 when we were introduced to her, and despite her name "Palin," she appears not to be related to Michael Palin, my favorite member of Monty Python. That would have been nice.

But her appearance on the *Today* show was not only good for ratings but it was very good for the conservative ideas that are so rarely promoted in the mainstream media. If NBC had any programming brains — which is not a given – they would invite Sarah Palin back to co-host the *Today* show again and again. NBC and the country would definitely be better for it.

April 9, 2012

WHAT A FEAT! LITTLE FEAT ROCKS NAPA, CALIFORNIA IN ITS U.S. CONCERT TOUR OPENER

Earlier this week a nearly sold-out audience in Napa, California, got together to satisfy its fetish for that strangely-named Southern rock and blues band that occasionally lapses into Dixieland jazz, Little Feat.[1] The band had before it two challenges: can the style still work after the passing of the band's founder and big toe, and current inspiration, Lowell George, and can the band come close to replicating the performance in its 1978 album *Waiting For Columbus,* arguably the best live album ever. The band met those challenges and overall Little Feat produced a delightful concert.

Little Feat still has one founding member, piano player Bill Payne, and three others, percussionist Sam Clayton, and guitarists Paul Barrere and Fred Tackett, who joined the band in 1973 for the album *Dixie Chicken.* In their concert they blended newer songs with the older classics. The new songs "Rooster Rag" and "Salome" show a departure from the earlier blues/jazz influence, and at times almost feel like folk songs.

I loved hearing the band sing "Fat Man In The Bathtub," a Little Feat classic. And percussionist Sam Clayton and drummer Gabe Ford capably kept the beat going on this percussion-heavy song. Also, "Spanish Moon" and "Time Loves A Hero" were both amazing. Not a foot in Napa's Uptown Theatre was left un-tapping.

One unexpected pleasure in this concert was the guitar work of Paul Barrere. All the musicians in the band were very good, but Barrere's guitar skills were a rare pleasure to hear and watch. Following the concert my wife and I debated as to whether Barrere was in the league of Eric Clapton.

I don't mean to be a heel, but as a loyal Little Feat fan I was hoping to hear more jazz. Instead of the saxophone, trumpet and clarinet ensemble that accompanied earlier hits like "Dixie Chicken" and "Mercenary Territory," Fred Tackett capably played his trumpet in a few of the songs. Bill Payne played great piano, which took up most of the slack.

But let's face it: the jazzy "Dixie Chicken" song is mostly a piano jazz and drum song with a full Dixieland jazz crescendo in the middle. So Bill Payne's piano playing mostly worked, even without the jazz accompaniment. Still, it would be nice to hear the jazz we all know so well in the original song.

The band also used "Dixie Chicken" as a time to cycle through breaks for the band members, and introduced a powerful bass riff that wasn't in the original song. For a die-hard Feat fan like me, it left me a little flat-footed.

And I would vote to add the song "Oh, Atlanta" to the concert play-list. "Oh, Atlanta" is such a classic Little Feat song that it just doesn't feel right to attend a Little Feat concert and not hear it. The lack of jazz instruments wouldn't affect this mostly piano and slide guitar song. Plus, as the city of Atlanta is a recent addition to the list of concert locations, you just know Atlantans will be clamoring to hear it.

Another plus to this concert: it was devoid of the usual liberal barbs that somehow manage to find themselves into movies, TV shows and rock concerts. The Dixie Chicks concerts a few years ago or the up-coming Bruce Springsteen tour seem to portray the message "non-liberals not welcome." Didn't happen here. "It's all about having fun," lead guitarist Paul Barrere told me before the concert.

And fun it was! The timelessness of most of the Little Feat songs was amazing. Think of it: here we were, listening to many songs that had been written in the early-to-mid-1970's and you just couldn't tell, besides the occasional lyric about "weed" or "joint," which seem tame compared to lyrics in today's songs. These Little Feat tunes truly are timeless.

Little Feat will blanket the US in this tour. A year from now Little Feat will hold another annual series of concerts in Jamaica. (And with a band named Little Feat you would think they would be playing at the Sandals resort in Jamaica, but not so.) The Jamaica gigs should be very newsworthy – extremely! — and Big Hollywood needs to send your's truly to cover these monumental concerts. It would be a tough assignment, but I'm up to it.

In conclusion, I have to say this to those Southern rock, blues and jazz fans in the remaining cities for this tour: I don't care how big your feet are, get in here and enjoy this concert by Little Feat!

March 19, 2012

PREPARE FOR THE END WITH *DOOMSDAY PREPPERS* TV SHOW

This just *has* to be a sign of the times. Record deficits and oil prices rising, and it could all get worse. So the National Geographic channel has begun airing a show named *Doomsday Preppers,* where viewers can watch end-of-the-world types prepare for the end.

Each episode highlights several people and their preparations for the end of the world, or, as they often put it, "when the stuff hits the fan." If you are a "doomsday prepper" the show has some pretty useful information, and if not, the show is still pretty entertaining.

Some of the calamities predicted by the preppers seem pretty far-fetched, like a shift in the earth's axis or an earthquake that divides the country's supply lines in half. But some of the calamities predicted are worth getting nervous about, like hyperinflation or a failure of the world financial system.

The preppers store or grow food, store water, generate their electricity, and prepare to defend themselves with handguns and home-made explosives. At the end of each segment, "experts"[1] grade each prepper's plans.

Some of the prepper plans are pretty impressive. One episode involved an Arizona family who keeps a pool/greenhouse, with chicken above fertilizing a pool that contains quickly-regenerating fish. A by-product, duckweed, purifies the water and generates fertilizer for the vegetable gardens.

Alright, it may be sensible, but still, aren't those folks just a little odd — kind of reminiscent of Ted Kaczynski? Sure enough, some of the interviews are filmed with just a hint of humor. And it is a hard to keep a straight face when a prepper is filmed buying something and the shop-owner asks them why they are buying the camouflage netting or handgun, and the prepper replies "why, to protect my family when the world ends, of course!"

The part of the segment that deals with guns and self-defense usually involves a chuckle or two. In one segment a housewife and her husband turn off the lights in their house and prowl around, pistols drawn, laser sights on and ready to shoot. A channel-surfer would have confused the scene for a re-run of *Mission Impossible.*

In another episode a lanky, shirtless guy in New England explains that he thinks guns are stupid. He feels that if thugs come to loot his place he will feed, charm them, and if need be, poison them. Anyone watching the show couldn't help but wonder how long a guy with this much naiveté and lack of weaponry would really last.

And what is the point of all the guns anyway? If there was a total breakdown of society, how long would these preppers really last against a nearby town full of starving people? In the Rodney King riots[2] in 1991, armed Korean shop-owners in Los Angeles managed to hold off armed looters for a few hours, but they didn't have a chance of holding out much longer until the National Guard showed up.

And when the preppers are taken seriously, as many clearly are, why do the preppers in this show discuss their secret stashes of food, much less brag about it on national TV? Now the whole town where they live knows where a storehouse of food is, just in case.

Still, some of the show's segments are helpful, like the New England lady who keeps bees and grows apples so that she will have honey and apple cider to barter. Or the North Carolina survivalist who buys vodka for barter or to use as explosives for self-defense. (For guys like me, any education on explosives is an easy sell.)

But there are some problems in the show. For example, one family turned their small suburban plot of land into a farm full of fruits and vegetables needed to survive if society breaks down. The family got good grades from the experts but this would have been a great time to discuss "hybrid" and "non-hybrid" seeds.

Seeds that are bought in hardware stores and nurseries are generally "hybrid," so that once the customer's crop of tomatoes or corn, for example, is grown and eaten, the customer has to go back to the store and buy more seeds for next year. Only "non-hybrid" or "heirloom" seeds can grow not only a full supply of vegetables this year, but also produce reliable seeds for next year. That is essential information, but it wasn't covered.

Other important issues are also missing. Rarely is the storage and purification of water discussed, and water is essential for *all* doomsday preparations.

But in general it is good to see a show interviewing people preparing for the end of the world. And the issue is a serious one. A recent scan through news headlines will show that people in the know suspect disaster is looming. Former White House Budget Director David Stockman was a recent example.[3] The federal government recently bought up a six-month supply of Mountain House emergency food, so it might know something.

So don't forget to watch *Doomsday Preppers* on Tuesday nights on the National Geographic channel to get a taste of the preparation we all need to make for whatever hits the fan.

March 12, 2012

MY DINNER WITH ANDRE REVIEW: THE ONLY ONE OF ITS KIND, FOR GOOD REASON

A few days ago I sat down to watch (finally!) the movie everyone was talking about back when I was too busy partying in college to watch. *My Dinner With Andre,* the 1981 movie starring Andre Gregory and Wallace Shawn. At the beginning of the movie the Wallace Shawn character shares some brief inner dialogue with the viewer, then he and the Andre Gregory character meet in a restaurant, sit down together and start talking.

All of a sudden, my wife had an asthma issue that needed immediate attention, possibly even a call to the hospital. I immediately phoned a doctor friend of ours and recounted the symptoms, while searching medical websites for advice. I kept another computer screen open on a medical chat-site, asking questions and comparing symptoms with others online.

Over an hour passed, the problem was diagnosed and pills taken that ended the problem for my wife. My wife was OK to go to bed and I turned off my computer, thanked our friend and online chatters for their advice. Still too stressed to go to bed, I sat back in front of the TV, which was still on but muted, so I un-muted the TV and resumed watching *My Dinner With Andre.*

And guess what? The same two guys were in the same restaurant, still talking! And it doesn't look as if anything has happened since the beginning of the movie, except maybe a change in the topics of conversation. But still...

I turned my computer back on and did some research. Could it really be that this movie is entirely about two guys sitting down in a restaurant and talking for almost two hours? That didn't sound right.

But it was true! For almost two long hours they just talked! And what were they talking about for so long? Nothing interesting. No juicy gossip about anyone famous or financial secrets from which the listener can profit. The Andre character had dropped out of New York theater society for a few years to travel the world and find himself. He recounted his worldwide travels and bizarre experiences with other theater types.

And Wallace Shawn's character was mostly relegated to being the listener, at times grunting whenever the Andre character needed to catch his breath. I could see spending a few minutes listening to his "I've-got-it-all-figured-out" self-deprecating schtick that he did so well[1] in *The Princess Bride,* but no such luck in this movie.

But the Andre character – what a windbag! He is an example of someone who wants to talk and talk and not listen. For the most part they have no interest in hearing anyone else talk. That was Andre. Unless the viewer is intimidated into being impressed with mildly-philosophical self-reflection, the whole conversation was pretty excruciating, especially for an action-junky like me.

In fact, these two characters sitting around and talking for almost two hours was kind of like the "E.F. Hutton" commercials made famous during those years, except in reverse. Instead of leaning forward to hear what was being discussed, if a listener nearby heard any part of the conversation they would quickly check their watch and realize that they had to leave. Quickly.

I know that two-hour conversations occasionally happen in real life, but why make a movie about one? Seriously, this movie didn't have any movement at all, except for the entry into and exit from the restaurant.

Sure, there are many intellectual films that are centered on conversations, where the plot turns on spoken words. But until *My Dinner With Andre,* there was at least some movement in such a movie. Even a walk.

Take for example the 1979 Woody Allen film *Manhattan. Manhattan* was a dialogue-centered movie with some movement and change of scenery. Towards the end of *Manhattan* the Woody Allen character realizes he misses his girlfriend and runs several blocks to see her. For those movie-goers who had just eaten dinner before watching this movie, this scene at least gave the movie-goer the feeling of having just gone on a walk. Kind of like the exhaustion viewers feel after watching

Pumping Iron or the hangover they feel after watching *Leaving Las Vegas.*

But the viewer feels no such feelings after watching *My Dinner With Andre.* After watching this movie my only feeling was claustrophobia. And I'm sure many other victims of this movie feel the same way.

If the *My Dinner With Andre* conversation-only formula was appealing, you can bet it would have been copied. See, back in the 1980's when *My Dinner With Andre* was made, probably more so than today, studios weren't shy about copying box-office winners. Witness the movies *Like Father Like Son* and its progeny. If you hadn't had enough of the adventures of kids and grown-ups trading places after watching *Like Father Like Son,* there was *Big, Vice Versa, 18 Again!,* and *Dream A Little Dream.* Similar themes and similar pay-offs. Same for all the beefcake/sword-and-sorcery movies like *Conan The Barbarian, The Beastmaster,* Lou Ferrigno's *Hercules,* and *Red Sonja.* The first one worked and made some good money, so similar movies were made with similar pay-offs.

But there were no copies or imitations of *My Dinner With Andre.* Who would copy such a lousy idea? Such a format would be relatively cheap: all you need is to rent a restaurant, hire a few extras as waiters, and pay a small amount to a couple of lead actors with the promise of numerous close-ups. If the idea had any redeeming qualities or commercial potential whatsoever, a rip-off *My Dinner With Andre* could be produced on a shoe-string. You could name it *My Brunch With Alvin.*

(Spoiler alert, not that it matters…) As *My Dinner With Andre* mercifully came to close, the Wallace Shawn character leaves the restaurant and takes a taxi home to his girlfriend, and his inner dialogue says "Debbie was home from work. And I told her everything about my dinner with Andre." At that point the wearied viewer yells at the TV or movie screen "…and tell her to avoid it!"

And that is the opinion of this reviewer. Do not watch this movie.

February 20, 2012

CHAPTER *4*

SILLIER THAN USUAL

Humor is mankind's greatest blessing
—**Mark Twain**

AN IDEA FOR A NEW MURDER MYSTERY SERIES: *PC DETECTIVE*

Murder mystery shows just aren't what they used to be. Long gone are the days when you have a murder committed, and it is solved by a mildly-disheveled *Columbo,* or the eccentric French detective Poirot in Agatha Christie's *Poirot.*

Oh that's right, Poirot is Belgian, not French. Sorry. But you get the point: nowadays murder mysteries are all over the place with their detectives. In *Monk,* the detective is obsessive compulsive. *Psyche* has a con man as a detective, and he claims to be psychic when he is merely very observant. Then there is *CSI,* in which is a murder is solved mostly by using physics and chemistry. *Bones* has a detective who has Asperger Syndrome. Sometimes *Doc Martin* solves mysteries in his medical practice – and he is a doctor who hates the sight of blood!

Such a growing field of sleuths deserves yet another entrant. And here is my idea: the politically correct detective. The idea is that political correctness, or "diversity," or "inclusion," or whatever you want to call it, would guide the thinking of the detective to such an extent that major turns in the plot of the show would hinge on the detective's idea of what is right, inclusive, encouraging of diversity, whatever.

"Ridiculous," you say? "It will never fly!" Have you read the news lately? Political correctness has injected itself into many otherwise normal national conversations. Recently, an MSNBC commentator suggested[1] that the US should not support Israel over Hamas terrorists because a poll showed that minorities and people of color are less supportive of Israel. And just last week, some developers of an iPhone app called "Sketchfactor" are being called[2] racist because their app guides users out of bad neighborhoods, which might also be minority neighborhoods. I could go on.

Political correctness is out there, and it distorts the thinking of a lot of people in many different situations. So, in the words of Teresa Heinz Kerry, our almost-First Lady from 2004, take your thoughts of this idea being ridiculous, and "shove it!"

My *PC Detective* show would open with a garden variety murder. The details really don't matter. Our protagonist would be a university sociology professor who is hired as a consultant by the local police to solve the crime.

A police liaison would approach the professor at the end of one of his class lectures, and the policeman would hear the final comment or two from the professor to the students. The professor would be heard echoing some worn-out liberal platitudes ("...so this demonstrates how Tea Party members are a bunch of racists," or "... so the findings of this latest study show conclusively that Republicans as a whole have smaller skull-size and therefore lower IQ's"). Then, the professor dismisses the class and reminds the students to read the next week's homework assignment. Next, the police officer meets with the professor and updates him on the facts of the murder.

Throughout the various twists and turns of the investigation, the detective/professor would find clues and either conclude that the murderer was a white male heterosexual Christian, or if any other possibilities exist, the detective would caution himself and the police against "profiling."

At some point a lower-level police officer – maybe an intern — would stumble across some definitive clue that clearly identifies the murderer, at which point the murderer instantly confesses and specifies a motive (that also happens a lot in popular murder mysteries).

Then the professor/detective would claim full credit and begin writing an article on the case (showing the importance of publication for academia).

There would be an epilogue, just like in some of the shows of the 1950's and 60's, in which the professor/detective talks directly to the audience. If the murderer is a NON-white male heterosexual Christian, the professor/detective blames racism, sexism, homophobia, etc. in society for the murder. If, on the other hand, the murderer IS a white male heterosexual Christian, then the professor blames the murder on the inherent hateful tendencies of this group of people. Obviously the epilogue would be tongue-in-cheek.

Although the ideas for this murder mystery series may be limited, here are some other ingredients to prolong the series:

Other protected groups: environmentalists, Prius or Volt drivers, vegetarians, vegans, union members, guilty white people, college professors, teachers, illegal immigrants, abortion providers, gay marriage supporters, and Elizabeth Warren supporters.

Other non-protected groups: Republicans, Walmart shoppers, cigarette smokers, oil company employees, stay-at-home moms, physicians, rich people, people who work on Wall Street, gun-owners, football fans, NASCAR fans, global warming skeptics, SUV drivers, abortion protesters, opponents of gay marriage, Rush Limbaugh listeners, and Sarah Palin supporters. Let's face it, all of these people are barely human anyway, so portraying them as vicious killers would not be a stretch.

There are several readers of my work who have written screenplays or who have had some success in show business. Feel free to use this idea, royalty-free. I could use a "shout out" from the writer every once in a while, but I would probably live if I get ignored. I'm pretty sure this idea will sell in Hollywood. So go for it!

August 11, 2014

RECYCLING AN INTERNET URBAN MYTH

Every once in a while, something comes to my attention on the Internet, and I think, "this is ridiculous. Do people really believe this?" Some stories are just too contrived — way too made-up to be taken seriously. And the final outcome of the story presented is just too self-contained and, well, just neat. Events in real life just don't end up like that.

But sometimes a tale gets forwarded to me by e-mail or I see it on social media and the story is just so over-the-top contrived that I can't help but to make a few changes and pass it along and see what happens.

That is what happened with the "rudeness on an airplane" story. The story I got had to do with a racist white woman who felt put upon when her assigned seat on an airplane was next to an African-American. I made a few changes to this, like changing the victim to an unidentified handicapped person, added to the whininess a little, and then enhanced the "comeuppance" part of it when the complaining woman has to sit next to an obese passenger, and – voila! – an Internet urban myth is born! Then I added a random photo of an airplane stewardess that I stole from the Internet, and I have now seen this modified story of "rudeness on an airplane" come back across my own computer screen, with some minor changes, two times since I made my changes and sent it out! This is really fun!

Below is my version of the "rudeness on an airplane" story that I sent out. Feel free to pass it on, and include an expression of outrage and hearty approval of the karmic justice on display here. According to the website Snopes, variations of this story have been making the rounds in e-mail and on the Internet since 1998. Let's breathe some more life into it!

Rudeness On An Airplane

A 50-something year old woman arrived at her seat on a crowded flight and immediately didn't want the seat. The seat was next to a handicapped man. Disgusted, the woman immediately summoned the flight attendant and demanded a new seat.

The woman said "I cannot sit here next to this, uh, person," gesturing to the handicapped guy.

The flight attendant said, "let me see if I can find another seat." After checking, the flight attendant returned and stated, "ma'am, there are no more seats in economy, but I will check with the captain and see if there is something in first class."

About 10 minutes went by and the flight attendant returned and stated "the captain has confirmed that there are no more seats in economy, but there is one in first class. It is our company policy to never move a person from economy to first class, but being that it would be some sort of scandal to force a person to sit next to an UNPLEASANT person, the captain agreed to make the switch to first class."

Before the woman could say anything, the pilot arrived and gestured to the handicapped man and said, "sir, if you would so kindly retrieve your personal items, we would like to move you to the comfort of first class, as we don't want you to sit next to an unpleasant person." Scattered applause could be heard among the other passengers nearby.

"Well, I never…" growled the lady. "At least I get a vacant seat next to me. These middle seats can get pretty cramped."

"Excuse me Mr. Pilot," said a nearby fellow passenger, looking like he weighed about 550 pounds. "If you don't mind, I would like to move to the seat next to that lady."

The pilot gestured to the open seat, "sure – be my guest."

"But…" whimpered the lady. The heavy guy settled in to the seat next to the lady, the love handles from his right side settling onto the arm-rest between the two seats and spilling over into her lap.

"Oh gross," said the lady, her face turning red.

This was too much for the surrounding crowd, which leapt to its feet with a thundering applause. The pilot had a big grin as he turned to go back to the cockpit.

If you are against discrimination against the handicapped, share this.

April 30, 2014

JOURNALISM SCHOOL CLASS OFFERINGS

Imagine my surprise! There I was, enjoying my lunch at a sidewalk cafe right across the street from a prestigious school of journalism. Suddenly a few feet away from me accumulated a group of journalism students, chatting, gossiping, talking about the latest student parties, all those fun things that make college years so fun. Just listening to them, for a few moments I was taken back to my years in college — what fun I had!

Anyway, these journalism students were on their way to a "brown bag lunch discussion" given by a member of the Pulitzer Prize committee! Wow! Very impressive, indeed.

After they left I noticed that one of them had accidentally dropped a list of current class offerings at this journalism school. As a news junky, I was interested in the focus of modern journalism, so I picked up the list of classes. Here is what I read:

Journalism 101: Mass Deception: How To Distract The Public And Advance The Democrat Agenda. Different news items can add up to a Democrat or a Republican victory in the day's news. This class will teach you how to retrieve and report only those news items that culminate in a Democratic victory for the day's news cycle.

Journalism 110: Conformity and Pack Journalism: once sneered at, the so-called "Mainstream Media" now provides guidance to reporting current events, quickens research, and provides career advancement for the journalist.

Journalism 120: Economic News Reporting: focusing on high numbers of homeless and lay-offs during Republican presidencies, rebounding economies and mass hirings during Democratic presidencies.

Journalism 130: The Genius of Joseph Goebbels: Repeat any narrative enough times and even the stupidest news-reader will begin to believe it. Clever political figures have adopted this approach, and if those politicians are liberals then we journalists need to follow.

Journalism 140: The "Journolist": the importance of a unanimous media front. Not only the news that is reported but even the buzzwords used by member journalists should match ("gravitas," "political stunt," etc.) If we journalists get our stories straight, the people will believe what we tell them, and we can reinforce each others' messages, paying dividends at the ballot box.

Journalism 150: How To Investigate And Demonize Republican Donors. Without such focused demonizing, the Koch Brothers, Foster Friess, Harold Simmons, and other prominent Republican donors might be seen as totally normal people. Dogged investigations and targeted demonizing can change that. Find ex-girlfriends with grudges, fired employees, public records like liens, judgments, and court records. For those records that are sealed, this course will teach the intrepid reporter how to get unsealed records that embarrass Republican donors. Extra digging and familiar officials in high places can reveal Republican donors' credit and IRS records, and anything else sealed by court orders. When no dirt can be found, it always helps to repeat a criticism made up in *The Nation* magazine.

Journalism 160: Blowing the Whistle on Whistle-blowers: How To Demonize Whistle-Blowers of Democratic Scandals. Laws protecting whistle-blowers were put in place to protect whistle-blowers of Republican scandals, not of Democratic scandals, because there aren't any Democratic scandals. Yet, some trouble-makers try to claim whistle-blower status and protections for calling Democratic officials on fabricated misdeeds. This class teaches the reporter how to blow the lid off of any whistle-blower protections of such trouble-makers.

Journalism 170: Selective Outrage: for example, screaming bloody murder about the Bush Administration's water-boarding of a few suspected terrorists and the ho-humming the drone-killings of hundreds of suspected terrorists and their friends and family-members by the Obama Administration. Unless we journalists focus our outrage, newsreaders run the risk of making up their own minds.

Journalism 180: Perils Of An Open Mic: last September, sneaky Republicans left a microphone turned on before Mitt Romney appeared for a press conference, enabling the world to hear reporters coordinating their "hostile" questions for the GOP candidate. This class will teach you what to look for to make sure such valuable coordinations go unnoticed.

Journalism 190: Role changes since the 1970's: long gone are the days where the journalist tries to get the facts while the White House claims there is no story, move on. Nowadays the public tries to get the facts while the journalist says that there is no story, move on. Will today's journalist be able to embrace these new roles without getting whiplash? This class will help.

Oh, and by the way, the brown bag lunch discussion that featured the member of the Pulitzer Prize committee, was entitled "Furthering A Lie Does NOT Necessarily Disqualify A Journalist From Receiving A Pulitzer Prize – the case of Walter Duranty."

Looks like those journalism students were learning their lessons well! This class list explains a lot!

June 27, 2013

A HEALTHCARE ALTERNATIVE TO PLANNED PARENTHOOD

The recent controversy regarding the Susan G. Komen Foundation and its decision to de-fund and then re-fund Planned Parenthood for breast exams got me thinking: there has to be another place for women to get breast exams besides going to Planned Parenthood. After all, in any given year, over 300,000 babies are killed inside Planned Parenthood clinics[1]. Truly a repellent organization. Fortunately, there is an agency already in charge of examining people all the time: the Transportation Safety Agency (TSA).

It is not as far-fetched as it sounds.

In only a few months Obamacare will kick in, and many doctors nationwide will be out of work. So why not have the TSA hire them to conduct breast exams on women and prostate exams on men before they board their flights? The traveler will not only be checked for weapons but will also be given a clean bill of health for breast, prostate, or other types of cancer.

And let's have a reality check here: it is only a matter of time before terrorists will begin to smuggle explosives up their rear-ends, so body-cavity searches will someday be required in order to board a plane. Why not have a group of professionally-trained doctors on hand, not only ready to search for weapons but also for pre-cancerous polyps in the large intestine while they are at it?

And having body-cavity searches before boarding an airplane will probably weed out 99.9% of all terrorists, so just by virtue of having such exams we will end terrorism on airplanes as we know it.

Of course, such searches will keep most non-terrorists from flying too. But what is wrong with that? Airplanes are too crowded anyway. Remember those nice, un-crowded airplane flights before airlines were de-regulated in the 1970's? This will be a way to return to those days.

And have you seen the searches that are already being done at the TSA security checkpoints nowadays? Do a Google search for "TSA"

This could be the TSA security checkpoint of the future. Security checks combined with prostate, colorectal and breast exams, all in one convenient location.

and then press the images tab, and you can see all sorts of invasive, kinky searches being done on the most harmless-looking people. For example, I just saw a slightly-overweight, balding white guy getting his genitals searched, and the TSA guy wearing latex gloves turned his palms to the outside, to pretend that he was not directly touching the guy's crotch. Right! Why not just hire doctors to do this search and let them directly touch the genitals, and give the traveler a testicular check-up while they are at it? That would be a win-win situation: safer travel and more regular testicular cancer screening!

Or how about that woman with her arms held out by her side, getting a full-frontal fondling of her breasts by the TSA agent? What is the difference between what she is experiencing versus a regular breast cancer screening exam? Not much. Except the woman in the Google image went on to her flight and had no idea if her breasts contained the beginnings of breast cancer. With specially-trained doctors and nurses at the checkpoint, checking not only for weapons but also for cancerous lumps in women's breasts, at least the women traveler will go to her flight knowing whether she needs a follow-up mammogram or is good for another year without needing another breast exam. All courtesy of the TSA.

And someday those follow-up exams can be located right next to the security check-point area! After the initial encounter with the TSA, mammograms and pap smears can be offered nearby, so that these follow-up tests can be conducted and still give the traveler time to make her flight.

Another advantage to doing bodily exams at security checkpoints is the fact that no one will claim they are being profiled. Let's face it: since 9/11 the passengers who look the most like Mohamed Atta and the rest are the ones who are most likely to be left alone by the TSA. But a new TSA security search coupled with, for example, a prostate exam, would be a medical procedure that would not only find weapons but would also find out if that traveler needed to have a follow-up cancer screening. Now, anyone looking like Mohamed Atta might complain if they have been *left out* of the security screening!

OK, that might be a little far-fetched, I admit it. But from the standpoint of the doctor-guard, withholding a security check/prostate exam and waving through someone is not letting that traveler out of a hassle, it is withholding from the traveler a benefit. So the doctor-guards will not even want to wave through any politically-correct class of people like Muslims, because skipping the security check would deny them a benefit. Why would any fair-minded person want to withhold from Muslims a benefit that everyone else is receiving? That wouldn't be fair, and in fact would be discriminatory! Quick — somebody give CAIR a call!

Yes, folks, this could be the way of the future. We better get used to seeing fewer agents in brown shirts and more doctors and nurses in white coats nearby our airport security checkpoints. It is good for security, good for our health, good for our national healthcare costs; heck, it's even good for the Susan G. Komen Foundation because it can de-fund Planned Parenthood again. Safer skies, safer breasts, safer prostates, safer colons. It is the TSA of the future!

February 6, 2012

THE LORAX MOVIE PRE-REVIEW

It was Thanksgiving just last week
"Lets go see a kid flick" I said to my daughter
"Yes Daddy," she answered. "Let's go see one quick!"

We checked on the web, for a movie we did seek
But sadly, so madly, the selection was bleak.
"*Arthur Christmas,* perhaps?" I contemplated.
Hmm, it says it's for kids, but PG it was rated.

It looked cartoony and colorful, no one swearing like sailors.
"But wait!" I thought suddenly, "what of the trailers?"
I stopped in my tracks, wasn't sure what to do.
I felt flummoxed, bamboozled, without even a clue.

My daughter's quite young, just a tiny tot.
So I worry about the trailers, I worry a lot.
You see, they advertise a coming movie
And the way they do this is simply not groovy.

They show the worst qualities, these trailers do.
If you saw them I'm sure you would agree with me too.
These trailers for PG films show violence and sex.
Violence and sex in these trailers is nothing new.

To the theater we headed, my daughter and I,
Where I watched each trailer, waiting to cover her eyes.
I tried to distract her with popcorn and candy,
So she wouldn't see anything disgusting or randy.

You would have to be a crazy, a quack, just plain nuts
To let your daughter see a trailer of a film that glamorizes teen sluts.
Or the latest Hollywood vivisection,
Of that I have a real objection.

When I'd had just enough and felt my blood pressure rising,
I saw on the screen something rather surprising.
"Oh good!" I exclaimed, "I can finally relax."
On the screen appeared a trailer for Dr. Seuss' *The Lorax.*
You can be sure when this movie comes out in the spring
The Dr. Seuss foundation will be hearing: Cha-ching!

Too early to review it, to slam it, poo-poo it?
I simply don't care, why should I first have to view it?
It's not a movie for kids but propaganda from "Big Green."
I'll explain what I mean.

Is de-forestation still a problem outside of Brazil?
(A rhetorical question: I know the drill.)

The trailer showed a world in which all trees are gone.
Instead of making me feel sad, it just made me yawn.

There are more trees being planted now than ever before.
Those "greenies," however, would just call me a right-wing whore.

You see, poor Dr. Seuss died in 1991,
And sadly since then he has been no fun.
The Lorax he wrote in 1970 when people were littering
These days folks are more likely to be Twittering.

Why can't movies just tell a story?
Something pleasant; nothing too gory.
Why are political views crammed down our throats?
If you ask me, that just loses votes.

And then there are kid movies that act like a leftist bully,
Including *Wall-E, Happy Feet,* and even *Ferngully!*
I know, I know, it could be worse by far.
One recent example is that film *Avatar.*

They annoy me with their perspective,
Their cheery, jeery, preachy corrective.
To me it just feels like a vicious invective.

See, I am tired.
Tired I am,
Tired of being propagandized to, again and again.

Why can't they bring back a different Dr. Seuss book?
You know, that popular one about that hammy cook?

He cooks with a different-colored ham.
The name's on the tip of my tongue. What is it? Damn...
It also has an egg in there, but I'll bet
I will never remember the name of it yet.

Truthfully, the book's name isn't that vital
I just want a movie with an honest title.

Don't kids get enough propaganda?
Can't they just be entertained by a giant panda?
We got enough of this stuff from *Captain Planet.*
We get it! "Don't take the earth for granite!"

You have to be careful with kid's movies these days,
Can't go to a movie even on holidays.
Can I get my money back for watching this ad?
My stomach is starting to feel pretty bad.

And I admit it, I'm starting to get pretty mad,
And not just a little, more than a tad.

It really is quite irritating,
The constant message they are advocating.
I want a non-political movie now, and I'm sick of waiting!

What's next? The virtues of occupying Wall Street?
Or maybe the joys of being a tax cheat?
Not for me I say, that's no cinematic treat!

So this movie, *The Lorax,* we should not attend.
There are plenty of other films I'd recommend.
For example, how about *It's A Wonderful Life?*
Or heck, even *Shrek* for my kid and my wife.

Let's teach these leftist movie producers a thing or two:
With our children's brains you simply don't screw.
So instead of that green propaganda you do
We will just stick with good old *Winnie The Pooh.*

November 28, 2011
Thanks to Nathan Beach and Mary Weber for their help with this column.

Dr. Seuss, holding a book.
He had such a kind and gentle look.

GEORGE BAILEY FOR PRESIDENT

Halloween is officially over and the next big holiday is Thanksgiving, followed by Christmas. But in our house, Christmas season has already begun and our family can't get enough of it. We have just put all the leftover Mounds and Almond Joy candy into storage[1] for next Halloween, and we have already begun watching our Christmas DVD's.

And since my last viewing of *It's A Wonderful Life,* I now have a nominee for our next president: George Bailey. Sure, he is a fictional character, but as a country we have done worse. And there is nothing in the Constitution that prohibits a fictional character like George Bailey from being president. Presumably he is a naturally-born U.S. citizen and over 35 years old, so he is good to go. He's even the brother of a war hero!

And in a 9+% unemployed America with a near-zero economic growth rate, George Bailey is just the man we need in the White House. This is what did it for me: that phone call scene between George Bailey, his soon-to-be fiancé Mary Hatch and his rich friend Sam Wainwright. Remember seeing that phone call, when George and Mary realized their love for each other? Actually, neither do I, because my glasses kept fogging up and I had allergy problems during that scene. But people who were able to view it tell me that Sam called Mary, and when he realized George was there he wanted to talk with George too. Having their faces so close to each other while listening to Sam on the phone, George and Mary noticed each other and emotions ran high.

During that moment their facial expressions showed not only their love for each other but their hesitancy to give in to it. Things were really touch and go. When George overheard Sam say something about setting up a new plastics factory in Rochester, George interrupted the mood entirely, and encouraged Sam to set up his new plastics factory in Bedford Falls instead, using the tool factory that had just shut down, which left "half the town out of work." George's love for Mary was actually put on hold in order to pitch a job deal for Bedford Falls!

That is what we need in our next president – someone who would put other things on hold and encourage investors to set up factories and hire employees and make a profit. George Bailey's attitude during those couple of seconds was part cheerleader, part Tony Robbins, part chamber of commerce member. In his actions and speech he basically said "set up your business here and hire our neighbors as employees and we can make you lots of money!" His attitude was win-win for the investor and for the employees.

Contrast that attitude with the attitude of President Obama and some of today's Democrats if they were part of the phone call:

President Obama: "Uh oh, you are a rich person, right Sam? You shouldn't be so much interested in setting up this plastics factory as you are in paying your fair share. Just as my billionaire friend Warren says, your tax rate should be a lot higher. There will be time to make profits, and there will be time to get bonuses — now is not that time. I do think at a certain point you've made enough money."

Elizabeth Warren, Democratic Senate candidate from Massachusetts: "that's right, Mr. Wainwright. If you are able to set up this factory, you will be employing people who were educated at public expense, in a factory owned by the bankruptcy court, and using the infrastructure financed by the City of Bedford Falls. You are really just an economic interloper. If you manage to make any profit at all with this plastics factory, you should be taxed at 100%"

Van Jones, former Special Advisor For Green Jobs: "Yeah, and if your new factory doesn't cap the salaries of its managers and use sustainable energy like solar and wind, I could see an 'Occupy Bedford Falls' right at your doorstep. Don't think we won't do it, mister!"

President Obama: "Say, you're not thinking of having a corporate jet for this plastics factory, are you?"

At that point in the conversation, Sam Wainwright would begin thinking of setting up his new plastics factory overseas. Maybe Shanghai Falls instead of Bedford Falls.

If George Bailey could answer those concerns, he would say none of them matter. Many people in Bedford Falls are unemployed, and a new plastics factory in Bedford Falls could employ them. If a rich person is behind the venture, George doesn't care. And George Bailey surely wouldn't want to discourage Sam Wainwright by mandating any maximum pay for factory managers, sustainable energy or higher taxes for the factory. And this is why I support George Bailey for president. Jobs are jobs, and we need the next president to focus on jobs with the same intensity as George Bailey.

And George's attitude will also go over well with business owners. Business owners like Sam Wainwright want to know that their plans to open or expand a business is something that will be welcomed and possibly encouraged by government, not discouraged, and certainly not regulated or taxed away. In George's case, he offers help if Bedford Falls jobs will be the result. Isn't that how it is supposed to happen?

And it pays off in an unexpected way at the end of the movie. Remember that when George is about to be thrown in jail and the townspeople start pitching in to pay off the deficiency at the Building & Loan, it is Sam Wainwright who sends a cable for $25,000, putting

Warren Buffett shares his concern with President Obama that the managers of the new plastics factory might somehow pay less in taxes than their secretaries.

Photo: Pete Souza/The White House

George's total way over the amount needed, and Clarence even gets his wings (how is that for a multiplier effect?). While watching that scene most women teared up or even wept out loud, but manly men like me had allergy problems, nothing more. Promise.

October 31, 2011

MY ENCOUNTER WITH "THE UNABOMBER"

Today is the sixteenth anniversary of the publishing of the "Unabomber Manifesto," a rambling 35,000 word anti-technology screed that contained enough writing-style clues that it eventually led to the arrest and guilty plea of Ted Kaczynski for the crimes of the Unabomber.

Publishing the Manifesto was a huge breakthrough for the investigators, because until that time the only main clue was that ridiculous police artist-sketch. Remember that drawing? Apparently this was the best a witness could give a police sketch artist after one of the earlier Unabomber bombings. The guy in the sketch looked like a white male, in his early 20's, weighing about 130-180 pounds, with dark hair, a mustache, some cool Aviator sunglasses, and a hooded sweatshirt with the hood covering his head. Basically, it could cover about 15% of the population of the US. And we were all told to be on the look-out for this guy! Just look at the sketch:

But this anniversary reminds me of my own encounter with "the Unabomber." Our paths almost crossed thanks to a police scanner that I had given my wife for Christmas back in the mid-90's, when we lived in Palo Alto, California.

Giving my wife a police scanner for Christmas was a strange gift, I know, but we were both curious, and I have never been a totally normal

FBI composite sketch of the Unabomer suspect

person anyway. Once we figured out how to use it we loved it. We had to get used to the police jargon and eventually we knew what the various numbers meant. We had to be careful to follow the rules, which are that if you hear of some police or fire event, you can go to the scene (like reporters do) but you must stay out of the way.

But this was Palo Alto, home to Stanford professors and homes with white picket fences, so there was rarely that much excitement coming through the scanner. Typically police officers were sent to arrest shoplifters, break up bar fights, that kind of stuff. Picture Andy Griffith.

My wife and I got in the habit of keeping the scanner in our car, as it at least provided more entertainment than just listening to the regular radio, and we could watch what the local police were up to. One time we overheard a call from the dispatcher to be on the look-out for a possibly-kidnapped 5-year old child at the nearby Stanford Mall. The police spent several minutes setting up a cordon so that no one could leave the mall without passing by a police officer who had a description of the missing child.

This was scary! I remember hearing this while driving, and my wife and I briefly considered driving to the mall nearby to help. We imagined ourselves driving to the mall parking lot just in time to see a kidnapper dragging the kid to a parked van, and all of a sudden our car screeched to a halt in his path. Then I would bravely jump out and yell "you take your hands off of that child, mister!"

As it happened, after about 20 long minutes one of the police officers involved called off the search and announced the child was found. As the officer reported what happened we could hear crying in the background, probably from the relieved mother of the missing child. We could hear the crying during several radio talks back and forth. Apparently this child had just wondered off and gotten *really* lost.

That was the most exciting call my wife and I overheard, until one Friday night on our way home from a movie. We heard the dispatcher alert police officers to the local Starbuck's Coffee Shop where someone phoned in a sighting of the Unabomber. The announcement was just like that: "a sighting of the Unabomber." No numbers or jargon of any kind.

Almost immediately several police officers called in for confirmation, and one of the officers openly laughed, but the dispatcher managed to stay serious. This was too much! And the Starbuck's on University Avenue! We were already nearby as we heard this! We had to go.

We figured there would be a traffic jam of police cars, so we thought we would just drive by and observe the commotion and go home. Instead, there wasn't a single police car there, and at the otherwise crowded Starbuck's, the parking space *directly in front* opened up. We parked and just sat there, watching.

Nothing happened! Of the crowd inside, we saw two ladies sitting at the front table, whispering to each other, openly suspicious of a guy standing in line for coffee. These ladies were real stereotypes; the type of busy-body ladies who spy on their neighbors and complain about the slightest infraction. And they weren't even any good at hiding their suspicions of the guy waiting in line. They kept looking out the front window, probably awaiting the police, and looking back at the guy standing in line.

And sure enough, the guy standing in line was a 20-something little white kid, weighing about 130 pounds, wearing jeans and a hooded sweatshirt, with the hood over his head. He looked around and he wore sunglasses – at night! I didn't notice a mustache either way. But I have to say, as Unabomber look-alikes go, he looked pretty good. And wearing sunglasses at nighttime is usually suspicious. Cool, but suspicious.

The problem was he was clearly in his early 20's, and we had heard of Unabomber bombings going back to the 1970's, when this guy was probably a toddler. It couldn't possibly be the Unabomber! After a few more minutes of no police cars or excitement, even the two women got bored and left.

A few months later we read about the Unabomber's Manifesto being published. From what we saw of this kid, he didn't look like the type to write 35,000 words of anything. But come to think of it, our guy actually looked a whole lot more like the Unabomber than did the real Unabomber. I think it was the sunglasses. Well, the hooded sweat-shirt, too.

But thanks to our police scanner, I crossed paths with a guy who really did look like the Unabomber as depicted in that police sketch. If you want some real excitement, get a police scanner. Those things are fun! And you never know what excitement will come your way, even in an otherwise boring neighborhood. Even Andy Griffith had an exciting case once.

September 19, 2011

THE JOY OF FEELING SUPERIOR

Some friends and I just went to a county fair in a nearby county, and we spent most of the occasion feeling superior to the locals. And it felt great.

This was the 40-60 something, hippie-guy and hippie-chick crowd, where terms like "sustainable" and "organic" filled the air, "harmony" and "hope" were advertized on one of the booths selling the tofu and crafts, and a folk-music band lamented the "corporate world" the singer had just left. Basically, the NPR crowd.

Part of the fun of it all was noticing all the internal contradiction of this hippie-dome. In walking around this fair, you had to carefully walk over plenty of thick, electrical wires delivering the evil electricity to the sellers who were selling their "sustainable" wares. A kiddy train made its way around the fair pulling hippie-kids with the use of a huge diesel-powered pretend locomotive. It passed me by and gave me a huge whiff of some "organic" diesel fumes. Who knows, maybe it was run on bio-diesel, but the smoke coming out of it didn't smell anything like cooking oil.

And check this out: one booth that caught our interest was some-thing selling goat products like cheese and soap. My wife has some experience in this area and asked the seller how she got around all that red-tape and high costs of getting certified. "Don't worry about all that," said the hippie-chick. I was distracted by the tattoo on her leg, but the tattoo was difficult to see because of her leg-hair. "Just sell at farmer's markets," she said, winking. My wife told her that you can be sent to jail if you sell dairy products without all the permits. "Hey, if you are really worried about all that you can always barter," she said. While that is true, even bartering illegal products can still land you in jail, which is not very sustainable.

Nearby was a booth advertizing cream that would remove wrinkles — guaranteed. All the late-night TV commercials hinting at stuff that removed wrinkles are smothered with disclaimers and fine-print. And as far I knew, the only way a cream could get rid of wrinkles was to somehow load you up with salt, so that your skin would swell, giving you a temporary wrinkle-fix. This booth just came right out and claimed it without any fine-print or disclaimers.

Not that I am even slightly-interested in getting rid of wrinkles, mind you. The appearance of age is hardly a concern of mine. Young people like me don't need to bother with trivialities like that. Really – it's the truth.

But at the wrinkle-cream booth, my friend's wife jumped at the chance to give it a try. And there is something almost convincing about applying such a cream and having the seller say stuff like "oh yes, it's starting to work. Amazing!" But then the sun heated up the perfume in the cream and my friend had to rush to the public restrooms nearby and rinse the cream off. She said it felt like sunscreen when the sun heats it up and burns your skin. I told her that she looked as if she had more wrinkles *after* applying the cream. (These are pretty good friends so I can get away with saying that.)

So that was our day. When we returned to Napa we heard from another friend tell of the glories of Napa County Fair's demolition derby. Now there is a true, *honest* event! You put all these old cars together in a football field and tell them to go at it, and the last car able to drive off wins. Kind of like the "smear the queer" jousting we did during elementary school recess. Sure, it is kind of pointless, but honest and BS-free. Napa County might be full of it in other areas, but it takes a certain down-home, honest county fair to get down and have a demolition derby, where probably nothing was "organic" or "sustainable." Mmmm, I'm suddenly craving garlic fries...

August 15, 2011

EPILOGUE

NOTES ON THE PASSING OF A
GOOD FRIEND

I t took a while, but as the years in middle school and high school progressed, I eventually got the memo that if you go out for the football team, you need to start football practice long before the first day of school, say, late July. If you show up the first day of school in late August and say "Coach, I am ready to begin practicing for the great Kinkaid Falcon football team," he will take you in, but you will be sidelined the whole season.

In eighth grade, that's what Clay Cravens and I did. We showed up to begin our football career on the first day of school, and we were sidelined the whole season. Clay and I spent a lot of time on the bench together. During the first few games we spent our time looking around, noticing the cheerleaders and generally watching the crowd of families and friends of the players who were told by the players to come and watch. We did not notice much of the games being played right in front of us.

As we were the only two perennial bench-warmers that year, Clay and I got to be good friends as we sat out the games together, talking and cracking jokes the whole time. If the Falcons were way ahead, which was rare, or way behind, which was more common but not all the time, the coach would let one or both of us into the game for awhile and then bring us back out.

I remember once coming home from a game and my mom asked me if she needed to wash my football uniform, and I told her that no, it was spotless, just as brilliantly purple, gold and white as before the game. She asked me, "how can that be? It has been raining for two weeks straight." I explained to her that I play football in such a way that I generally don't get muddy, or even get onto the ground. My dad said he didn't think that was possible to do while being an offensive lineman.

Clay probably went through the same curious conversations in his household, so as the season progressed, he and I decided to muddy up our uniforms before we left the game. That way, our uniforms would no longer be the cleanest uniforms at the end of the game. Clay and I would put mud all over our own uniforms and help each other with those hard-to-reach spots on the back of our uniforms.

We also decided to leave our helmets on while we sat out the game on the bench, so that as everyone left the game and noticed our filthy uniforms, they would assume we had played most of the game. No one would remember our faces as the two guys who were sitting on the bench the whole game. Even the players on our team were confused, because they didn't remember seeing us on the field but saw that our uniforms were dirtier than theirs. I remember that after one game,

The late Clay Cravens and your humble author, at a high school reunion in June, 2011.

Bridget O'Toole Purdie

Clay's and my uniforms were so muddy that our uniforms couldn't be told apart from a team that had all black colors on their uniforms.

Our league was mostly made up of other prep schools, so we were pretty evenly-matched. Occasionally there would be a situation where our team would have the ball several plays inside the other team's 10-yard line, and sometimes our team would score a touchdown after such an effort. After that happened, our team members would go to the sidelines and jog or walk to the mid-field area and await the coach's instructions on the kick-off, or whatever next the team would do. During the team's migration back to the mid-field sidelines, the families and friends in the stands and the cheerleaders would congratulate the team members, cheering them on and giving the players high-fives. It was a "victory lap" even though it was just 40 yards on the sideline.

Clay came up with the idea that in those rare times when our team would be inside the other team's 10-yard line, he and I would make our way down the sideline, helmets still on, and wait for the touchdown. Then we would take off our helmets and position ourselves in the very front of the team as it made its way back to mid-field, accepting all the congratulations and high-fives of the cheerleaders and people in the stands. Clay and I had a great laugh as we accepted all the congratulations that were rightfully due to others who had risked their lives for that touchdown.

This is when I learned the concept of "false modesty" from Clay, as he would seemingly discount all the congratulations that were hurled his way, even though he was in front of the pack, smiling and waving to everyone. He would say things like "oh, thanks, but really I couldn't have done it without ..." and he would gesture to other players. The people in the stands and the cheerleaders didn't know the difference.

By the end of the season, Clay and I realized we actually had the best of both worlds. We didn't need to risk our bones or joints in the dangerous game that was 8th grade football, but we managed to get most of the glory for any successes our team had. And, our uniforms were so dirty that no amount of bleach could have gotten out the ground-in mud that had dirtied our uniforms so badly, so our parents left us alone.

A few days ago when I heard that Clay has passed away, I was shocked, and in fact I still am. I am also confused when I see the picture of Clay's smiling face next to the word "obituary." Last year I saw Clay at a reunion and he and I posed for a picture together. People told me that Clay's smile was the same smile they had always seen on Clay, and I agree. In fact, I will always remember Clay as a very cheerful, happy person, always eager to do something goofy or amusing, like claim credit for other football player's sacrifices while falsely denying the glory that he got.

That was classic Clay Cravens: he was in the position of either sitting on the bench or making the best of a bad situation and having a little fun. As always, he chose the fun. All of his friends and loved ones will miss Clay, but we know he is in Heaven, adding to the life and humor there with his silly antics.

Clay, we already miss you tremendously, and we thank you for your friendship, love and humor through the years. We look forward to being with you again, when we can all have many more silly laughs together. Goodbye for now, my good friend.

ACKNOWLEDGMENTS

This is the part of the book where I either rub it in that I got this book published despite many nay-sayers who said it wouldn't happen ("ha ha! You didn't think it would happen but here it is!"), or thank those who have encouraged me through thick and thin.

But mine is one of those strange situations where, whenever I announced my intention of publishing a book, most people would just say "oh," shrug their shoulders and talk about something else. Boredom sets in, I guess. I probably hang around a lot of people who are not too impressed or disgusted either way with publishing a book. The good news is that at least my friends know what a book is, so they deserve *some* credit. So there's that. And besides, I'll settle for a neutral opinion over a negative one any day.

But let me blather on a little anyway, to thank those who were at least mildly tolerant of the idea.

Most of the columns in this book were the product of my freelance columnist work, and I owe a big thanks to the many editors at online publications with whom I have worked. People who accepted my columns and published them for all the world to see and criticize. Not much is written about these people, the unsung heroes of the online publishing world. But receiving 30-40 submissions every day (I'm guessing), and synthesizing them down to about five to eight columns that will be published the next day is quite a tough job. Many times these editors even include their own daily columns!

There are others, but these especially deserve a shout-out: Shane Vander Hart at Caffeinated Thoughts, Thomas Lifson at American Thinker, and Christian Toto at Big Hollywood (now at Hollywood in

Toto). It is amazing the time and attention to detail that the editors of these and other online publications are able to bring to their websites, all day, seven days a week. Normal people would be way too lazy and undisciplined to do this job.

And it may not have been the type of Internet work that was intended, but I hereby wish to thank the various northern California courthouses that provide free Internet services, allowing me to do some quick research and writing between court hearings. The Redwood City courthouse, in particular, has such comfortable chairs and strong, free Internet signal that the place is almost worth a special trip, even if I have no pending legal matters in that courthouse!

I also wish to thank Sel P for the cover art. Sel was very talented and immensely patient with my various artwork ideas and changes – even in mid-stream! He can be reached at sel.designroom@gmail.com. Typesetting credit goes to the steady skills of Gowsala T, who can be reached at gowsalat@yahoo.in. In fact, the whole country of India deserves a shout-out for the help of its citizens on this book. I did not do this on purpose, but the cover art and interior formatting and typesetting were all done in India. Ciyarsa! (That means "cheers!" in Hindi.)

In fact, if you are buying this book by calling an 800-number, chances are that you will be dealing with someone in an Indian call center. Tell them Tom says "hi!"

I also wish to thank Patricia Rash, my cousin-in-law and former English professor at King University, and Ellen Tsagaris, my cubicle-mate at my first job out of law school and current English professor at Kaplan University, who proof-read this book. Let's face it: the conversational tone of column-writing nowadays can be jarring for anyone trained in the grammarian sciences. I might not have taken all their grammatical suggestions, but Drs. Rash and Tsagaris persevered, and I appreciate their advice.

I also wish to thank my wife Martina and daughter Rachel. Their on-going support has made all the difference, not only with proof-reading columns, but also with organizing thoughts and providing tips on honing the jokes here so that they ark just right. My step-kids

Nathan Beach and Mary Weber also helped with the Dr. Seuss humor piece (which was actually a frank discussion about the nasty movie trailers that are shown to audiences who come to see G-rated movies). Rhyming, especially in the style of Dr. Seuss, was never my strong suit. My own, unaided Dr. Seuss column would surely have been given the boot. See what I mean?

And despite the occasional silliness of my writing, these columns were the result of much prayer.

I hope you enjoyed reading this book. I certainly enjoyed writing it. If enough people buy this book, there will be more. So you, dear reader, will be partly to blame.

Tom Thurlow
Napa County, California
November 1, 2014

NOTES

Chapter 1

Perry Indictment Not Thought Through

1. https://www.youtube.com/watch?v=s7y7oJ266qI
2. http://austin.twcnews.com/content/news/296555/lehmberg-to-stay-in-office--judge-denies-petition-for-removal
3. http://kxan.com/2014/08/18/texans-for-public-justice-has-filed-dozens-of-complaints-against-republicans/
4. http://www.npr.org/templates/story/story.php?storyId=130508181
5. http://www.houstonchronicle.com/news/politics/texas/article/Grand-jurors-offended-by-Perry-suggestion-5699285.php?cmpid=twitter-premium&t=fed90ac52829895b84
6. http://mediatrackers.org/national/2014/08/20/perry-grand-juror-active-democratic-party-delegate-jury-proceedings
7. https://twitter.com/davidaxelrod/status/500634429367533568
8. http://nymag.com/daily/intelligencer/2014/08/rick-perry-indictment-is-unbelievably-ridiculous.html
9. http://www.powerlineblog.com/archives/2014/08/liberal-texas-newspaper-debunks-dems-attack-on-rick-perry.php
10. http://www.mystatesman.com/news/news/democrats-cprit-perry-narrative-leaves-out-some-de/ng49Z/?icmp=statesman_internallink_textlink_apr2013_statesmanstubto mystatesman_launch#dc5364f7.3660112.735464

Was The "Ship Of Fools" Incident A Set-Up? And If Not, Why Not?

1. http://wattsupwiththat.com/2014/01/02/now-that-the-ship-of-fools-is-safe-in-antarctica-tough-questions-need-to-be-asked/
2. http://pjmedia.com/eddriscoll/2013/12/14/yet-another-final-countdown-expires/
3. http://www.cfact.org/2013/09/19/gullible-green-sailors-trapped-in-the-arctic/
4. http://pjmedia.com/eddriscoll/2013/12/14/yet-another-final-countdown-expires/
5. http://www.amazon.com/Breakthrough-Guerilla-Expose-Fraud-Democracy-ebook/dp/B00A27XDZU/ref=sr_1_5?ie=UTF8&qid=1389680845&sr=8-5&keywords=o%27keefe
6. http://www.youtube.com/watch?v=P5p70YbRiPw&feature=youtu.be

7. https://www.indiegogo.com/projects/help-us-return-to-mawson-s-antarctic-hut-the-home-of-the-blizzard

Healthcare Prison Blues

1. http://entertainment.time.com/2013/11/07/watch-carrie-underwood-and-brad-paisley-rip-obamacare-apart-at-the-cmas/

Meanwhile, On Al Jazeera America ...

1. http://www.petitionbuzz.com/petitions/dropaljazeera
2. http://www.jpost.com/Features/Front-Lines/Qatari-power-and-irresponsibility-set-to-continue-318030
3. http://www.reuters.com/article/2013/09/01/us-egypt-protests-jazeera-idUS BRE97S0ZL20130901
4. http://www.youtube.com/watch?v=SIkrQGz5ats
5. http://www.meforum.org/3147/al-jazeera#_ftn64
6. http://www.nytimes.com/2007/11/12/opinion/12cohen.html?_r=0
7. http://www.examiner.com/article/al-jazeera-terrorist-mouthpiece-or-credible-news-organization
8. http://www.journalism.org/2013/09/16/how-al-jazeera-tackled-the-crisis-over-syria/
9. http://www.telegraph.co.uk/news/worldnews/middleeast/qatar/10022759/Qatar-playing-with-fire-as-it-funds-Syrian-Islamists-in-quest-for-global-influence.html
10. http://www.discoverthenetworks.org/groupProfile.asp?grpid=6233

Five Game-Changing Questions On Obamacare

1. http://dailycaller.com/2012/01/06/labor-unions-primary-recipients-of-obamacare-waivers/
2. http://firstread.nbcnews.com/_news/2011/10/14/8325174-obama-administration-halts-part-of-health-care-law
3. http://hotair.com/archives/2013/07/29/obama-not-even-pretending-he-has-legal-authority-to-delay-the-obamacare-employer-mandate/
4. http://www.businessinsider.com/obama-voted-against-debt-ceiling-increase-2006-2013-1
5. http://thehill.com/homenews/administration/324981-white-house-adviser-compares-republicans-to-terrorists
6. http://beta.congress.gov/bill/113th/house-bill/1780
7. http://youtu.be/N8Jfku9aL_c
8. http://reason.com/blog/2013/09/25/the-dodgy-new-hhs-report-on-obamacare-pr?utm_source=feedburner&utm_medium=feed&utm_campaign=Feed%3A+reason%2FHitan dRun+%28Reason+Online+-+Hit+%26+Run+Blog%29
9. http://www.cbsnews.com/8301-505144_162-57604782/study-insurance-costs-to-soar-under-obamacare/
10. http://thehill.com/blogs/healthwatch/health-reform-implementation/317205-hhs-announces-obamacare-navigators

11. http://thehill.com/blogs/healthwatch/health-reform-implementation/307821-celebs-you-might-see-promoting-obamacare
12. http://www.nbcnews.com/id/53125456/ns/local_news-reno_nv/#.UkpMFYasiSq

Obamacare On The Balcony

1. http://youtu.be/uv7-LVFgd8U
2. http://thehill.com/blogs/healthwatch/health-reform-implementation/307821-celebs-you-might-see-promoting-obamacare
3. http://www.washingtonpost.com/blogs/post-politics/wp/2013/05/29/louisiana-democratic-chair-opposition-to-obamacare-is-about-race/
4. http://www.realclearpolitics.com/epolls/other/repeal_of_health_care_law_favor oppose-1947.html#polls
5. http://www.humanevents.com/2013/07/19/thanks-to-obamacare-doctor-shortages-set-to-quintuple/
6. http://articles.chicagotribune.com/2013-05-15/news/chi-emanuel-to-shift-retired-city-workers-to-obamacare-20130515_1_retired-city-workers-health-care-health-insurance
7. http://blog.heritage.org/2013/07/02/obamacare-impact-another-insurer-leaves-california-market/
8. http://www.usatoday.com/story/news/politics/2013/09/23/aca-family-glitch-issues/2804017/
9. http://www.politico.com/story/2013/08/hhs-obamacare-navigators-95575.html
10. http://capwiz.com/nteu/issues/alert/?alertid=62634726&type=CO&utm_source=Illinois+Policy+Institute&utm_campaign=7790111647-0613_ecompass&utm_medium=email&utm_term=0_0f5a22f52c-7790111647-10830129
11. http://beta.congress.gov/bill/113th/house-bill/1780
12. http://youtu.be/1LRcLMScEqo
13. http://youtu.be/N8Jfku9aL_c
14. http://www.nationaljournal.com/domesticpolicy/obama-s-affordable-care-act-looking-a-bit-unaffordable-20130829
15. http://www.forbes.com/sites/theapothecary/2013/09/23/its-official-obamacare-will-increase-health-spending-by-7450-for-a-typical-family-of-four/

2013: The Year Privacy Died

1. https://www.aclu.org/national-security-technology-and-liberty/massive-nsa-phone-data-mining-operation-revealed
2. http://online.wsj.com/news/articles/SB10001424127887324299104578529112289298922?mg=reno64-wsj&url=http%3A%2F%2Fonline.wsj.com%2Farticle%2FSB10001424127887324299104578529112289298922.html
3. http://www.huffingtonpost.com/2013/05/09/warrantless-searches-email-fbi-email_n_3248575.html
4. http://www.thesmokinggun.com/documents/woman-arrested-for-obama-bloomberg-ricin-letters-687435

5. http://online.wsj.com/news/articles/SB10001424127887324299910457853380228
9432458?mg=reno64-wsj&url=http%3A%2F%2Fonline.wsj.com%2Farticle%2
FSB10001424127887324299104578533802289432458.html

6. http://www.washingtonpost.com/investigations/us-intelligence-mining-data-from-
nine-us-internet-companies-in-broad-secret-program/2013/06/06/3a0c0da8-cebf-
11e2-8845-d970ccb04497_story.html

7. http://www.nationalreview.com/article/350599/information-revealing-service-ian-tuttle

8. https://www.google.com/url?sa=t&rct=j&q=&esrc=s&source=web&cd=1&cad=rja
&ved=0CDAQFjAA&url=http%3A%2F%2Fwww.nytimes.com%2F2009%2F01%2
F20%2Fus%2Fpolitics%2F20text-obama.html%3Fpagewanted%3Dall&ei=yKm2Ub
qsO-SE0QHcy4CIBQ&usg=AFQjCNET-DlRmHLwoNLRLOLY1GoJJ__GZQ&

9. http://www.usnews.com/news/articles/2013/05/23/obama-global-war-on-terror-is-over

10. http://www.nationalreview.com/corner/350505/no-copbad-cop-mark-steyn

11. https://www.google.com/url?sa=t&rct=j&q=&esrc=s&source=web&cd=1&
cad=rja&ved=0CDAQFjAA&url=http%3A%2F%2Fwww.washingtonpost.
com%2Fblogs%2Fpost-politics%2Fwp%2F2013%2F05%2F21%2Fconservat
ive-group-true-the-vote-sues-irs-over-being-subject-to-heightened-scrutin

12. http://dailycaller.com/2013/05/13/flashback-romney-donor-vilified-by-obama-cam-
paign-then-subjected-to-2-audits/

13. http://www.washingtonpost.com/blogs/federal-eye/wp/2013/05/14/
irs-released-confidential-info-on-conservative-groups-to-propublica/

14. http://www.politico.com/story/2013/05/nom-wants-hearing-after-irs-flap-91266.html

15. http://dailycaller.com/2013/06/10/what-do-they-know-about-you-an-interview-with-
nsa-analyst-william-binney/2/

16. https://www.networkworld.com/community/blog/hope-9-whistleblower-binney-
says-nsa-has-dossiers-nearly-every-us-citizen

17. http://hotair.com/archives/2013/06/06/lindsey-graham-hey-im-glad-the-nsa-is-collect-
ing-americans-phone-records/

18. http://www.breitbart.com/Breitbart-TV/2013/06/07/Ignored-NSA-Whistleblower-Vindi-
cated-Said-Months-Ago-Everyone-in-US-Under-Virtual-Surveillance

19. http://www.cbsnews.com/8301-201_162-57584695/lawmakers-move-to-limit-
domestic-drones/

20. http://www.nytimes.com/2013/02/16/technology/rise-of-drones-in-us-spurs-efforts-to-
limit-uses.html?pagewanted=all

21. http://www.govtech.com/e-government/102484274.html

22. http://blogs.lawyers.com/2010/08/law-enforcements-newest-tool-google-earth/

The IRS Audited Our Adoption Expenses TWICE

1. http://townhall.com/tipsheet/katiepavlich/2013/05/20/dojs-witch-hunt-against-true-
the-vote-n1601527

2. http://www.usnews.com/news/politics/articles/2013/05/22/gop-questions-irs-scrutiny-
of-anti-abortion-groups

3. http://www.scribd.com/doc/142066752/Congress-Receives-Irrefutable-Evidence-of-
IRS-Harassment-of-Pro-Life-Organizations

4. http://www.taxpayeradvocate.irs.gov/userfiles/file/Full-Report/Most-Serious-Problems-Adoption-Credit-Delays.pdf
5. http://www.taxpayeradvocate.irs.gov/userfiles/file/Full-Report/Most-Serious-Problems-Adoption-Credit-Delays.pdf

IRS Scandal Follows Old Obama Illinois Pattern

1. http://www.cnn.com/2008/POLITICS/05/29/obamas.first.campaign/
2. http://articles.chicagotribune.com/2004-03-17/news/0403170332_1_blair-hull-gery-chico-blacks-and-liberal-whites
3. http://edition.cnn.com/2004/ALLPOLITICS/06/25/il.ryan/
4. http://dailycaller.com/2013/05/16/the-ominous-obama-nixon-comparisons-begin-to-pile-up/
5. http://www.foxnews.com/politics/2013/05/14/lawmakers-say-irs-targeted-dozens-more-conservative-groups-than-initially/
6. http://youtu.be/BSwnWW-y48c
7. http://townhall.com/tipsheet/katiepavlich/2013/05/20/dojs-witch-hunt-against-true-the-vote-n1601527
8. http://www.examiner.com/article/anonymous-irs-official-everything-comes-from-the-top
9. http://online.wsj.com/article/SB10001424052702304723304577368280604524916.html
10. http://www.foxnews.com/politics/2012/07/24/romney-donor-bashed-by-obama-campaign-now-target-two-federal-audits/
11. https://www.google.com/url?sa=t&rct=j&q=&esrc=s&source=web&cd=5&cad=rja&ved=0CEwQFjAE&url=http%3A%2F%2Fdailycaller.com%2F2013%2F05%2F14%2Ffrank-vandersloot-im-not-the-only-major-mitt-romney-donor-audited%2F&ei=z_ebUZvzNcGViQL_54DgDw&usg=AFQjCNEwTJ9Jp-zypq7
12. http://www.latimes.com/news/nationworld/nation/la-na-fbi-reporter-20130521,0,661230.story
13. http://www.imdb.com/title/tt0074119/quotes

The Clinton Scandal Playbook And Benghazi

1. http://edition.cnn.com/ALLPOLITICS/1996/news/9609/18/travelgate/index.shtml
2. http://www.washingtonpost.com/wp-srv/politics/special/whitewater/stories/wwtr950227.htm
3. http://edition.cnn.com/US/9601/travel_office/
4. http://www.washingtonpost.com/wp-srv/politics/special/whitewater/stories/wwtr950227.htm
5. http://www.nytimes.com/1996/01/08/opinion/essay-blizzard-of-lies.html
6. http://articles.latimes.com/1995-11-17/news/mn-4111_1_white-house-official
7. http://www.nydailynews.com/archives/news/dems-day-hil-hit-travelgate-role-article-1.868474
8. http://www.nytimes.com/2012/10/03/world/africa/requests-for-bolstered-security-in-libya-were-denied-republicans-say.html?_r=1&

9. http://freebeacon.com/blowing-the-lid-off-benghazi/

10. http://www.nytimes.com/2012/10/22/us/politics/explanation-for-benghazi-attack-under-scrutiny.html?pagewanted=all

11. http://articles.latimes.com/2012/sep/20/news/la-pn-obama-defends-embassy-security-20120920

12. http://www.washingtonpost.com/politics/president-obamas-2012-address-to-un-general-assembly-full-text/2012/09/25/70bc1fce-071d-11e2-afff-d6c7f20a83bf_story.html

13. http://abcnews.go.com/International/deadly-anti-us-riots-pakistan-obamas-ad-denouncing/story?id=17291751

14. http://articles.latimes.com/2012/sep/22/world/la-fg-pakistan-rioting-20120922

Monty Python And The Sequester

1. http://www.youtube.com/user/MontyPython

2. http://www.youtube.com/watch?v=MIaORknS1Dk

3. http://www.politico.com/story/2013/02/sequestration-poll-republicans-to-be-blamed-most-87914.html

4. http://firstread.nbcnews.com/_news/2013/03/05/17197602-white-house-cancels-tours-citing-sequester?lite

5. http://www.msnbc.com/the-last-word/seriously

6. http://mic.com/articles/30788/another-education-program-bites-the-dust-because-of-sequester-cuts

7. http://www.mcclatchydc.com/2013/04/02/187502_sequestration-may-mean-hard-times.html?rh=1

8. http://www.cbsnews.com/news/budget-cuts-hurt-schools-in-military-communities-hard/

9. http://www.usatoday.com/story/travel/flights/2013/02/27/air-traffic-controllers-amp-up-sequester-warnings/1950427/

10. http://www.washingtonpost.com/blogs/the-fix/wp/2013/04/29/republicans-even-out-sequester-blame-game-with-faa-furloughs/

11. http://dailysignal.com/2013/02/24/chart-of-the-week-sequestration-cuts-2-4-percent-out-of-total-spending/

12. http://www.usgovernmentspending.com/federal_budget_fy13

13. http://money.cnn.com/2012/02/10/news/economy/obama_budget/index.htm

Panic In Detroit

1. http://www.youtube.com/watch?v=Rf0fmqWS-kI&feature=youtu.be

2. http://www.whitecastle.com/

3. http://www.mlive.com/news/detroit/index.ssf/2010/02/survey_a_third_of_all_detroit.html

4. http://usnews.nbcnews.com/_news/2012/04/24/11376348-detroit-may-let-abandoned-buildings-burn-film-documents-firefighters-tough-times?lite

5. http://www.nytimes.com/2012/11/11/magazine/how-detroit-became-the-world-capital-of-staring-at-abandoned-old-buildings.html?pagewanted=all&_r=0

6. http://www.businessweek.com/articles/2013-03-06/faq-the-takeover-of-detroit
7. http://www.freep.com/article/20130103/NEWS01/301030088/Audit-shows-Detroit-has-327M-deficit
8. http://www.nytimes.com/2011/11/19/us/detroit-to-lay-off-9-percent-of-public-work-force.html?_r=0
9. http://ballotpedia.org/wiki/index.php/Detroit_Public_Schools_employee_salaries
10. http://www.freep.com/article/20120809/COL33/308090096/Stephen-Henderson-Intolerable-waste-in-Detroit-s-Water-Department
11. http://www.michigancapitolconfidential.com/17404
12. https://in.yahoo.com/?p=us

President Buchanan Redux

1. http://www.whitehouse.gov/sites/default/files/omb/budget/fy2013/assets/hist07z1.xls
2. http://www.cbo.gov/sites/default/files/cbofiles/attachments/08-24-BudgetEconUpdate.pdf
3. http://www.usnews.com/news/articles/2012/11/19/how-the-nations-interest-spending-stacks-up

Obama's Political Capital

1. http://www.washingtonpost.com/blogs/post-politics/wp/2013/01/31/hagel-mccain-clash-over-iraq-surge/
2. http://www.washingtonpost.com/blogs/post-politics/wp/2013/01/31/ted-cruz-confronts-chuck-hagel-on-2009-al-jazeera-interview/
3. http://www.powerlineblog.com/archives/2013/02/is-the-white-house-more-worried-that-hagel-wont-be-confirmed-or-that-he-will-be.php
4. http://www.nationalreview.com/corner/337790/jack-lew-s-campaign-deception-jeff-sessions
5. http://www.cnbc.com/id/100366609/Source_Obama_to_Name_Lew_Treasury_Secretary
6. http://stmedia.startribune.com/documents/Ltr.SenJudComReJones.PDF
7. http://washingtonexaminer.com/article/2512436#.UJQYj2fDtF8
8. http://thecaucus.blogs.nytimes.com/2010/10/25/in-appeal-to-hispanics-obama-promises-to-push-immigration-reform/
9. http://articles.latimes.com/2010/oct/07/news/la-pn-obama-base-20101008
10. http://www.cbsnews.com/news/obama-to-gop-i-won/

The GOP Needs A General Grant

1. http://transcripts.cnn.com/TRANSCRIPTS/1301/24/pmt.01.html
2. http://www.gutenberg.org/ebooks/2517?msg=welcome_stranger#link2H_4_0022
3. http://nbcpolitics.nbcnews.com/_news/2013/01/14/16505804-obama-chides-gop-on-debt-limit-we-are-not-a-deadbeat-nation?lite
4. http://www.washingtonpost.com/blogs/the-fix/wp/2013/01/16/how-president-obamas-executive-orders-on-guns-might-doom-a-big-bill/

5. http://www.nytimes.com/2013/01/21/us/politics/obamas-second-inaugural-speech.html?pagewanted=all&_r=1&

6. https://www.stlbeacon.org/#!/content/28356/voices_ward_fredericksburg_120612

7. http://www.youtube.com/watch?v=oLo0Jwj03JU&feature=youtu.be

Acknowledge The Plan

1. http://everytown.org/

2. http://www.youtube.com/watch?v=hxRlpRcorEU&feature=youtu.be

3. http://www.imfdb.org/wiki/Main_Page

4. http://content.time.com/time/arts/article/0,8599,2019689,00.html

5. http://www.examiner.com/article/jamie-foxx-on-killing-white-people-new-movie-how-great-is-that

6. http://www.kgw.com/story/local/2014/10/06/12405148/

7. http://www.mysanantonio.com/news/local_news/article/Two-wounded-in-theater-shooting-4122668.php

8. http://www.cbsnews.com/news/police-off-duty-cop-saved-lives-in-mall/

9. http://www.washingtontimes.com/news/2012/dec/31/open-letter-to-joe-biden-on-guns/

Silver Linings

1. http://www.supremecourt.gov/opinions/07pdf/07-290.pdf

A Call For Full Disclosure In The Gun Control Debate

1. http://www.cbsnews.com/news/schumer-newtown-could-be-tipping-point-for-gun-control/

2. http://www.politico.com/story/2012/12/feinstein-schumer-push-changes-on-gun-laws-85135.html

3. http://hotair.com/greenroom/archives/2009/07/22/chuck-schumer-is-better-than-you/

About Those Absentee Politicians

1. http://firstread.nbcnews.com/_news/2012/11/28/15518240-congress-to-make-history-but-for-the-wrong-reason#comments

2. http://www.weeklystandard.com/blogs/obama-plays-golf_662260.html

3. http://politicalticker.blogs.cnn.com/2012/06/17/golfer-in-chief-hits-100th-round-as-president/

4. http://www.reuters.com/article/2012/03/26/us-nuclear-summit-obama-medvedev-idUSBRE82P0JI20120326

The One Warren Buffett Tax Hike Proposal You Will Never See

1. http://www.nytimes.com/2012/11/26/opinion/buffett-a-minimum-tax-for-the-wealthy.html?_r=1&

Some Fair Reassurance

1. http://www.youtube.com/watch?v=oLo0Jwj03JU&feature=youtu.be
2. http://fairmodel.econ.yale.edu/vote2012/computev.htm
3. http://yaledailynews.com/blog/2012/09/25/fair-predicts-close-race/

Biden Helps The Supply-Side Cause

1. http://www.npr.org/2012/10/11/162754053/transcript-biden-ryan-vice-presidential-debate
2. http://www.freesound.org/people/Halleck/sounds/29938/
3. http://www.youtube.com/watch?v=jH0yfGAyKbA&feature=youtu.be
4. http://www.youtube.com/watch?v=qmHdqWPB_S8&feature=youtu.be
5. http://www.bls.gov/data/
6. http://edition.cnn.com/2001/ALLPOLITICS/03/12/kennedy.jfk/index.html
7. http://www.nytimes.com/2012/09/05/us/politics/transcript-of-bill-clintons-speech-to-the-democratic-national-convention.html?pagewanted=all&_r=0

No On Napa County's Measure U

1. http://ballotpedia.org/wiki/index.php/Napa_County_Angwin_General_Plan_Amendment_Initiative,_Measure_U_(November_2012)
2. http://www4.angwin-ecovillage.com/
3. http://www.saveruralangwin.org/index.html
4. http://napavalleyregister.com/news/opinion/mailbag/help-protect-our-rural-character/article_4ad4afba-0c59-11e2-abf3-001a4bcf887a.html
5. http://napavalleyregister.com/news/local/pacific-union-college-still-considering-sale-of-land/article_c682ae50-9be3-11e1-a6d4-001a4bcf887a.html
6. http://www.youtube.com/watch?v=RS0KyTZ3Ie4&feature=related
7. http://nvcwinery.ewinerysolutions.com/index.cfm?method=homepage.showpage
8. http://www.countyofnapa.org/WorkArea/login.aspx?fromLnkPg=1

When Something Is Described As "Complicated"

1. http://abcnews.go.com/Politics/OTUS/transcript-bill-clintons-democratic-convention-speech/story?id=17164662&page=3#.UFAelo3N9cQ
2. http://www.nytimes.com/2012/09/08/us/politics/a-day-later-its-still-the-economy.html?partner=rss&emc=rss&utm_source=twitterfeed&utm_medium=twitter

Colorado Democrat Redistricting May Have Left Opening For Republican Underdog

1. http://www.denverpost.com/news/ci_19477875
2. http://lundberg2012.com/
3. http://www.polisforcongress.com/
4. http://projects.washingtonpost.com/congress/members/P000598

5. http://votesmart.org/interest-group/933/rating/5942
6. http://www.opensecrets.org/pfds/summary.php?CID=N00029127&year=2010
7. http://www.chec.org/
8. http://www.opensecrets.org/races/summary.php?id=CO02&cycle=2012
9. https://secure.piryx.com/donate/H5NVm9th/Lundberg-for-Congress/

Brace Yourself For The Paul Ryan Smears

1. http://www.theonion.com/articles/romney-murdered-jonbenet-ramsey-new-obama-campaign,29114/
2. http://www.youtube.com/watch?v=Nj70XqOxptU&feature=youtu.be
3. http://www.cnbc.com/id/48170576/Romney_Campaign_Rejects_Felony_Remarks
4. http://articles.chicagotribune.com/2012-08-10/opinion/ct-edit-ad-20120810_1_priorities-usa-action-gst-steel-joe-soptic
5. http://politicalticker.blogs.cnn.com/2012/08/07/ad-linking-romney-to-death-of-the-wife-of-a-laid-off-steelworker-not-accurate/?iref=allsearch
6. http://www.washingtonpost.com/blogs/fact-checker/post/new-anti-romney-ad-same-steelworker-tougher-message/2012/08/07/ac9afe2c-e0ab-11e1-8fc5-a7dcf1fc161d_blog.html
7. http://www.washingtonpost.com/blogs/fact-checker/post/new-anti-romney-ad-same-steelworker-tougher-message/2012/08/07/ac9afe2c-e0ab-11e1-8fc5-a7dcf1fc161d_blog.html
8. http://www.politico.com/politico44/2012/08/team-obama-says-they-dont-story-of-man-who-stars-of-131462.html
9. http://www.foxnews.com/politics/2012/08/08/obama-campaign-aide-accused-lying-over-controversial-anti-romney-ad/
10. http://www.npr.org/2012/07/14/156785337/week-in-news-the-swiftboating-of-mitt-romney
11. http://www.cbsnews.com/news/wealthy-gop-donor-sheldon-adelson-sues-jewish-political-group-for-libel/

Mia Love: The GOP's Rising Star In Utah's 4th Congressional District

1. http://love4utah.com/
2. http://www.eenews.net/tv/videos/1319/transcript
3. http://abcnews.go.com/Politics/OTUS/mia-love-bl
4. http://abcnews.go.com/Politics/OTUS/mia-love-black-conservative-mormon-gop-house-candidate/story?id=16203847#.UCCS503N9cQ
5. http://www.rightwingnews.com/interviews/an-interview-with-mia-love/
6. http://www.sltrib.com/sltrib/politics/54357832-90/budget-candidate-crisis-debt.html.csp
7. http://news.yahoo.com/blogs/ticket/meet-mia-love-black-conservative-mormon-running-congress-175550501.html
8. http://www.dailykos.com/story/2012/01/11/1053962/-A-Clean-2-2-Utah-Dem-Gerrymander

9. http://www.opensecrets.org/races/summary.php?id=UT04&cycle=2012
10. http://cookpolitical.com/
11. https://mialove.nationbuilder.com/donations1

Chik-fil-A And Double Standards

1. http://www.bpnews.net/38271
2. http://www.bostonherald.com/news/opinion/op_ed/view/20220727poultry_excuse_mayor_radical_imam_ok_but_not_chick-fil-a
3. http://www.addictinginfo.org/2012/06/12/catholic-bishops-in-uganda-voice-support-for-kill-the-gays-bill/

President Obama Channels Don Rickles

1. http://www.youtube.com/watch?v=Uzf4yjphgf8&feature=youtu.be

Elena Kagan: The Obamacare Recusal That Wasn't

1. http://nymag.com/daily/intelligencer/2012/03/white-house-defends-stammering-solicitor-general.html
2. http://www.dailymotion.com/video/x7jswx_my-cousin-vinny-opening-statement_fun
3. http://codes.lp.findlaw.com/uscode/28/I/21/455
4. http://www.judicialwatch.org/files/documents/2011/mrc-kagan-docs.pdf
5. http://www.judicialwatch.org/press-room/press-releases/new-documents-show-supreme-court-justice-elena-kagan-s-comments-obamacare-legislation/
6. http://50-57-133-148.static.cloud-ips.com/files/documents/2011/doj-kagan-docs-11102011.pdf#page=2
7. http://www.judicialwatch.org/files/documents/2011/mrc-kagan-docs.pdf
8. http://www.nytimes.com/2001/08/14/us/three-abstain-as-supreme-court-declines-to-halt-texas-execution.html?src=pm

Why The Elizabeth Warren Controversy Continues

1. http://www.bostonherald.com/news/opinion/op_ed/view/20220518lizs_goose_is_cooked_no_morsel_of_truth_in_her_indian_identity
2. http://www.nytimes.com/2012/06/03/us/politics/elizabeth-warren-seeks-to-revive-senate-campaign.html?_r=2&hpw&
3. http://www.washingtonpost.com/blogs/the-fix/post/assessing-elizabeth-warrens-wounds/2012/06/04/gJQANrTODV_blog.html
4. http://elizabethwarren.com/issues

Hey Californians: Go To Tahoe!

1. http://arc.asm.ca.gov/budgetfactcheck/
2. http://ballotpedia.org/wiki/index.php/Jerry_Brown%27s_California_Tax_Increase_Initiative_(2012)

3. http://ballotpedia.org/wiki/index.php/Molly_Munger's_California_State_Income_Tax_Increase_to_Support_Education_Initiative_(2012)
4. http://www.ocregister.com/common/archives/?blog_slug=jan&post_id=36215
5. http://www.lao.ca.gov/reports/2011/calfacts/calfacts_010511.aspx#zzee_link_2_1294170707

Ted Cruz, The Tea Party's Bunker-Buster

1. http://www.epa.gov/captrade/
2. http://humanevents.com/2012/04/17/house-blocks-epa-from-banning-lead-in-ammunition/
3. http://www.fws.gov/southwest/es/DSL.html
4. http://www.politico.com/politico44/2012/03/hhs-spells-contraception-coverage-rule-options-117734.html
5. http://www.nytimes.com/2011/12/10/business/labor-board-drops-case-against-boeing.html
6. http://www.supremecourt.gov/opinions/07pdf/07-290.pdf
7. http://www.scotusblog.com/wp-content/uploads/2008/03/06-984.pdf
8. http://www.youtube.com/watch?v=F5m6lhwOT60&feature=youtu.be
9. http://www.youtube.com/watch?v=_Ojd13kZlCA&feature=youtu.be
10. http://www.youtube.com/watch?v=a1cSl-RJLLc&feature=youtu.be
11. http://dewhurstfortexas.com/latest-news/dewhurst-continues-lead-campaign-repeal-obamacare
12. http://www.fec.gov/data/CandidateSummary.do?format=html&election_yr=2012
13. http://dewhurstfortexas.com/endorsements
14. http://www.statesman.com/news/news/opinion/cruz-politifact-got-it-wrong-dewhursts-wage-tax-wa/nRkjk/
15. http://www.dallasnews.com/news/politics/headlines/20120112-senate-rivals-attack-dewhurst-in-debate.ece?ssimg=428501
16. http://www.tedcruz.org/wp-content/uploads/2012/02/2005-05-10-WSJ-taxes.pdf
17. http://prattontexas.podomatic.com/entry/2012-02-16T17_31_03-08_00
18. http://napawhinecountry.com/californias-proposed-tax-hikes/
19. http://www.fec.gov/data/CandidateSummary.do?format=html&election_yr=2012
20. http://www.publicpolicypolling.com/main/2012/04/cruz-closing-in-on-dewhurst.html
21. http://www.tedcruz.org/endorsements/

The Plague Of Financial Ruin

1. http://napavalleyregister.com/news/local/they-lost-their-home-and-business-but-not-their-faith/article_b5b2e356-7bb8-11e1-8a5b-0019bb2963f4.html
2. http://www.endhomelessness.org/library/entry/the-state-of-homelessness-in-america-2012
3. http://blogs.census.gov/2011/09/13/households-doubling-up/
4. http://teressamorris.com/

The Perils Of A Live Microphone

1. https://www.youtube.com/watch?v=PlXK8o70Se0&feature=youtu.be
2. http://www.cbsnews.com/videos/1979-salt-ii-treaty-signed/
3. http://www.nytimes.com/2010/11/10/opinion/10bolton.html?_r=2&scp=2&sq=john%20 bolton%20yoo&st=cse&
4. http://thehill.com/blogs/congress-blog/foreign-policy/213813-cuts-to-sm-3-missile-funding-send-wrong-message-to-iran
5. http://www.spacenews.com/policy/pentagon-shifts-sm-3-for-european-missile-defense.html
6. http://freebeacon.com/turner-to-obama-what-flexibility/
7. http://www.telegraph.co.uk/news/worldnews/wikileaks/8304654/WikiLeaks-cables-US-agrees-to-tell-Russia-Britains-nuclear-secrets.html
8. http://www.nytimes.com/1998/05/18/us/clinton-says-chinese-money-did-not-influence-us-policy.html
9. http://www.forbes.com/2009/08/27/ted-kennedy-soviet-union-ronald-reagan-opinions-columnists-peter-robinson.html

Newt's Apollo 13 Candidacy

1. http://youtu.be/hrko6ru9AFc
2. https://www.youtube.com/watch?v=kMhpP0DFlPA&feature=youtu.be
3. http://napawhinecountry.com/the-old-newt-is-back/
4. http://foxnewsinsider.com/2012/01/17/transcript-fox-news-channel-wall-street-journal-debate-in-south-carolina/
5. https://www.youtube.com/watch?v=ka0LMt5ciRc&feature=youtu.be
6. http://www.whitehouse.gov/the-press-office/2011/12/06/remarks-president-economy-osawatomie-kansas
7. http://www.hannity.com/show/2012/01/17
8. http://www.cbsnews.com/news/south-carolina-primary-exit-polls-2-3rds-say-debates-mattered/

The Old Newt Is Back

1. https://www.youtube.com/watch?v=VRXfXgBjfkA
2. https://www.youtube.com/watch?v=rUp3vhMSfZE
3. http://www.latimes.com/nation/politics/politicsnow/la-pn-gallup-poll-20111121-story.html
4. https://www.youtube.com/watch?v=6_rL8U6cCnU
5. https://www.youtube.com/watch?v=90Q8nn3RDyE&feature=related
6. http://www.mediaite.com/tv/newt-gingrich-declares-im-going-to-be-the-nominee/
7. https://www.youtube.com/watch?v=9lg61qIpstY&feature=youtu.be
8. https://twitter.com/#%21/JonahNRO/status/155418003519971328
9. http://www.washingtonpost.com/opinions/a-worthy-challenger/2012/01/05/gIQAGeRfdP_story.html
10. http://youtu.be/FlDR_fmaYm8

11. http://www.clubforgrowth.org/pr/?postID=1008
12. http://www.rushlimbaugh.com/daily/2012/01/10/gingrich_goes_perot_on_romney
13. http://fivethirtyeight.blogs.nytimes.com/2012/01/11/romney-looks-strong-in-south-carolina-and-beyond/
14. http://edition.cnn.com/2009/TECH/space/07/17/moon.landing.hoax/index.html?_s=PM:TECH
15. http://www.americanthinker.com/2011/11/newt_is_no_gecko.html

Don't Mess With West Texas Or Eastern New Mexico

1. http://www.pillsbury.com/Products/Cookies/Refrigerated-Cookies
2. http://napawhinecountry.com/dear-fish-and-wildlife-service/
3. http://www.regulations.gov/#%21documentDetail;D=FWS-R2-ES-2010-0041-0001
4. http://cornyn.senate.gov/public/index.cfm?p=NewsReleases&ContentRecord_id=13d0c8bc-932e-42d9-8887-34ab5dbc2681&ContentType_id=b94acc28-404a-4fc6-b143-a9e15bf92da4&Group_id=24eb5606-e2db-4d7f-bf6c-efc5df80b676
5. http://ceed.utpb.edu/energy-resources/petroleum-library/permian-basin-statistics/
6. http://www.eia.gov/
7. http://ceed.utpb.edu/energy-resources/petroleum-library/permian-basin-statistics/
8. http://www.regulations.gov/#%21documentDetail;D=FWS-R2-ES-2010-0041-0001
9. http://www.nytimes.com/2007/09/02/us/02delta.html
10. http://abclocal.go.com/kfsn/story?section=news/local&id=6734504
11. http://abclocal.go.com/kfsn/story?section=news/local&id=6734504
12. http://www.sacbee.com/2011/07/21/3783726/delta-smelt-population-up-wet.html
13. http://www.knoxnews.com/business/tellico-dam-still-generating-debate
14. http://www.reuters.com/article/2011/04/25/idUS46562358120110425
15. http://articles.latimes.com/2011/jul/16/business/la-fi-bryson-profile-20110716
16. http://www.businesswire.com/news/home/20110411006983/en/BrightSource-Energy-Closes-Financing-Ivanpah-Project
17. http://www.kcet.org/updaily/socal_focus/environment/mojaves-desert-tortoise-not-endangered-by-solar-project-says-feds-34533.html

Newt Is No Gecko

1. http://www.latimes.com/nation/politics/politicsnow/la-pn-gallup-poll-20111121-story.html
2. http://www.salon.com/2011/03/08/gingrich_divorce_hospital_cancer/
3. http://www.creators.com/conservative/jackie-gingrich-cushman/setting-the-record-straight.html
4. http://www.cbsnews.com/news/gingrich-ive-had-moments-of-regret-in-personal-life/
5. http://www.washingtonpost.com/wp-srv/politics/govt/leadership/stories/012297.htm
6. http://www.nytimes.com/2011/11/17/us/politics/newt-gingrich-on-defensive-over-freddie-mac-fees.html?pagewanted=all
7. http://www.youtube.com/watch?v=qi6n_-wB154
8. http://hotair.com/archives/2011/11/09/newt-that-pelosi-ad-was-a-bad-idea-huh/

9. http://articles.latimes.com/2011/may/15/news/la-pn-gingrich-ryan-medicare-20110515

10. http://www.desmoinesregister.com/section/documentcloud%26dckeyword%3D253688-gingrich-contract-with-america_digest/

11. http://www.nytimes.com/2011/10/24/us/politics/mitt-romney-changes-his-tone-on-flat-tax-plans.html

12. http://www.commentarymagazine.com/2011/11/08/gop-romney-entitlement-reform/

13. http://www.washingtonpost.com/politics/as-governor-romney-worked-to-reassure-liberals/2011/11/02/gIQAookxgM_story_1.html

14. http://2012.republican-candidates.org/Romney/Gun-Control.php

15. http://www.boston.com/politicalintelligence/2011/10/romney-makes-new-shift-global-warming-position/aBMsQrPwV3bxnFZHLRNPwO/index.html

16. http://www.nationalreview.com/corner/280922/romney-s-ethanol-position-evolving-katrina-trinko

17. http://politicalticker.blogs.cnn.com/2011/10/25/romney-avoids-weighing-in-on-ohio-union-fight/

18. http://www.lumrix.net/health/Massachusetts_health_care_reform.html

19. http://online.wsj.com/news/articles/SB100014240529702039143045766276838188892932?mg=reno64-wsj&url=http%3A%2F%2Fonline.wsj.com%2Farticle%2FSB10001424052970203914304576627683818892932.html

20. http://www.washingtonpost.com/blogs/the-fix/post/newt-gingrichs-war-on-republican-debate-moderators/2011/11/10/gIQAiy558M_blog.html

21. http://video.cnbc.com/gallery/?video=3000056477

22. https://www.youtube.com/watch?v=6LMT8-o-mpc

23. http://www.weeklystandard.com/blogs/gingrich-occupy-wall-street-go-get-job-right-after-you-take-bath_609253.html

24. https://www.youtube.com/watch?v=u5qSiO_maTs

25. https://www.youtube.com/watch?v=zrQHcMucLVU

Mitt Romney: 2012's Gerald Ford

1. http://pjmedia.com/instapundit/

2. http://washingtonexaminer.com/opinion/columnists/2011/04/sunday-reflection-when-jimmy-carter-your-best-case-scenario-youre-trouble

3. http://caucuses.desmoinesregister.com/2011/10/29/cain-romney-lead-new-iowa-poll/

4. http://www.rasmussenreports.com/public_content/politics/elections/election_2012/election_2012_presidential_election/new_hampshire/election_2012_new_hampshire_republican_primary

5. http://swampland.time.com/topline-results-of-oct-20-25-2011-cnntimeorc-poll/

6. http://miamiherald.typepad.com/nakedpolitics/2011/10/cnn-florida-poll-shows-mitt-romneys-the-man-to-beat.html

7. http://www.archives.gov/exhibits/charters/constitution_amendments_11-27.html

8. https://www.youtube.com/watch?v=c5e8FvDQcSg

9. http://www.youtube.com/watch?v=JULw8qsnHcY

10. http://www.nytimes.com/2011/10/24/us/politics/mitt-romney-changes-his-tone-on-flat-tax-plans.html

11. http://www.forbes.com/sites/aroy/2011/11/05/mitt-romneys-vaguely-promising-plan-for-entitlement-reform/
12. http://www.washingtonpost.com/politics/as-governor-romney-worked-to-reassure-liberals/2011/11/02/gIQAookxgM_story_1.html
13. http://2012.republican-candidates.org/Romney/Gun-Control.php
14. http://www.boston.com/politicalintelligence/2011/10/romney-makes-new-shift-global-warming-position/aBMsQrPwV3bxnFZHLRNPwO/index.html
15. http://www.nationalreview.com/corner/280922/romney-s-ethanol-position-evolving-katrina-trinko
16. http://www.lumrix.net/health/Massachusetts_health_care_reform.html
17. http://online.wsj.com/news/articles/SB10001424052970203914304576627683818892932?mg=reno64-wsj&url=http%3A%2F%2Fonline.wsj.com%2Farticle%2FSB10001424052970203914304576627683818892932.html
18. http://forums.hannity.com/showthread.php?t=2340101

Where Is The Urgency?

1. http://www.washingtonpost.com/politics/republican-debate-transcript/2011/10/11/gIQATu8vdL_story.html
2. http://www.traderjoes.com/guides/wine-guide.asp
3. http://www.politifact.com/truth-o-meter/statements/2010/jan/29/jeb-hensarling/rep-hensarling-says-annual-deficits-under-republic/
4. http://www.time.com/time/magazine/article/0,9171,2013826,00.html
5. http://www.cbo.gov/doc.cfm?index=12316&zzz=42013
6. http://www.treasurydirect.gov/NP/BPDLogin?application=np
7. http://www.cbo.gov/doc.cfm?index=12316
8. http://www.cbo.gov/doc.cfm?index=12316
9. http://www.roadmap.republicans.budget.house.gov/
10. http://napawhinecountry.com/?p=10
11. http://english.pravda.ru/opinion/columnists/27-04-2009/107459-american_capitalism-0/
12. http://www.ace.mu.nu/
13. http://politisite.com/2011/10/17/cnn-wlrc-western-republican-leadership-conference-presidential-debate-information-october-18-2011/

Governor Perdue Does Stand-up

1. http://projects.newsobserver.com/under_the_dome/was_perdue_joking_you_decide_listen_here#storylink=misearch
2. http://media2.newsobserver.com/smedia/2011/09/28/10/28/11veHD.So.156.mp3
3. http://instantrimshot.com/index.php?sound=rimshot&play=true
4. http://hotlineoncall.nationaljournal.com/archives/2011/07/bloodbath-for-n.php
5. http://www.americanthinker.com/2011/07/sauce_for_the_gerrymander.html
6. http://www.cbsnews.com/news/gop-keeps-house-seat-in-nevada-special-election/

7. http://www.nytimes.com/2011/09/14/nyregion/ny-democrats-try-to-avoid-upset-in-special-election.html?pagewanted=all
8. http://quoteinvestigator.com/tag/famous-last-words/

The Life Alert President

1. http://www.gallup.com/poll/113980/Gallup-Daily-Obama-Job-Approval.aspx
2. http://www.rasmussenreports.com/public_content/politics/obama_administration/daily_presidential_tracking_poll
3. http://www.bls.gov/news.release/empsit.nr0.htm
4. http://www.gallup.com/poll/148889/Economic-Confidence-Plunges-Past-Two-Weeks.aspx
5. http://www.salon.com/news/politics/war_room/2008/02/14/clinton_change/index.html
6. http://www.politico.com/news/stories/0811/61720.html
7. http://videoshare.politico.com/singletitlevideo_chromeless.php?bcpid=309045726001&bckey=AQ~~,AAAAAETmrZQ~,EVFEM4AKJdT-Wv9cQWadwt8FUbtX2ID_&bctid=1116793416001
8. http://www.politico.com/politico44/perm/0811/call_uncle_sam_5c130fdd-0e34-4b04-99e1-3d923ea3919e.html
9. http://www.politico.com/news/stories/0811/61720.html

Chapter 2

Football Player Shoots Off Mouth, Unites Previously-Ambivalent Fans Behind Opposing Team

1. http://napawhinecountry.com/george-bailey-for-president/
2. http://www.youtube.com/watch?v=bkTq__jd4I4&feature=youtu.be

The Sanctimony Tax

1. http://pjmedia.com/instapundit/
2. http://pjmedia.com/instapundit/158554/
3. http://www.politico.com/blogs/click/2012/09/eva-longoria-romney-and-i-dont-need-tax-breaks-134788.html
4. http://www.nytimes.com/2012/11/19/opinion/krugman-the-twinkie-manifesto.html?_r=1&

Confessions Of A Shopkick Detractor

1. http://www.shopkick.com/

"Bus Beat-Down" Videos

1. http://www.youtube.com/watch?v=w6KFWiidiJo&feature=youtu.be
2. http://www.youtube.com/watch?v=Yjr44CgJy7c&feature=youtu.be
3. http://www.youtube.com/watch?v=DeVF8W_ezNQ&feature=youtu.be

Chapter 3

Persecuted Movie Review: Thanksgiving Turkey Comes Early

1. http://www.theatlantic.com/politics/archive/2014/04/mozillas-gay-marriage-litmus-test-violates-liberal-values/360156/

Man Of Steel: Chock Full Of Christian Dog Whistles

1. http://www.imdb.com/title/tt0335345/?ref_=fn_al_tt_2
2. http://www.imdb.com/title/tt0377992/?ref_=fn_al_tt_1

Julie Borowski Interview, Part 1

1. https://www.youtube.com/user/BillWhittleChannel
2. https://www.youtube.com/user/StevenCrowder
3. https://www.youtube.com/user/TokenLibertarianGirl
4. http://julieborowski.wordpress.com/
5. https://www.youtube.com/watch?v=hvmzCMT-4Q4&feature=share&list=UUzIjg5vIfBGcdyLWu6lhXxw
6. https://www.youtube.com/watch?v=_jJQJRKnu2I&feature=share&list=UUzIjg5vIfBGcdyLWu6lhXxw
7. https://www.youtube.com/watch?v=nASPjBVQkQk&feature=share&list=UUzIjg5vIfBGcdyLWu6lhXxw

Julie Borowski Interview, Part 2

1. https://www.youtube.com/user/BillWhittleChannel
2. https://www.youtube.com/user/StevenCrowder
3. https://www.youtube.com/user/TokenLibertarianGirl
4. http://julieborowski.wordpress.com/
5. https://www.youtube.com/watch?v=hvmzCMT-4Q4&feature=youtu.be
6. https://www.youtube.com/watch?v=cR83DUW_92Y&feature=youtu.be
7. https://www.youtube.com/watch?v=5QGDJhXznrU&feature=youtu.be
8. https://www.youtube.com/watch?v=G9VjmHpsMxw&feature=youtu.be
9. https://www.youtube.com/watch?v=o6G3nwhPuR4&feature=youtu.be
10. https://www.youtube.com/watch?v=wAkdHzpXXo0&feature=share&list=UUzIjg5vIfBGcdyLWu6lhXxw
11. https://www.youtube.com/watch?v=o6G3nwhPuR4&feature=youtu.be

12. http://www.amazon.com/The-Tyranny-Cliches-Liberals-Cheat/dp/1595231021/ref=sr_1_1?ie=UTF8&qid=1369268276&sr=8-1&keywords=tyranny+of+cliches
13. http://www.breitbart.com/Big-Government/2012/11/16/gop-reaps-its-abandonment-of-limited-government

Addicts Can Learn New Lessons From An Old Movie: *Stuart Saves His Family*

1. http://online.wsj.com/news/articles/SB10001424127887324081704578235443281579414?KEYWORDS=franken&mg=reno64-wsj&url=http%3A%2F%2Fonline.wsj.com%2Farticle%2FSB10001424127887324081704578235443281579414.html%3FKEYWORDS%3Dfranken
2. http://www.aa.org/?Media=PlayFlash
3. http://www.na.org/
4. http://www.na.org/

James Bond: Super Spy, Life Coach

1. http://www.amazon.com/Bond-50-Complete-Collection-Blu-ray/dp/B006U1J5ZY/ref=sr_1_1?s=movies-tv&ie=UTF8&qid=1348550533&sr=1-1&keywords=james+bond
2. http://www.amazon.com/gp/mpd/permalink/m3TA9R1YH562JL/ref=ent_fb_link

Carolla and Prager: The Newest Odd Couple Click On Stage

1. http://napawhinecountry.com/my-dinner-with-andre-review-the-only-one-of-its-kind-for-good-reason/
2. http://pragertopia.com/
3. http://adamcarolla.com/
4. http://www.prageruniversity.com/

Palin's Privilege

1. http://pjmedia.com/tatler/2012/04/03/sarah-palin-guest-hosts-today-probably-not-for-the-last-time/?singlepage=true
2. http://www.hollywoodreporter.com/live-feed/jon-stewart-slams-sarah-palin-today-show-guest-host-308187
3. http://www.huffingtonpost.com/2012/04/09/bryant-gumbel-embarrassed-palin-today_n_1411907.html
4. http://www.youtube.com/watch?v=0VElmb1ttOM&feature=youtu.be
5. http://www.amazon.com/Firing-William-Buckley-Presidential-Hopeful/dp/B007QAFSLI/ref=sr_1_14?s=movies-tv&ie=UTF8&qid=1334032030&sr=1-14
6. http://www.slate.com/articles/news_and_politics/explainer/2008/02/why_did_william_f_buckley_jr_talk_like_that.html

What a Feat! Little Feat Rocks Napa, California In Its U.S. Concert Tour Opener

1. http://www.littlefeat.net/

Prepare For The End With "Doomsday Preppers" TV Show

1. https://www.practicalpreppers.com/ABOUT-PRACTICAL-PREPPERS/National-Geographic.html
2. http://www.nytimes.com/1992/05/03/us/riot-los-angles-pocket-tension-target-rioters-koreatown-bitter-armed-determined.html?pagewanted=all
3. http://usatoday30.usatoday.com/money/economy/story/2012-03-03/david-stockman-says-economic-disaster-lurks/53339644/1

'My Dinner With Andre' Review: The Only One Of Its Kind, For Good Reason

1. http://www.youtube.com/watch?v=9s0UURBihH8&feature=youtu.be

Chapter 4

An Idea For A New Murder Mystery Series: *PC Detective*

1. https://www.youtube.com/watch?v=8dGmtFyapho&feature=youtu.be
2. http://colorlines.com/archives/2014/08/want_to_avoid_black_neighborhoods_theres_an_app_for_that.html

A Healthcare Alternative To Planned Parenthood

1. http://www.plannedparenthood.org/files/4013/9611/7243/Planned_Parenthood_Services.pdf

George Bailey For President

1. http://napawhinecountry.com/halloween-guide-for-dieting-parents/

INDEX

Made in the USA
Charleston, SC
01 December 2014